Higher Education Policy Series 45

Changing Relationships between Higher Education and the State

Edited by Mary Henkel and Brenda Little

Jessica Kingsley Publishers
London and Philadelphia

First published in the United Kingdom in 1999 by

Jessica Kingsley Publishers Ltd,
116 Pentonville Road,
London N1 9JB,
England

and

325 Chestnut Street,
Philadelphia, PA 19106, USA.

www.jkp.com

Copyright © 1999 Jessica Kingsley Publishers

Library of Congress Cataloging in Publication Data

A CIP catalogue record for this book is available from the Library of Congress

British Library Cataloguing in Publication Data

Henkel, Mary

Changing relationships between higher education and the state. - (Higher education policy ; 45)

1. Higher education and state - Europe

I.Title II. Little, Brenda

378.4

ISBN 1-85302-644 1 hb ✓
ISBN 1-85302-645X pb

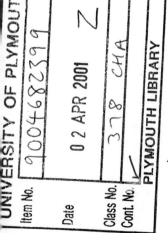
Printed and Bound in Great Britain by
Athenaeum Press, Gateshead, Tyne and Wear

Contents

List of Figures

List of Tables

Preface and Acknowledgements

This book is the outcome of a series of six international seminars convened in London during 1996 and 1997 to examine changing relationships between the state and higher education in a European context. The editors are grateful to the Economic and Social Research Council for a grant which made it possible to bring higher education researchers from a total of seven countries (Austria, France, Germany, Finland, Norway, Sweden and the UK) together with other academics, including some coopted by government into intermediary bodies, institutional leaders and members of senior management teams in universities, members of academic interest groups, policy makers and representatives of the media. The seminar series was planned and organised by John Brennan and Brenda Little (replacing Peter deVries) of the Open University's Quality Support Centre and Maurice Kogan and Mary Henkel of Brunel University's Centre for the Evaluation of Public Policy and Practice. The series provided opportunities for analysis from a range of national, professional, institutional and disciplinary perspectives; for gathering empirical evidence from several countries; and for the exchange of analyses and perspectives between actors implicated in various ways in the relationships between the state and higher education.

The editors acknowledge the invaluable help provided by Deana Parker of the Quality Support Centre in getting the various seminar papers 'into shape' for this publication. For permission to reprint copyright material the editors gratefully acknowledge the following: Some of Chapter 10 develops material included in an article in the journal *Perspectives,* with the kind permission of the Taylor and Francis Group. Chapter 11 originally appeared in *Higher Education Management 10,* 2. It is printed here with the kind permission of OECD. Chapter 3 was previously published in the *European Journal of Education.* Throughout this volume, we refer to the major review chaired by Sir Ron Dearing in the UK. He is now Lord Dearing.

Mary Henkel and Brenda Little

CHAPTER I

Introduction

Mary Henkel and Brenda Little

Reappraising the relationship

Powerful ideological and economic movements have forced nations across the world to reappraise the relationships between the state and a range of public institutions in the latter part of the twentieth century. This book focuses on the relationships between the state and one specific set of public institutions, namely higher education institutions.

The book arises from a series of seminars conducted during 1996 and 1997. The seminars moved between broad issues of political, social and economic theory and close-grained study of instruments of change and their consequences for the inner life of academic institutions and the careers of their students. The empirical material was weighted towards the UK[1], but participants were throughout conscious of the need to assess the influence of global forces upon national developments against that of national histories and individual societies' constructions of institutional relationships (Musselin in Chapter 3); and to respect the power of historic tradition and organisational memory to incorporate, if not wholly to resist, change.

A primary aim of the seminars, and now the book, was to provide conceptual structures and heuristic devices within which comparative analyses of the relationships between higher education and the state can be made by readers. But only cursory reflection on

---

1 During the course of the seminar series, a National Committee of Inquiry into Higher Education had been set-up in the UK. The Committee, chaired by Sir Ron Dearing, was charged with making recommendations to the government about the future shape and direction of UK higher education for the next twenty years.

our topic is required to make it clear that it contains no fixed points of reference. The metaphor of a framework for analysis would probably be misleadingly reassuring. The context is one in which not only have the relative stabilities in the balance of power or of exchange relationships between the state and higher education been disturbed (Neave and van Vught 1991) but also political, economic and epistemological change (Välimaa Chapter 2) are combining to compel reappraisal of concepts and structures of thought that are most taken for granted in discussions of the politics of higher education: concepts of the state; the definition and value of advanced knowledge; the authority of higher education institutions over knowledge (Jones and Little Chapter 7); the idea of exchange between two partners, the state and higher education.

Both the state and higher education have different meanings in different theories and traditions and encompass a bevy of institutions, actors and interests. The perspective of political science in which the state is usually equated with a set of institutions or a form of government (Vincent 1994) is that broadly adopted in this book but it may not match the conceptions of all its readers, or even all its contributors. For some the state, and higher education too, are predominantly normative concepts, representing ideals of social order, forms of knowledge or basic values.

Historically, neither the state nor higher education has stood still. The changes *in* the state, as well as *in* higher education during the last two decades have been powerful generators of the changes in the relationship *between* them. Burton Clark's triangle of influences (state, market, professional) upon higher education is a dominant analytic device in higher education literature. But for most of the twentieth century, analysts of European higher education have been able to focus primarily on the duality of state-professional influences. Social demand, even where it has resulted in a massive rise in student numbers, has not necessarily disturbed this dual relationship (see Neave and van Vught 1991). However, during the last 20 years, governments have, in different degrees, embarked on more fundamental change in response to a broader set of challenges to their capacity to support and govern their public institutions. Definitions of the boundaries and relationships between the state and the market have begun to alter.

A new public management has emerged in which market mechanisms and modes of thinking and practice have been incorporated into the public sector (Bleiklie 1994, 1996; Meek and Wood 1996): competition, contracts, incentives, quality assurance, performance indicators, managerialism. Public institutions have been opened up to the influence, direct advice and appraisal of private organisations, notably management consultants. User evaluation and consumerism have been introduced to the public sector, and, together with managerialism, have, in some cases, been seen as a means of reducing the power of professionals in state organisations. In the UK, industrialists have been given key roles in the governance of intermediary bodies in higher education, as well as in universities. Across Europe, more or less strenuous efforts have been made to reduce the financial dependency of higher education institutions on the state and to encourage new levels of collaboration in the production and transmission of knowledge between academics, the private sector and governments.

It remains the case that no higher education institution can survive wholly independently of the state. But the possibilities of university privatisation have been put on the agenda in Europe. The power of the purse in the relations between higher education and the state, while dominant, is no longer unequivocal. The limits to the capacity of the state to generate the resources to sustain higher education institutions have, during the last two decades, been more extensively and explicitly acknowledged.

Massification, a prime cause of the escalating expense of higher education, has generated other instabilities, not least in the dual nature of the state–higher education relationship. Massification signifies and generates the economic and political salience of higher education to a hugely increased range of stakeholders. It also entails institutional diversification (Välimaa Chapter 2).

Massification and institutional diversification

These last two trends have implications for the role of the law in the regulation of higher education by the state. We have seen the replacement of legal homogeneity by negotiated co-ordination of diversity (Musselin Chapter 3) or by performance conditionality (Neave 1996; Välimaa Chapter 2) within a more general shift from process control to product control (Neave and van Vught 1991). Reliance upon universal, uniform frameworks is giving way to systems that can accommodate and encourage diversity, discretion and, perhaps, entrepreneurialism. State regulation is widely giving way to institutional self-regulation.

In the UK, the maverick in Europe, massification and economic and political salience have, in one sense, had the opposite effect. For the first time, in the 1980s, higher education came within the compass of the law (Kogan 1996). The law, however, provided a framework of authority within which multiple modes and mechanisms of control were encompassed and the rhetoric of the self-regulating institution was sustained, even if the financial and normative structures established by government exert powerful constraints.

However, along with the debate about the reality of self-regulation, undoubtedly the pivotal role of the institution has emerged as a key point of convergence across Europe: its role in terms of maintaining some semblance of autonomy, and in terms of its mediating effects on institutional and academic behaviour in response to external pressures. Hence the choice in this volume to devote one section to the institution and its management (Cuthbert, Kogan and Smith *et al.*).

The role of massification and diversification in the dilution of the dual nature of the relationship between the state and higher education is only one aspect of their significance. They represent, too, a loosening of the association of higher education with the sustainment of a nation's high culture and with the responsibility of higher education in the selection of élites seen in the past as needed for the maintenance of society. They therefore cut into two important kinds of power accorded higher education by the state, socio-political and ideological power (Salter and Tapper 1994).

Massification and diversification are also part of an apparently decisive shift towards the economic instrumental justification for higher education, as the beliefs take hold that knowledge is the most important engine of wealth production in society and that this knowledge must encompass leading-edge research as well as technological application; the diffusion of information through computerisation; and a variety of cognitive and social skills. In this context the evaluative criterion of social usefulness becomes more powerful. In an environment in which knowledge is increasingly developed in the context of application (Gibbons *et al.* 1994), Välimaa (Chapter 2) suggests that universities are required to redefine themselves. They may need to pull up their roots in Humboldtian ideals of autonomy and reform themselves into 'pragmatic' institutions. In that case, it can be argued that the stage is set for the triumph of values of utility, of knowledge weighed in terms of its exchange value, and of higher education as a sub-system of the economy, judged in terms of its efficiency or 'performativity' (Lyotard 1979).

Perhaps most fundamentally, massification and diversification involve the admission into higher education of forms of knowledge that test the boundaries and distinctions between higher and other forms of education. They do so in the context of a twentieth century epistemological revolution, in which knowledge itself has become essentially contestable. Postpositivist and postmodern undermining of concepts of truth, of universal knowledge criteria and the authority of certain forms of knowledge over others have huge implications, when combined, paradoxically, with belief in knowledge as the engine of economic productivity and power.

Role of higher education in societies

Such undermining constitutes a challenge to what has been termed 'higher education essentialism': the idea that higher education entails a particular and intrinsically exclusive conception of knowledge, mediated by strong internal control and adherence to epistemic rules of inquiry and testing, logic, use of evidence, norms of conceptual and theoretical rigour and creativity, and the disinterested pursuit of truth. In turn, that challenge puts a question mark against a long taken for granted function of higher education, as the guardian of valid knowledge in a society and of how it is defined.

> As the apex of the educational hierarchy, higher education makes the decisions on how knowledge should be organised and what status should be attached to different knowledge areas ... any significant change in the content or boundary of a knowledge area has to be sanctioned by higher education if it is to carry lasting weight. (Salter and Tapper 1994, p.4)

The centrality of theories of knowledge and knowledge production for the role of higher education in societies and therefore for the relationship between higher education and the state is reflected in several chapters in this book. For example, Sjölund (Chapter 11) and Välimaa (Chapter 2) show how policy changes at the level of government and its notions of regulation and at the level of the university and its ideals are integrally linked with changes in the conditions in which knowledge is produced. Jones and Little (Chapter 7) demonstrate how in the UK, the boundaries between higher education and employment are becoming blurred. 'Learning in the workplace is being pulled towards academic values' and even given academic credibility by the award of academic qualifications, at the same time as higher education is 'being pushed in the direction of relevance' and employment credibility. Smith, Scott, Bocock and Bargh (Chapter 15) draw attention to higher education's loss of monopoly over the production of knowledge in demand from society.

These developments represent significant shifts in the balance of power and exchange between higher education and the state. But they also indicate change in the structure of those relationships. They point analysts away from dualities. The state has not only incorporated aspects of the market into its own institutions; it has, to different degrees in different national settings, propelled universities into various forms of market relationships in which other players or stakeholders are involved. The arena in which higher education's future is being forged is highly pluralist, even if its overall contours remain structured and constrained by the state. It is an arena in which different kinds of user are flexing their muscles and indeed in which distinctions between users and providers are becoming less clear. This can be seen in the extent to which governments and higher education institutions alike are responding to employers' views about the adequacy of higher education's products, in the form of graduates.

Within this context of significant shifts in the balance of power and exchange between higher education and the state, polarities become less potent tools of analysis. Contrasts between the liberal and the economic ideologies of higher education (Salter and Tapper 1994), between autonomous and popular (Trow, quoted in Smith *et al.* Chapter 15) or autonomous and pragmatic (Välimaa Chapter 2) functions of universities, or between mass and élite forms of higher education may be maintained as analytic devices but only in awareness that polarities, or even continua, quickly dissolve, at minimum into ambiguities and frequently into complex multiplicities.

This is illustrated vividly by Kogan in an exploration of the foundations of relationships between higher education and governments which sets the scene for the seminar series.

Higher education has always pleaded for exceptional arrangements for its control on two assumptions which pull in different directions. First, high quality higher education requires autonomy in the performance of its prime functions. Second, it cannot … survive without the funds that only nation states can find. … In effect, however, the playing out of the first assumption reveals striking ambiguities, the autonomy of institutions from state control is a far different thing from the autonomy of individual academics. A third set of arguments conditioning the relationship is the need of society for the products of higher education, trained and educated people and new knowledge. This sets terms on the autonomy that is allowed for the sake of good knowledge generation and on the conditions under which governments feel they ought to fund it. (Kogan 1996, p.1)

The structure of the book[2]

All that said, we seek here to provide a minimal structure within which readers can themselves work on, or play with, some of these complexities. It is based on the idea of normative or ideal models of the relationships between higher education and the state, and their implications for what happens at different levels of higher education: those of the central authorities, the institution, the basic unit and the individual. (Becher and Kogan 1992; Välimaa (Chapter 2)). If the dynamic between the centre and the institution is dominant in the book, the implications for basic units, individual academics and students are also a strong concern.

Within a political science perspective, there are two ideal models. The classic model which has existed in most systems, but by no means covering all the institutions within them, has been that of the self-regulating higher education institution which sustains its own values and ways of working. Stated in maximum terms the academy's desired state was one in which 'academic autonomy, whether defined and guaranteed by law, by financial independence or by customary tolerance, is thus the necessary safeguard for the free and unfettered

---

2   In this section we draw on a paper prepared for the first seminar in the series by Maurice Kogan 'Relationships between higher education and the state: overview of the issues', ESRC seminar 15 May 1996. Open University/Quality Support Centre.

discharge of every university's primary duty, which is to permit intellectual non-conformity as the means of advancing knowledge' (Templeman 1982).

The contrast is that of the dependent institution, characterised by higher degrees of dependence and sponsorship. Its objectives might be set externally, or it can be an institution which, because it is unable to sustain itself on its own academic reputation, depends on financial support and other forms of sponsorship.

A spectrum of relationships between the state and higher education can then be envisaged across the divide between the two ideal models: from self-regulation and an exchange relationship with sponsors through to sponsorship-dependency and a hierarchical relationship with sponsors. These relationships are then regulated through a number of different mechanisms, viz. legal controls/bureaucratic rules; financial controls; normative/evaluative influences/structures; competition/contracts: such mechanisms result in a range of modes of governance, viz. managerial; collegial-professional; market; state control. Thus, in bringing this selection of papers together into a book, we have grouped them in a way which reflects Kogan's model of the range of relationships regulated through a number of mechanisms and their resultant modes of governance.

Our first two chapters provide a range of perspectives to the discussion of types of relationships. Välimaa discusses the changes in national strategies towards self-regulated institutions operating within a diverse system of higher education in terms of the social dynamics of a massified system in postindustrial society. For Välimaa, governmental policy objectives geared to increasing diversity result in vertical stratification between institutions and thus pose significant challenges for the management of universities. Musselin (Chapter 3) then contrasts the relationships that exist within France and within Germany. Continental European countries have ensured that the university was incorporated in the national bureaucracy, with the function of holding together the disparate interests of the disciplinary bases (Neave 1985). However, Musselin's chapter starkly contrasts the relationship between higher education and the state in France with that in Germany. Whilst the latter conforms to the 'norm' for continental systems, the French central administration sustains a trans-university notion of national faculties – thus denying the existence of 'the university' as an entity in its own right. The introduction in France of a contractual policy between the Ministry and higher education aimed to change the relationship, and Musselin concludes that the new policy has resulted in part in the State agencies adopting a more centralised style, albeit with central agencies promoting differentiation among the universities within a national framework.

The UK government's approach to higher education (as evidenced through various policy changes) has shifted from an exchange relationship to a sponsorship-dependency relationship: and we should acknowledge the possible 'range' of sponsors. For example, we cannot talk of the changing nature of the relationship without also considering the changing nature of the relationship between higher education and the world of work. Teichler (Chapter 4), for example, notes that in the 1960s, many countries and their governments believed that a growing investment in higher education would contribute significantly to economic wealth. Thus, government policies relating to higher education have been concerned with macro policies e.g. access to, and size of, overall higher education systems and broad categories of provision. However, we also see (particularly in the UK) government policies becoming concerned with micro policies affecting the style and content of higher education, partly in response to employers' perceptions about the adequacy, or otherwise, of graduates' knowledge, skills and attributes (see Jones and Little Chapter 7).

We have four chapters on the theme of higher education and work. Teichler provides an international overview, analysing the current dynamics in the changing relationships between higher education and the world of work in terms of job prospects for graduates, massification of higher education, growth in the 'knowledge society', rapid technological change and its impact on the structure of industry and services. Whilst acknowledging that the systematic knowledge base of the relationships between higher education and work is limited, he notes that what evidence there is does point in the direction of higher education becoming 'more useful for the world of work', although according to the Humboldtian ideal 'a significant distance might be most productive for society'. He concludes that whilst it is difficult for higher education to strike a balance between links to, and distance from, the world of work, such controversies should not be deplored. Rather what is needed is more in-depth knowledge of the needs of society by all those responsible for higher education. The remaining chapters covering this theme are all UK based. Connor (Chapter 5) addresses the impact of supply changes on graduate employment, and considers the extent and nature of any graduate supply-demand imbalance, especially in terms of qualitative mismatches between the skills and attributes of the graduates being produced and the requirements of employers. Teichler has noted 'the more knowledge becomes a productive force, the more higher education is expected to be evidently productive' (Chapter 4). But this in turn increases concerns about undue instrumental pressures on higher education. Moreover, whilst government policies have focused on macro-policies geared, in part, to expanding higher education systems, such expansion has brought with it concerns about 'overeducation'. Dolton and Vignoles' chapter (Chapter 6) reviews some of the growing literature on graduate (under)utilisation in the labour market and considers whether there is in fact a problem of 'overeducation' in terms of presumed industrial and employment demands.

Others have noted a widespread concern that intellectual enhancement for all and equality of opportunity are being given up for presumed industrial demands (see, for example, Taylor 1997, cited in Teichler Chapter 4). Certainly within the UK, with the publication of the Dearing report, we see a shift in the purposes of higher education towards serving the needs of the economy, in contrast to the purposes identified thirty years previously (when the Robbins committee enquiring into the nature of higher education emphasised the opportunities for individual development). In the final chapter on this higher education and work theme, Jones and Little (Chapter 7) consider particular UK government initiatives which have sought to promote a closer interaction between higher education substantives (i.e. the style and content of the higher education curriculum) and the world of work. At the same time as developments were afoot to move to a position whereby academe would accept learning derived from the workplace as equally valid as that delivered through more traditional processes, the more widespread Enterprise in Higher Education initiative was geared towards pushing the higher education curriculum more towards the values and attitudes of the world of work. Of course, such curriculum development initiatives cannot be seen as forms of control as such.

Our next set of chapters, relating as they do to funding mechanisms, including elements of competition and contracts, are very much about forms of control. In a thought-provoking analysis of the problems of, and policies for, the funding of higher education in the UK, Williams (Chapter 8) provides a multi-dimensional framework in which a range of arguments about the finance of higher education can be assessed.

He ends by identifying the relationship between different forms of funding (transfers to institutions and transfers to students) and different modes of higher education management. He suggests that in the context of mass higher education, governments have reacted against the shortcomings of the collegial and bureaucratic management associated with the channelling of funds to institutions.

The arguments for channelling funds through students and for an associated shift towards market-oriented policies and management are pursued by Barnes. He contends that in this way a benign balance of power between the various stakeholders can be achieved. The autonomy of higher education institutions (a *sine qua non* for their proper functioning, in his view), student choice, diversification and quality in higher education can all be advanced through his proposals. 'Higher education should charge economic fees and government should offset these wholly, mainly or in part by student bursaries which would be linked to the offer of a place and to continued satisfactory progress by a student towards a recognised qualification. Recurrent funding other than for research would be abandoned.' (Chapter 9).

Whilst Barnes argues for market-oriented policies to achieve a balance of power, elsewhere Kogan has noted that '...UK governments have shown considerable mastery of the use of constructive ambiguity, in both maintaining the legal independence of universities whilst creating frames within which independence is functionally constrained' (1996, p.5). The specific mechanisms put in place to fund research activity within universities can be seen as a particular example of such constraints. In his discussion of the impact of the 1992 Research Assessment Exercise in England, McNay (Chapter 10) notes with concern the tendency of such exercises to push institutions in certain directions which might be inimical to other policy directives. In her analysis of the strategic management of research within Swedish universities, Sjölund (Chapter 11) discusses the tension between the university as an autonomous body and controls exercised on that body by external funding agencies, private and public. Increased freedom to attract more resources to a university brings into question the ways in which that university maintains its academic value system and autonomy under such new circumstances. Sjölund's study shows how Swedish universities have sought to create stable and autonomous, yet flexible, organisations.

Research selectivity exercises for distributing public funds are just one example of the evaluative influences currently impacting on higher education institutions. The introduction of national systems and procedures to evaluate, to control and to improve the quality of higher education has been a feature in most European countries in the last few years. Two chapters look specifically at the impact of such systems on academic and institutional life. In Chapter 12, Brennan provides an overview of evaluation of higher education in Europe, exploring the controversies which surround evaluation and quality assessment activities, primarily in terms of the values inherent in such evaluation procedures and the extent to which these values threaten existing academic values. In their comparative study of responses of academe to quality reforms in England and in Sweden, Bauer and Henkel (Chapter 13) note that although institutional structures and strategies have become more critical to the health of higher education, academic values and disciplines remain a formidable force.

Having considered how higher education systems are responding to externally-imposed evaluative mechanisms, we then look more closely at the internal workings of higher education institutions and the effect of government policies on institutional practice. How institutions respond to external changes, and how their responses become structured in terms of internal organisational and power structures is the focus of Kogan's chapter on the interface between academics and administrators (Chapter 14). In discussing their distinctive roles in terms of tasks, values, knowledge and power, Kogan raises a number of issues arising from universities' increasing dependency upon central academic bureaucracies. Smith *et al.* (Chapter 15) note that, internationally, deregulation is being used by governments as a way of promoting new forms of institutional self-regulation which are responsive to the priorities set by government. Within higher education systems, university vice-chancellors occupy a pivotal position between the centrally determined policy framework and the self-governed university. Smith *et al.* examine the changing roles of university vice-chancellors in the UK and discuss the nature of executive leadership in a university setting. They suggest that earlier collegial models of leadership have now been replaced by a new model which emphasises 'managerial skills that are both bureaucratic and entrepreneurial' (Chapter 15). Cuthbert (Chapter 16) then offers a personal perspective on how institutional practice in one UK university has been affected by changes in government higher education policy. He argues that in order to understand the process of change in higher education it is necessary to recognise that institutional management *per se* plays a significant part in making choices and exercising influence at the institutional level.

The dominant theme running throughout the chapters is that of diversity – diversity of institutions, diversity and instability in the graduate labour market, diversity of knowledge production and transmission. Having started the book with a chapter discussing diversity in terms of the social dynamics of a massified system in a postindustrial society, and acknowledging the pivotal role of the institution *per se* as a key point of convergence across European systems of higher education, it is right and proper that we return to a consideration of institutional diversity at the end of our book. Thus, Watson (Chapter 17) takes a look at the discourse on diversity in British higher education, and considers the arguments underlying many of the recommendations set out in the Dearing report with a view to establishing some broad policy dimensions for the higher education system as a whole, against which key institutional types can be identified.

References

Becher, T. and Kogan, M. (1992) *Process and Structure in Higher Education.* London: Routledge.

Bleiklie, I. (1994) *The New Public Management and the Pursuit of Knowledge*, LOS senter Notat 9411, University of Bergen.

Bleiklie, I. (1996) 'Rendering unto Caesar ...: on implementation strategies in academia', Paper presented at the annual CHER conference, Turku, June 27–30, 1996.

Kogan, M. (1996) 'Relationships between higher education and the state: Overview of the issues', Paper presented at ESRC Seminar 15 May 1996. Quality Support Centre/Open University.

Meek, V. Lynn and Wood, F. (1997) *Higher Education Governance and Management: an Australian Study,* Evaluations and Investigations Program, Higher Education Division, Department of Employment, Education, Training and Youth Affairs.

Neave, G. (1985) 'Higher education in a period of consolidation: 1975–1985.' *European Journal of Education 20*, 2–3.

Neave, G. (1996) 'Homogenisation, integration and convergence: the cheshire cats of higher education analysis.' In V.L. Meek, L. Goedegebuure, O. Kivinen and R. Rinne (eds) *The Mockers and the Mocked: Comparative Perspectives on Differentiation, Convergence and Diversity in Higher Education.* Trowbridge: Pergamon and IAU Press.

Neave, G. and van Vught, F. (1991) *Prometheus Bound: The Changing Relationship Between Government and Higher Education in Western Europe.* Trowbridge: Pergamon Press.

Salter, B. and Tapper, T. (1994) *The State and Higher Education.* Essex: The Woburn Press.

Templeman, G. (1982) 'Britain: A Model at risk' CRE-Information (Second Quarter, 1982)

Vincent, A. (1994) 'Conceptions of the state.' In M. Hawkesworth and M. Kogan (eds) *Encyclopaedia of Government and Politics.* London: Routledge, Vol.I.

CHAPTER 2

Managing a Diverse System of Higher Education

Jussi Välimaa

Introduction

Managing a diverse system of higher education is a challenging topic in the sense that both the management and the diversity of the higher education system are multidimensional as social phenomena. I will approach the issue from an academic rather than from a managerialist perspective. The main reason for this approach emerges from the nature of the problem itself. First, there is a need to define the nature of a diverse system and describe the dynamics of differentiation and its counterforce, integration, before we can reflect on its management. In addition, the change of national steering strategies towards self-regulated and autonomous universities needs to be discussed in relation to the social dynamics of a massified higher education system in postindustrial society. Second, after having laid down the foundations for understanding a diverse system, there arises a need to elaborate on what the challenges of management are at the various levels of a higher education system. The chapter is structured accordingly: I will begin with a discussion on the change in the university's social role in postindustrial society. I will then define the main concepts, after which I will discuss management issues in a diverse higher education system.

The change in the university ideal

Pragmatic university ideal

The circumstances of higher education institutions have changed remarkably during the last two decades, changing fundamentally the relationship between higher education institutions and their environment. The most important contextual factor in this change is the massification of higher education systems (Trow 1974). The massification should not, however, be understood only in a mechanical way as a description of the expansion of students, faculty, and higher education institutions, but in a cultural way as a series of multiple modernisations (Scott 1995). The key components of massification are not only the expansion of the system, but also institutional diversity, organisational complexity, and academic heterogeneity (Bargh, Scott, Smith 1996). Therefore, crucial in the massification process is the fundamental change in the social dynamics of higher systems. In the mass higher education system, society (and the government as its representative) as the main funder of higher education has economic, political, and moral justification to use its power to steer national systems of higher education, even though steering itself has become a complex matter because of massification. For the same reasons, the influence of international organisations (like the EU) is less direct. Therefore, massification also indicates an emergence of a new moral code into the relationship between higher education institutions and their environment.

The conditions of knowledge production are, in turn, challenged by the changes in society. The postmodern condition has strengthened the justification for a multiplicity of voices to open up gender and minority perspectives in social sciences and new political dimensions in public life. Furthermore, in postindustrial society new industrial production structures and practices have made enterprises more heavily dependent on the new information technologies (Dill and Sporn 1995; Reich 1991). As to higher education, it has been suggested that a new form of knowledge production is emerging alongside the traditional, familiar one. As Gibbons (1994) and others have suggested, the parameters for the new production of knowledge are set in the context of application, and the nature of research changes into transdisciplinary problem solving that aims at useful outcomes. It seems that even the Humboldtian dichotomies between basic and applied research, that is 'pure' vs. 'dirty', or between theory and practice are no longer adequate. Essentially, they are no longer adequate because the dynamics of knowledge production are different. In a university existing in a social context of application (negotiations, interests, reflexivity) it is not relevant to ask whether research accumulates disciplinary-based knowledge, but whether it is useful for society.

In this environment the traditional Humboldtian idea of the universities orienting outwards from society has met with both a financial and a moral crisis. As a reflection of the new situation, traditional universities are suffering from a lack of public trust and a lack of funding (Bérubé, and Nelson 1995; Fairweather 1996). In the new university frame, which I call the pragmatic university, there is a need to redefine the aims, goals and ethics of research from a new perspective that is not rooted in the Humboldtian ideals of an autonomous university, but in relation to the practical relationship between society, business enterprises and the academic world. In a pragmatic university the relationship between universities and society as well as the dynamics of knowledge production are more strongly interconnected than in the traditional Humboldtian university, because disciplinary principles (Toulmin 1992) are challenged by practical orientations of higher education institutions. Externally, the changes in the university–society relationship reflect on the idea that the social role of universities is seen in economic terms as part of the industrial production of the advanced nations. Pragmatic universities are expected to be productive and efficient higher education institutions with high social accountability and quality of education. Internally, the changes in the university–society relationship have influenced the conditions of academic work creating new dynamics in knowledge production.

In addition to these changes in the production of knowledge the clienteles of higher education institutions have multiplied. According to Burton Clark (1995), 'mass, even universal, access in place or on its way means that not only are there more students but more different types of students'. Following the same rationale, there are not only more graduates going on to the job market, 'but more different types of graduates are being prepared for more diverse occupational specialities' (Clark 1995).

Policy change: from central steering to self-regulation

The steering policy of higher education systems has changed from centrally planned steering towards self-regulated universities since the 1980s. According to Neave 'the central tenet of legal homogeneity' helped the normalising state to ensure equity and equality of higher education, but it made system changes difficult, because the change had to be equally and systematically spread across the entire system. This seems to be one of the main reasons why many European countries have engaged in the deregulation of higher education systems. During this process the previous principle of legal homogeneity has given way to performance conditionality (Neave 1996). As to steering instruments, governments have emphasised the use of economic incentives. This way the power of the purse has been strengthened at the cost of steering through legislation. The evaluative state, in turn, in its firm ideological belief in the blessing of deregulation and market forces has been convinced that these together will provide more stimulus to institutions to innovate and find a particular niche in a more competitive higher education market (Meek *et al.* 1996). Marketisation has been used to describe this development of a more competitive environment within higher education. At the system level it refers to governmental policies to build up a market-like culture and resource allocation systems, whereas at the institutional level it refers to competitive behaviour that has been stimulated between and within institutions (Bargh *et al.* 1996).

In the cultural contexts of massification and marketisation the processes of differentiation and diversification of higher education are looked upon favourably, because it is assumed that a diverse higher education system will be more responsive to a variety of social needs and expectations. Furthermore, it is normally assumed that market mechanisms are a good way to increase the diversity in and among higher education institutions. However, before we can proceed with the analysis we need to stop and discuss more deeply the intellectual devices referred to in the above: differentiation, diversification, and diversity.

Contextualising differentiation, diversification, diversity, and integration

The differences between the concepts of differentiation, diversification, and diversity have been analysed by Huisman (1995). According to Huisman, differentiation and diversification are processes in which variation and difference increase in a given (biological) system. Diversity, in turn, is their measurement at any particular point in time. Thus, differentiation and diversification are dynamic concepts, whereas diversity is a static one. These definitions can be traced back to the biological sciences, and especially to Darwin's theories on the development of species. After having analysed the intellectual history of these concepts, Huisman correctly notes that these concepts are not easy to use in higher education studies, even though they have been used (and abused) in a number of studies. The main theoretical difficulties are related to the fact that these biological concepts would require the use of other biological concepts (species, organisms, biological structures and functions) which are, however, irrelevant or impossible in the social sciences (Huisman 1995, in Goedegebuure *et al.* 1995).

Huisman is convincing in his analysis of the contents of the concepts. The author becomes, however, less convincing when he analyses the reasons why these originally biological concepts have not been utilised in empirical social research. The main problem with the author's analysis is that he focuses his attention on the (biological) roots of concepts and not on their relationship with the social phenomena which they aim to explain in social sciences. Therefore, these concepts become more like metaphors than intellectual devices to be used in the analysis of society, or a part of it. It seems that we easily miss the point if we are interested in the metaphorical use of concepts instead of understanding the nature of the problem that required their development. As to differentiation, we should not only follow the biological roots of this concept, but analyse why and how it was taken into use in social sciences, and especially how Emile Durkheim introduced it into the social sciences (Durkheim 1984). According to Collins (1994) Durkheim's basic question was: What holds society together? In order to answer this question he explained the nature of social change with the help of two interconnected social forces: differentiation and solidarity. In this sociological analysis the processes of both differentiation and integration are important and interconnected because they explain the same phenomenon: social change (Giddens 1995). Huisman, however, does not seem to get to this point, because he is mainly interested in differentiation, diversification, and diversity as independent (biological) concepts that should be operationalised in empirical research (Huisman 1995). In the Durkheimian sociological tradition, these concepts were not used to explain the evolution of societies as species, but to explain what kind of social forces have produced cohesion in societies in different historical periods. Therefore, despite the similarities in the concepts, the biological and sociological reasons for using these concepts have been very different. In the Durkheimian tradition, differentiation and integration have been used as intellectual devices to explain the emergence of a modern society, whereas in the biological sciences they have been used to understand the evolution of life through natural selection.

The interconnectedness of the processes of differentiation and integration has been noted by other authors as well. Burton Clark has illustrated and explained this interplay in national systems of higher education. In answering the Durkheimian basic question, Clark has defined integrative social forces in higher education with the help of three ideal types: market, state, and academic oligarchy (Clark 1983). These categories are useful, for as Williams (1995) has stated, 'Clark's triangle' is not just a model to describe the claims of competing interest groups, but also a representation of different value systems and different ideas of higher education. In addition, Guy Neave (1996) has drawn attention to the fact that the increase of differentiation in higher education challenges the social forces of integration and vice versa, noting that it is 'a continual process of oscillation between the polar extremes', as Meek *et al.* (1996) have interpreted him.

The causes of differentiation

In modern higher education research there seem to be two different but complementary theoretical perspectives to explain the causes of differentiation (see Meek *et al.* 1996). According to the traditional one, developed by Burton Clark, the expansion of knowledge is the engine of differentiation in the academic world. It leads to an increase of new disciplines and academic fields and to the specialisation, and consequently, to the fragmentation of the academic profession, challenging the forces of integration. In this way Clark's ideas follow the Durkheimian rationale: the increase of knowledge leads to the division of labour, and the division of labour is the source of differentiation. Therefore, differentiation on the disciplinary dimension is 'arguably many times greater than differentiation on the institutional dimension', as Clark (1996) puts it. It has also been noted that there is a relationship between the internal dynamic of knowledge production and the way in which modern society pursues knowledge. This internal dynamic inevitably results in subject specialisation and disciplinary fragmentation (Meek *et al.* 1996). These processes are, quite naturally, neither automatic nor purely academic, because governments may influence, and have influenced, these processes through higher education policy making.

Another contribution to the analysis of a diverse system is a combination of three organisational theories: population ecology, the resource dependency perspective, and institutional isomorphism (van Vught 1996). The author compiles different organisational theories beginning with the assumption that universities and other higher education institutions may be defined as an open system that is continuously in interaction with the environment in terms of resource inputs (students, faculty, money, etc.) and product outputs (services, research results, graduates etc.). Through this interaction institutions are tied to society economically, politically and locally as well as nationally. Useful in this frame of analysis is also the notion that resource competition is an essential part of the relationship between higher education institutions and their environment (van Vught 1996). Differentiation is, in turn, caused by higher education institutions' attempts to adapt to their environment through finding their own niche in a market-like situation (Meek *et al.* 1996).

To sum up the above discussion I will define a diverse system of higher education in relation to the massification of higher education. A modern, diverse higher education system is a complex system that consists of many higher education institutions with extensive and heterogeneous student populations, large number of academics, and an increasing number of disciplines and academic fields. It is characterised by a variety of tasks and social responsibilities as well as simultaneous interplay between the forces of differentiation and integration. For these reasons whether the structure of a national higher education system bears the label of a unified, stratified, binary, or dual system (Teichler 1988) is not critical. What is critical is that all systems are responses to complexity as Scott (1995) puts it. From the perspective of management the diverse systems consist of a variety of professional norms and values and of complex organisational structures with different organisational models coexisting like archaeological layers (Bargh *et al.* 1996; Becher, Henkel, Kogan 1994).

Differentiation and marketisation as policy goals

I have briefly referred to different theoretical approaches that explain why higher education systems differentiate both through the expansion of knowledge leading to specialisation and through adaptation to their environments. For policy makers, diversity appears normally as a positive and favourable goal, because it is supposed that a diverse system can more easily respond to various societal needs and expectations. The shift from central steering to self-regulation ideas makes it easy to assume that diversity increases the range of choices for students, opens up higher education to all of society, provides social mobility, enables and protects specialisation, and meets the demands of an increasingly complex social order (Birnbaum 1983; Stadtman 1980 in Goedegebuure *et al.* 1996).

Supporting the diversity of national higher education systems seems to have been one of the most important goals of western policy makers during the last decade (Goedegebuure *et al.* 1996). Normally policy makers assume that market mechanisms are the optimal way to increase the diversity in the national systems. The evaluative state has created these market forces through competition for bonus money and research funding which are more or less connected with quality assessments (Meek and O'Neill 1996; Fulton 1996). This suggests that the idea of competition is both a steering instrument and a policy objective.

Together with the change in the strategies of public policy making, the practices of policy-making have found support in liberal ethics rooted in the firm belief that competition will make public institutions more efficient. However, there are both practical and theoretical problems with this kind of neo-liberal argument, because there exists no single market in higher education but many (Clark 1983). In addition to this traditional notion, a serious theoretical problem is caused by the fact that there are no 'natural' market forces in many fields of public institutions, including the traditional European higher education system. Therefore, governments have faced the need to create (or play) market forces (Dean 1997). The role of the state is, however, problematic because essentially the state is a moral community ensuring principles of social behaviour through laws and norms more than an economic community aiming at making a profit. Therefore, governments may adopt different policies, and consequently, depending on policy goals, they may have many different roles as a market force in the higher education field. Relying on Clark's 'triangle of tension', Williams has defined four different roles the state may play in the higher education field (Williams 1995). First, the state may be a 'referee mediating between the opposing forces of supply and demand, ensuring fair play. Alternatively, the state may see its role as that of promoter of the game. It provides the facilities and sets the rules in order to achieve some purpose that transcends the market.' Third, the state may 'throw its weight behind the consumers, or again, in the extreme case, it may act as a monopsony buyer of higher education services acting as a single proxy consumer' (Williams 1995, pp.172–173). Theoretically, this provides one example of the principal-agent problem as formulated by economists. Namely, as Williams (1995) has put it, it is the question of: how does the principal, the government, get the agents, the higher education institutions, to carry out its wishes?

I suggest that this theoretical principal-agent problem has resulted in national policies in which official rhetoric (increasing institutional autonomy through deregulation) and actual politics (decreasing institutional autonomy through the power of the purse) strongly contest each other. Consequently, the social environment for higher education institutions has become uncertain and unpredictable because the use of competition as a steering instrument does not say anything about the criteria used. Depending on the policy objectives, the criteria may vary from year to year. And they do vary, as the British (Fulton 1996), the Australian (Meek and O'Neill 1996), and the Finnish experience show. As a result, institutions try to predict governmental policies in order to be able to profit from the criteria used in the future (Fulton 1996).

It seems that the use of competition as a steering instrument does, in fact, reinforce hierarchical stratification between institutions instead of promoting diversity in the national systems. This way the policy aiming to promote differentiation easily changes into the policy promoting stratification. In Kogan's definition, stratification refers to 'the differences in levels as typified by purposes, status and resources between institutions' (Kogan 1996). It seems that governments that have declared their intention to be more selective in funding research to support quality and efficiency (and to promote differentiation) do not see, or want to see, that they most probably end in supporting and creating stratification in the system.

In addition to national policies, the internal processes of the higher education system follow their own dynamics. According to empirical research, institutions imitate the most successful institutions in an uncertain and unpredictable environment. This imitating behaviour may bring convergence and integration into national higher education systems. Academic drift, thus, works towards integration, resisting governmental policies promoting diversification (Meek and O'Neill 1996). In addition, Fulton (1996) has pointed out that a differentiated higher education system will not exist, if a unified value system exists. Referring to the British case he suggests that polytechnics and universities shared a unified value system that led polytechnics to imitate the structures and functions of universities, which, in consequence, led to the discontinuation of the binary system. In the UK, government policies have strengthened stratification in the system profiting the leading research universities. 'The sharpest example of government funding reinforcing stratification is indeed UK' (Kogan 1996).

For these reasons the processes of differentiation and policies promoting stratification are closely tied together. For the purposes of this chapter I will not make a clear distinction between differentiation and stratification, because from the perspective of institutional management these processes together reinforce marketisation, creating a socially unpredictable environment for pragmatic universities.

Management in a diverse environment

So far I have described the parameters for institutions existing in a postindustrial society, where governments have put their faith in increasing institutional autonomy through deregulation, and in national steering based on market-like mechanisms normally manifested in competition. In return societies are expecting higher education institutions to be more efficient with improved quality and higher input for the national economies. Massification and marketisation characterise the reality in which most Western higher education institutions and systems are functioning or towards which they are moving. In this kind of postindustrial, postmodern, and mass higher education system, unpredictability and uncertainty are the best known environmental parameters for higher education institutions.

In the following I will try to change my perspective from that of a critical academic to a more managerial approach. In this section my task is to reflect on the challenges met by, and the instruments applied by, management at the various levels of a higher education system. Management, in my vocabulary, represents the interest of knowledge that focuses attention on uniformity in institutional practices and on efficiency in academic actions. In this sense, it represents an integrative social force in the academic world. The levels described by Becher and Kogan will structure my analysis (Becher and Kogan 1992). I will utilise this model as an ideal type of a massified Western higher education system in a postindustrial and postmodern environment.

1. Central authority

In the Western countries, the main challenge for central authorities is to create or simulate market structures in higher education (Dill 1997). Normally, the promotion of competition is the way to simulate market-like behaviour. In this way the idea of competition is both a steering instrument and a policy objective. The normal policy instruments consist of economic incentives, quality assurance agencies, and understanding students as a market force.

Incentives

Incentives may be based on selectivity in research funding, where institutions are rewarded on the basis of their research performance. The extreme example is provided by the UK. Another form of incentives is the institutional bonus money through which the central authority rewards institutional performance on the basis of academic output. In Finland the main indicator is the output of academic degrees (Välimaa 1994).

Quality assurance agencies

Quality and efficiency of higher education are the catchwords adopted by most governments, and normally they are also interconnected. From the perspective of management it seems to be true that quality assessment improves institutional efficiency. Most governments (over 70 in 1997) have thought it important to establish or support national quality assessment agencies (Brennan 1997). In the evaluative state these agencies serve as instruments in national higher education policy making, because they provide information on the quality of education and research. For central authorities this is very relevant information. Quality assessment agencies may be directly connected with the funding of higher education (Australia) or research (UK), or their connection may be less direct (The Netherlands, Finland).

Students as a market force

The definition of students as a market force is related to quality assessment agencies through the issue of the quality of academic programmes. Therefore, as a steering challenge, central authorities may foster market competition by providing students with sufficient information through programme quality assessments. In addition to these instruments, governments have strong influence on institutional behaviour through student support systems, as Fulton (1996) and Williams (1995) have discussed.

2. Institutions

The use of competition as a steering instrument in the simulation of market forces has had serious consequences for the management of higher education institutions. According to Williams (1995) changes in the mechanisms of public funding have had more impact on the marketisation of higher education than changes in the sources of funding. In addition, the funding lines of higher education institutions have multiplied, causing new challenges to money allocations inside the institutions as well. Consequently, the environment of higher education institutions has become more competition-oriented. Especially in countries like UK, Australia and Finland, where the funding of basic functions is (or will be) separated from the funding of research, it has created more unpredictability and uncertainty for the institutions. The unpredictability of institutional environments has, in turn, created challenges to create university structures that emphasise flexibility and adaptability (Dill and Sporn 1995b). This challenges the institutional leadership as well, because 'to live in the market and to focus on comprehensiveness requires more local organisation and more local leadership than exist under strong state control', as Clark (1995) puts it. In addition to changes in the environment of institutions, the internal dynamics of higher education institutions are changing. According to an international survey, the differences among disciplinary departments and other basic units are growing (Clark 1993 in Clark 1995). These developments require, in turn, strategic decisions at the institutional level, because in the market-like environment there can be both losers and winners (Clark 1995).

According to Dill and Sporn (1995b), the 'network' university seems to be the most promising solution for a university struggling for survival in circumstances of high competition and complexity. Network organisation provides an efficient way to manage exchange in an organisation. As a result, in a network university, management has greater flexibility and adaptability. Strategic choices between programmes and activities will increase efficiency and reduce costs. Decision making, in turn, aims at vertical and horizontal integration in addition to decentralised decision-making structures. The authors believe that a network university would allow the exchange of 'thick information' and creates the best potential for adaptability and innovation (Dill and Sporn 1995b).

These changes are already taking place in universities. In a study conducted at the University of Jyväskylä, we noted that the ideal type of 'good administration' has changed during the 1990s (Välimaa, Aittola, Konttinen 1997). Before the 1990s the aim of good administration was to maintain the status quo: everything should follow the old routines, whereas the 'new' mode of administration, or rather management, stresses ability to change. The old administrative ideals emphasised steering based on obedience to laws and statutes, whereas new management is more interested in steering the institution through money allocations. The old administration mode was strongly hierarchical, whereas the new ideal stresses flexibility, reactive, and dynamic elements. It is also more willing to start new projects and carry out faster development projects. Naturally, the description of the above ideal types does not necessarily indicate that radical changes have occurred in the daily routines. However, being faithful to the Weberian idea of ideal types (Sadri 1994) it means that the aims of good management have changed towards more reflective and flexible ideas. In this sense, the complexity and unpredictability of a political, economic and social environment has set new parameters for both internal administration and management.

Whether the new university will be called a network university or something else remains to be seen. However, institutions need to respond to the new challenges to be able to interact with their environment successfully. Important challenges in this adaptation are: how to cooperate with private enterprises; how to find new clientele (normally students); and how to find new funding sources.

3. Basic units

Managing basic units as they adapt to new circumstances meets somewhat different challenges. The most important new dimension is created by the institutional framework. Basic units face competition and cooperation challenges with other basic units inside their own university and with other disciplinary-based basic units nationwide and sometimes even globally. This situation leads to competition and cooperation locally, nationally, and, indeed, globally to secure sufficient resources in the competition with other discipline-based units. It also requires the creation of attractive profiles both in teaching (to attract new students) and in research (to get research grants).

According to Hill and Turpin (1995), within higher education institutions the societal slogans of quality and efficiency have been introduced to basic units with the help of a new managerial style. This style which emphasises cost-efficiency, productivity and quality of academic institutions, may be called managerial culture. Essential is that the new managerial culture challenges the disciplinary principles in basic units. These are, in turn, strongly related to academic cultures and the territories that academic tribes inhabit (Becher 1989). Hill and Turpin (1995) maintain that managerial culture changes the dynamics of the academic communities and the influences on preconditions of academic work, and thus, knowledge production. Therefore, an essential challenge seems to be: how to secure the academic quality of research and teaching?

4. Individuals

In a pragmatic university, the traditional categories of researcher and teacher based on academic work of researching and teaching are no longer sufficient, because academics have had to develop multidimensional working profiles (Clark 1993, in Clark 1995). In the new environment academics need to take into account the selling of their expertise in the market place inside and outside universities. Therefore, marketing and consultation are becoming more important. I maintain that the change of the content of work also influences the understanding of oneself as an academic and influences the academic identities (Välimaa 1995); it seems that salesman and consultant are new additions to the traditional titles of teacher or researcher.

At the individual level, therefore, the changes in the environment set new parameters for academic identity. In the postindustrial, postmodern, massified, and pragmatic circumstances, the criteria for academic expertise emphasise the ability to adopt a multiple personality rather than sticking to the traditional *habitus* of an academic. In this sense it is parallel to what postmodern writers have described as nomadic identities. This contains positive elements as well. As Bauman (1996) has noted, 'the modern "problem of identity" was how to construct an identity and keep it solid and stable, the postmodern "problem of identity" is primarily how to avoid fixation and keep the options open'.

Conclusions

There is no doubt that during the recent decade governments around the globe have put their trust in market forces. According to Meek and O'Neill, 'policy makers seem to believe that market-like competition rather than centralised state control makes the conduct of higher education more efficient and effective' (Meek and O'Neill 1996). This policy change may be interpreted as a reaction to former welfare state policy that aimed at securing equity and equality through central planning. In the neo-liberal critique central steering is seen as bureaucratic and inefficient (Dean 1997). It may also be defined as an attempt to make national higher education systems more responsive to the needs of society. In both regards increasing diversity has been seen as an essential policy objective. However, it seems that this policy objective is hard to reach with the help of the policy instruments applied, because in addition to increasing diversity it increases stratification between institutions. As Fulton has pointed out, we have 'the makings of an institutional hierarchy – a system of vertical stratification – which can and easily does militate against the kind of horizontal diversity, the wide range of institutional missions, that a diversified mass student market presumably needs' (Fulton 1996).

In this chapter I have tried to reflect on what kind of requirements these contradictions in policy making and the changes in the environment have set to the management of higher education institutions. What seems to be important is that the relationship between higher education institutions and society emphasises reflexivity which 'in political terms means accountability rather than autonomy, and, in the context of markets, interaction rather than insulation', as Scott (1995) puts it. Simultaneously, universities are developing as open intellectual systems in close interaction with society at large. The most important challenges for the management of pragmatic universities are twofold: first, there is a constant need to predict both governmental policies and changes in the environment, and second, management should ensure the academic foundations of relevant research in order to be able to show good performance both in research and teaching.

References

Bauman, Z. (1996) 'From pilgrim to tourist – or a short history of identity.' In S. Hall and P. du Gay (eds) *Questions of Cultural Identity*. London: Sage.

Bargh, C., Scott, P. and Smith, D. (1996) *Governing Universities. Changing the Culture?* Bury St Edmunds: SRHE & Open University Press.

Becher, T. (1989) *Academic Tribes and Territories, Intellectual Enquiry and the Cultures of Disciplines*. Bury St Edmunds: SRHE & Open University Press.

Becher, T. and Kogan, M. (1992) *Process and Structure in Higher Education*. London and New York: Routledge.

Becher, T., Henkel, M. and Kogan, M. (1994) *Graduate Education in Britain*. Higher Education Policy Series 17. London: Jessica Kingsley.

Bérubé, M. and Nelson, G. (1995) 'Introduction: a report from the front.' In M. Bérubé and G. Nelson (eds) *Higher Education Under Fire*. New York: Routledge.

Birnbaum, R. (1983) *Maintaining Diversity in Higher Education*. San Francisco: Jossey-Bass.

Brennan, J. (1997) 'Authority, legitimacy and change: the rise of quality assessment in higher education.' *Higher Education Management 9*, 1, 7–29.

Clark, B.R. (1983) *The Higher Education System, Academic Organisations in Cross-National Perspective*. Berkeley and Los Angeles: University of California Press.

Clark, B.R. (1993) *The Research Foundations of Graduate Education: Germany, Britain, France, United States, Japan*. Berkeley: University of California Press.

Clark, B.R. (1995) 'Complexity and differentiation: the deepening problem of university integration.' In D.D. Dill and B. Sporn (eds) *Emerging Patterns of Social Demand and University Reform: Through a Glass Darkly*. Trowbridge: IAU Press and Pergamon.

Clark, B.R. (1996) 'Diversification of higher education: viability and change.' In V. Lynn Meek and L. Goedegebuure, O. Kivihen and R. Rinne (eds) *The Mockers and Mocked: Comparative Perspectives on Differentiation, Convergence and Diversity in Higher Education*. Guildford: Pergamon and IAU Press.

Collins, R. (1994) *Four Sociological Traditions*. New York and Oxford: Oxford University Press.

Dean, M. (1997) *Neo-Liberalism as Counter-Enlightenment Cultural Critique. A Contribution to the Symposium on the Displacement of Social Policies.* University of Jyväskylä, Finland, January 1997.

Dill, D.D. (1997) *Evaluating the 'Evaluative State': Implications for Research in Higher Education.* Keynote Address presented at the CHER Conference, Alicante, Spain, 18–20 September 1997.

Dill, D.D. and Sporn, B. (1995) 'The implications of a postindustrial environment for the university: an introduction.' In D.D. Dill and B. Sporn (eds) *Emerging Patterns of Social Demand and University Reform: Through a Glass Darkly.* Trowbridge: IAU Press and Pergamon.

Dill, D.D. and Sporn, B. (1995b) 'University 2001: what will the university of the twenty-first century look like?' In D.D. Dill and B. Sporn (eds) *Emerging Patterns of Social Demand and University Reform: Through a Glass Darkly.* Trowbridge: IAU Press and Pergamon.

Durkheim, E. (1984) *The Division of Labour in Society.* With an introduction by Lewis Coser, translated by W.D. Halls. Hong Kong: Macmillan.

Fairweather, J.S. (1996) *Faculty Work and Public Trust. Restoring the Value of Teaching and Public Service in American Academic Life.* Boston: Allyn and Bacon.

Fulton, O. (1996) 'Differentiation and diversity in a newly unitary system: the case of the UK.' In V.L. Meek and L. Goedegebuure, O. Kivinen, R. Rinne (eds) *The Mockers and the Mocked: Comparative Perspectives on Differentiation, Convergence and Diversity in Higher Education.* Guildford: IAU Press and Pergamon.

Gibbons, M., Limoges, C., Nowotny, H., Schwartzman, S., Scott, P. and Trow, M. (1994) *The New Production of Knowledge.* London: Thousand Oaks, New Delhi: Sage.

Giddens, A. Introduction. In A. Giddens, (ed) *Emile Durkheim: Selected Writings.* New York: Cambridge University Press (first published 1972).

Goedegebuure, L., Meek, V.L., Kivinen, O. and Rinne, R. (1996) 'On diversity, differentiation and convergence.' In V.L. Meek, L. Goedegebuure, O. Kivinen and R. Rinne (eds) *The Mockers and the Mocked: Comparative Perspectives on Differentiation, Convergence and Diversity in Higher Education.* Guildford: IAU Press and Pergamon.

Hill, S. and Turpin, T. (1995) 'Cultures in collision: the emergence of a new localism in academic research.' In M. Strathern (ed) *Shifting Contexts, Transformations in Anthropological Knowledge.* London and New York: Routledge.

Huisman, J. (1995) *Differentiation, Diversity and Dependency in Higher Education.* Utrecht: Lemma.

Kogan, M. (1996) 'Diversification in higher education: differences and commonalities.' In J.-P. Liljander (ed) *Erilaistuva Korkeakoulutus* (Differentiation in Higher Education). Jyväskylä: Institute for Educational Research.

Meek, V.L. and O'Neill, A. (1996) 'Diversity and differentiation in the Australian unified national system of higher education.' In V.L. Meek, L. Goedegebuure, O. Kivinen and R. Rinne (eds) *The Mockers and the Mocked: Comparative Perspectives on Differentiation, Convergence and Diversity in Higher Education.* Guildford: Pergamon and IAU Press.

Meek, V.L., Goedegebuure, L., Kivinen, O. and Rinne, R. (1996) 'Conclusion.' In V.L. Meek, L. Goedegebuure, O. Kivinen and R. Rinne (eds) *The Mockers and the Mocked: Comparative Perspectives on Differentiation, Convergence and Diversity in Higher Education.* Guildford: IAU Press and Pergamon.

Neave, G. (1996) 'Homogenization, integration and convergence: the Cheshire cats of higher education analysis.' In V.L. Meek, L. Goedegebuure, O. Kivinen and R. Rinne (eds) *The Mockers and the Mocked: Comparative Perspectives on Differentiation, Convergence and Diversity in Higher Education.* Guildford: Pergamon and IAU Press.

Reich, R. (1991) *The Work of Nations: Preparing Ourselves For 21st Century Capitalism.* New York: Alfred A. Knopf.

Sadri, A. (1994) *Max Weber's Sociology of Intellectuals.* New York & Oxford: Oxford University Press.

Scott, P. (1995) *The Meanings of Mass Higher Education.* Bury St Edmunds: SRHE & Open University Press.

Stadtman, V.A. (1980) *Academic Adaptations: Higher Education Prepares for the 1980s and 1990s.* San Francisco: Jossey-Bass.

Teichler, U. (1988) *Changing Patterns of the Higher Education System. The Experience of Three Decades.* Higher Education Policy Series 5. London: Jessica Kingsley.

Trow, M.A. (1974) 'Problems in the transition from élite to mass higher education.' In *Policies for higher education.* Conference of Future Structures of post-Secondary Education. Paris.

Toulmin S. (1992) *Cosmopolis, The Hidden Agenda of Modernity.* Chicago: The University of Chicago Press.

Välimaa, J. (1994) 'A trying game: experiments and reforms in Finnish higher education.' *European Journal of Education 29,* 2, 149–163.

Välimaa, J. (1995) *Higher Education Cultural Approach. Jyväskylä Studies in Education, Psychology and Social Research.* Jyväskylä: University of Jyväskylä.

Välimaa, J., Aittola, T. and Konttinen, R. (1997) 'The impacts of quality assessment: the case of Jyväskylä University.' Accepted for publication in the *Higher Education Management.*

Van Vught, F. (1996) 'Isomorphism in higher education? Towards a theory of differentiation and diversity in higher education systems.' In V.L. Meek, L.

Goedegebuure, O. Kivinen and R. Rinne (eds) *The Mockers and the Mocked: Comparative Perspectives on Differentiation, Convergence and Diversity in Higher Education*. Guildford: Pergamon and IAU Press.

Williams, G. (1995) 'The marketization of higher education: reforms and potential reforms in higher education finance.' In D.D. Dill and B. Sporn (eds) *Emerging Patterns of Social Demand and University Reform: Through a Glass Darkly*. Trowbridge: IAU Press and Pergamon.

CHAPTER 3

State/University Relations and How to Change Them

The Case of France and Germany

Christine Musselin

Introduction

This chapter will focus on the issue of steering higher education in public systems. First, we shall present some of the results of the empirical studies we carried out in France and Germany at the end of the 1980s and in the early 1990s on the bodies that are responsible for higher education. We shall thus be able to show that there is a specific (national) type of relation between the state bodies and the universities in each country and that it differs greatly. Hence, we shall argue that state/universities interactions have national bases that must not be seen in terms of culture, but rather as societal (in the sense of Maurice *et al.* 1982) constructions of relationships.

Yet, even if rather stable modes of regulation can be found in these interactions, changes may occur. In the second part, we shall present a policy developed in France, as from 1989, to change the nature of the relations between the state and the universities by funding through negotiation (*contractualisation*) certain exchanges between the different partners. We shall use these recent French developments to reflect on how higher education systems may be changed.

Steering higher education in France (before 1989) and in Germany

Erhard Friedberg and I came to the issue of the intervention of the state in higher education after a first comparative empirical study of two French and two German universities in which we examined the relations between the faculty members and the administration, and the ways in which decisions were taken (especially by the official university bodies), and resources were allocated. First, our findings showed that German professors identified strongly with their institutions and considered their university as an entity to which they were committed and loyal. This is much less the case with French academics. Second, German decision-making committees are much more respected than their French counterparts. They are indeed 'able' to take decisions, to ask for changes, or even, in some cases, to reject a project proposed by the departments.

One of the explanations we found for these differences was the way in which faculty are recruited. In Germany, the recruitment of a professor leads to bargaining procedures[1] that mainly concern the amount of resources the professor will receive for teaching and research. In other words, the university invests in a faculty member and, in return, the latter is more committed to his institution. Hence, we stated that the types of relations that exist between the university and the academic profession (as a market-place) influence the internal functioning of the university structures (Musselin 1987; Friedberg and Musselin 1989a, b).

This led to a second wave of field work. If there is close interaction between the university and the faculty, then state intervention in higher education has to deal with this dual aspect: universities on the one side, and the academic profession on the other. This is why we studied the French and German state bodies responsible for steering higher education: the central administration in France and the Land agencies in Germany. We therefore carried out a first study on the French bodies in 1987 and the same study in 1988 and 1989 in regional Ministries (*Landministerium fur Wissenschaft und Kunst*) in Germany and then compared the two (Friedberg and Musselin 1992, 1993; Musselin *et al.* 1993; Musselin 1992).

---

1   Negotiations for the recruitment of new faculty take place at three levels. First, with the recruiting university, second with the minister of the Land (of the recruiting university), and last with the candidate's own university.

Brief presentation of the competencies of state bodies responsible for higher education in France and Germany

Having given the background to this empirical work, we shall now very briefly describe the state bodies in France and Germany to stress the differences between the two countries.

In France, the *loi de décentralisation* of 1982 did not concern higher education, which remained under the control of the state. No responsibilities were given to the local governments yet, the latter pay great attention to higher education and are intervening to a greater extent in the financing of higher education (Filâtre 1993), despite the 1982 law! In 1987, when we carried out our first study, universities were under the direct responsibility of the Ministry for Research and Higher Education. The management of French universities was entrusted to five directorates, overseen by a general directorate (DGESR, General Directorate for Higher Education and Research): the DESUP (Directorate for Higher Education) whose two main functions were the agreement on curricula (*habilitation*) leading to national diplomas[2] and the planning of the development of universities; the DPES (Directorate for Higher Education Staff); the SAF (Service for Administration and Budgets) that allocated financial resources based on impersonal criteria[3]; the DR (Directorate for Research)[4]; and the Directorate for University Libraries.

In Germany, responsibility for higher education is shared between the Federal State (*Bund*) and the local States (*Länder*). The first defines the general framework whereby the *Länder* can develop their regional law on higher education. The *Bund* is also involved 50 per cent

---

2   In France, most diplomas are 'national'. When a faculty member wants to create a new course that will be sanctioned by a national diploma (for instance, a DEUG, a Licence or a Maîtrise), he must write a project and submit it to the Ministry which then decides if it corresponds to the model that defines the minimal content of a specific type of diploma in a specific subdiscipline. This course is then habilité (officially agreed upon). This is the procedure we shall call habilitation in this article.

3   The budget allocated to the universities was calculated through a programme allocation process called GARACES. For a precise description of this process and a critical analysis of its effects, see the report by Y. Fréville (1981). A more positive description of GARACES was given in an article written by one of its main instigators, G. Allain (1986).

4   It only deals with 'purely' university research, as opposed to research carried out in institutes which are part of national research institutions, such as the CNRS, INRA, INSERM.

in the decisions and in the funding of new buildings, new campuses and heavy science equipment. But each *Land* is responsible for the allocation of budgets and positions and for agreements on new curricula. It is also involved in the recruitment of professors. The formal structures of each *Landministerium für Wissenschaft und Kunst* differ but, in addition to the classic responsibilities, such as 'staff', 'budgeting', 'higher training' and 'research activities', there is a division between administrators called *Hochschulreferenten* (literally 'university correspondents'), who are responsible for a specific university and who act as 'go-betweens' with the Ministry, and the universities.

Hoping that this brief overview of the formal structure in each country will suffice, we shall now summarise the main results of our field work in both countries.

A logic by discipline in France; a logic by organisation (university) in Germany

In the first research we carried out on universities, we stressed the weak governing ability of French universities (Musselin 1987; Friedberg and Musselin 1989a). The study of state bodies led us to the conclusion that this weakness was somewhat reinforced by a central administration that 'denied' the existence of 'universities' in France. The formal structure of the Ministry, internal procedures, the relations between the different offices and between the directorates split the universities into different problem areas (training, staff, budgeting, research, libraries) and, within these, into disciplines (thus, for instance, in the DPES, one office was responsible for the faculty staff in humanities, the other for the faculty staff in science). Nowhere was a university considered as an entity. In this fragmented structure, the dominating logic of action (except in the DR which had its own logic) was based on the *habilitation* of curricula: resources to be allocated (present or future) were calculated according to the *habilitations* of diplomas and budget increases were generally based on the creation of new curricula. As the procedures for these *habilitations* were discipline-based, the calculation of the budgets was also discipline-based. Therefore, to reflect on the university as a whole made no sense, when reasoning by disciplines and cycles[5] was the norm. In a way, except for the resources based on square metres, a university budget was no more than the sum of the resources allocated (through bureaucratic criteria) to each curriculum after *habilitation*.

Conversely, universities in Germany are fairly integrated organisations, with a stronger institutional position[6], and are considered true partners by the Ministry. The *Hochschulreferent* plays a crucial role in interactions between the ministry offices and the university. He has usually known 'his' university for many years and, when the president presents him with a project that has been agreed upon by the university decision-making committees, he defends it before the other ministry offices[7] that manage the necessary resources (research funds, budget, positions). He also 'transmits' the ministry policy to the university. He is where the different aspects of university management converge. The logic of the disciplines is therefore much weaker than in France.

Administration and the academic profession

A second important difference between the two countries lies in the interplay between the state and the academic profession in decision making.

The description above of the French system corresponds to the traditional representation of France as a centralised country. And so it is. But centralisation does not mean that the state bodies are in a strong position. In fact, most of the crucial decisions taken by the central administration (i.e. decisions concerning the *habilitation* of curricula,

5   In France, university studies are divided into three cycles. The first lasts two years and generally leads to the DEUG. The second also lasts two years: the first year leads to the Licence and the second to the Maîtrise. Then, students may enter a third cycle of studies, generally in order to obtain a DESS or a DEA after a further year's study. If they obtain the latter, they are entitled to study for a doctorate.

6   In German universities there is not the competition of the grandes ecoles in training the élites. They still follow the Humboldtian tradition (while French universities have only existed in their present form since 1969) and are less fragmented than the French universities.

7   We should of course nuance this for each Land we studied. In Niedersachsen and Baden-Württemberg, the interactions followed this pattern. In Nordrhein-Wesfalen, it was not as strong because the offices that manage the resources were trying to establish direct contacts with the universities and were beginning to weaken the position of the Hochschulreferenten.

positions, research funds, etc.) are submitted to experts of the various disciplines who are chosen by the Ministry – which means that with each ministerial change the names of the experts change! The evaluations and advice given by these experts, who belong to the academic profession, are the basis on which the administration[8] makes its decisions. The influence of the administrative staff is thus rather weak: they have very limited legitimacy and try to gain more by basing their decisions on the advice of scientific advisers. The problem is that these experts are not representative of the profession: they are not elected, and their 'choice' is always a mix between partisan and scientific reward.

This seemed so 'normal' to us that, when we interviewed German administrative staff in the *Landministerium,* we were very surprised by the absence of academic experts on whose expertise one could rely to take decisions. There are almost no relations between the Ministry of the *Land* and the German academic profession in matters of decision making concerning positions, curricula or research. But conversely, the Ministry has a rather direct influence on the state of the academic market-place, since it participates in recruitments by allocating (or not) extra funding to the university that wants to 'attract' an eminent faculty member with a large recruitment budget. The *Hochschulreferent* assesses the selected candidate and decides whether it is worth making him an attractive offer.[9] Hence, the interplay between the state and the profession differs from one country to another (Musselin 1994) and the independence of the administration *vis-à-vis* the academic profession may vary considerably.

8   Administrative chief executives are often chosen among faculty members. They have generally been university presidents. They also change when there is a ministerial change. In this case, they may return to their university as a 'normal' faculty member.

9   The university itself finds some resources (mostly by redistributing) to make an offer but, when it fears it will not be sufficient to be attractive, it asks the ministry for financial help.

Synoptical decision making in France; 'case by case' decision making in Germany

The third main characteristic of state intervention is the basis on which decisions are taken.

In France, most of the procedures were synoptical, that is, decision making was organised in national procedures that, in theory, allowed for comparisons between similar situations. All was structured so that state bodies could manage such comparisons with the help of the academic experts. Let us take the case of the *habilitations* for curricula until 1989. Every four years, each diploma in the same type of discipline was examined simultaneously with the same diplomas of the same discipline in all universities. For instance, every licence in science was evaluated for *habilitation* or *re-habilitation*. The comparison of the situations, not the specificity of each situation, led to decisions. Thus, work in the state bodies was organised around a double periodicity: an annual one that concerned budgets, the publication of positions, recruitment and promotion bodies, and the suppression, creation, and vacancy of positions; and one every four years which concerned the *habilitation* of curricula and university research funds.

The formal structure we described above was rather appropriate for such synoptical decision making, since it allowed choices to be made out of context. Because the management of the universities was split into directorates that had their own sector of activities and responsibility, it was not really possible for each specialised office (for example, that of the science faculty members) to take into account the impact of its decisions on other domains (for example, the effects of the vacancy of a position on a curriculum or on research in the university concerned). The scope for comparison was largely confined to its specific area of responsibility (i.e. in this case staff and positions in science) and all the more so, since the number of management applications[10] for the whole of France did not make it possible to take into consideration the competing interests of each university. Thus, the specificity of each situation disappeared behind

10   As an example, let us quote this extract from an interview:

'For the last recruitment procedures, we advertised 2200 positions to which 14,000 candidates applied. We organised 127 juries (...) There were two referees for each candidate and we sent the publications of each candidate to their referees. It meant managing 28,000 mailings.'

a formal structure that divided the reality into areas of responsibility without allowing for the emergence of poles of decision that could integrate the interests of the universities and those of the Ministry. Nobody was able to assume the complex context of a particular issue. The compartmentalisation created by the dispatching of responsibility, the number of files to be processed, and the respect of national norms, converged to justify a synoptical way of taking decisions.

In Germany, on the contrary, decision making is primarily non-synoptical. Case-by-case decision taking prevails. There are no planned re-examinations of the curricula and no federal procedures that deal with all recruitments simultaneously (recruitments occur when a position becomes vacant). Each request/project from a university is examined for itself. The criteria for decisions are centred on the relevance of the project for the university concerned. The fact that a similar project has been developed in a nearby university will obviously be taken into account and may be used as an argument to reject it. But there is no procedure for the simultaneous examination of all similar requests. Each decision is taken according to the specific situation of the university and each request offers an opportunity to renegotiate with the *Landministerium*.

This decision-making process is encouraged by the two points developed above. First, the logic by organisation and the *Hochschulreferenten*'s function: as they represent a university, the latter are not in a position to compare the same kind of projects. Furthermore, in order to defend 'their' university before other offices that could have this synoptical perspective, the best strategy for them[11] is to stress the excellent and specific characteristics of the project they are defending. Second, the absence of academic experts does not permit a transversal view based on disciplines.

---

11 Another realistic strategy for them is to avoid projects that are difficult to defend: that is one of the reasons why they encourage the faculty members and the university staff to inform them about any possible future project at a very early stage so as to estimate its chances of success.

Targeted incentives policy in France; integrated actions in Germany

This fourth result could also be presented as a direct consequence of the previous ones. In France, because of the relative weakness of the central administration to impose changes on the universities, the favourite means of action used by the state bodies to steer the system as a whole was, with the exception of the creation of new rules, the launching of national incentives policies (Musselin 1992). Rather than case-by-case management and reaching specific arrangements with each university, the central administration proposed targeted national orientations in which the universities had to integrate their projects to obtain the extra resources allocated for these orientations. This could be summed up in slogans such as 'create a *magistère*[12] and you will have funds for it' or 'renew your first two-year cycles and you will get more resources'. This, of course, was used to try to introduce pedagogical innovations, but also for more routine cases. For instance, each *habilitation* campaign was used as an opportunity for the Ministry to set its priorities and to incite universities to formulate their *habilitation* projects in a certain way if they wanted a positive answer.

So, reflections on change and initiatives were the prerogative of the State bodies, even if the universities could then decide to subscribe to them or not. The definitions of a general framework and of national norms were then used as a reference for the synoptical confrontation and comparison of the projects.

In Germany, the action of the *Länder* seems much less divided. The presence of the university in the Ministry through the strong links established with the *Hochschulreferenten* and case-by-case decision making favoured a much more integrated and negotiated form of management.

National styles of steering higher education?

What we tried to show above was that state intervention and the relations of the state with the universities present national patterns. Stable modes of regulation can be found behind the diversity of the many interactions between both levels and they constitute a

12   A new national diploma created in 1985.

framework within which some actions will seem legitimate and others not; within which some decisions will be taken and others not; within which some actors will be relevant and others not; and within which some aspects will be taken into account and others not.

These constants greatly influence the nature and content of the relation between the State and the universities. In other words, they reveal interdependencies. For instance, the fact that the activity of the French Ministry is built on a logic of disciplines and of *habilitation* of diplomas maintains[13] the organisational weakness of French universities: they have (had) no incentives to engage in more collective action and to develop a stronger shared identity, and the best way to obtain resources from the Ministry is to present disciplinary projects.

These modes of regulation also show that the relations between the state and the universities are not a matter of chance. They have been built over time and reflect a balance point between different actors which has a certain continuity. The fact that they seem to be a kind of sedimentarisation of the past and that they have been built on systemic interdependencies explains why they are rather stable and why, when reading the work of historians on higher education, what they describe does not sound strange to us but, on the contrary, finds some echo. But this should not lead us to believe that the present modes of regulation in national higher education systems are determined by the past. In fact, the actors in these configurations inherited from the past are not their prisoners: they are only limited by them. That is why these configurations can evolve and change if we understand change as follows: first, the nature and content of the relations may change (for instance, the negotiation-based relations between the *Länder* and the universities in Germany could become weaker or more bureaucratic); second, the logic we have identified in the relationships may vary. From this point of view, the analysis of the policy developed by the French Ministry as from 1988 seems to be an opportunity for change in France. This is the point we shall develop now.

---

13   We say 'maintains' in order to avoid either 'is due to' or 'is the cause for'. We do not know which was the consequence of the other. We can only offer the following hypothesis: as state agencies developed by the end of the 1950s/ early 1960s at a time when the specialised colleges were the backbone of the French university system, they probably reproduced discipline-based organisation and the logic that they maintained after the Faure Law (1968) which instituted pluridisciplinary universities in France.

Principal changes induced by the contractual policies

In May 1988, after the re-election of François Mitterrand as President of France, a new government was formed under the responsibility of Michel Rocard who made education a priority. The Ministry of Education was entrusted to Lionel Jospin who was responsible for training from kindergarten to university. He called on Claude Allègre, a well-known physicist and long-time friend, to become his Special Adviser for Higher Education (Allègre 1993). In September 1988, the beginning of the academic year threatened to be difficult because of the great rise in student numbers. Jospin announced to the French Conference of University Presidents (CPU) that he wanted to establish a different relationship, emphasising negotiation between the State and the universities, and that four-year contracts would therefore be implemented between the latter and the central bodies.

In May 1989, the departments in charge of higher education in the Ministry were restructured. One of the new bodies, the DPDU (Direction for the programming and the development of universities) was mandated (among other things) to implement the policy of funding through negotiation. As such, there is nothing very novel about this. In France, new governments always appoint new ministers who often change the previous formal structure. Yet, this time, the change was more than a mere ritual. It seems to us that the policy of funding through negotiation implemented in 1988 was also an attempt to modify the previous form of government intervention in French higher education. Obviously, the policy of funding through negotiation did not completely reverse the logic of disciplines, the presence of the academic profession, synoptical decision making, and the targeted incentives policy. But there were enough changes to begin to speak of a new art of government. Let us now present the main changes that occurred and that we observed, since we were able to repeat the 1987 study a few years later, in order to compare the situations both past and present. Another research study, which focused more on the policy of funding through negotiation, completed these first efforts.[14]

What is meant by 'funding through negotiation'?

As we said above, one of the main objectives of the policy of funding through negotiation was to introduce more bargaining relationships between the central administration and the universities. But this policy remains above all a state initiative. This does not mean that the state wanted to disengage itself: rather, it tried to improve the situation and to 'better govern' it. Thus, the change was not a question of less interventionism but of replacing traditional ways of acting by new ones. The new Ministry therefore decided to extend the contractual relations that had been introduced at the beginning of the 1980s to allocate research funds to the universities[15] to the university budget. For reasons that would be too long to explain here, the process of funding through negotiation for the general budget was developed separately from the research budget. Furthermore, the philosophy and objectives of each of these two processes were very different. That is why we shall only speak of contracts that do not concern research.

The idea behind funding through negotiation was to allocate resources on a different basis and to be able (1) to rebalance the situation among the universities and (2) to give more leeway without formal decentralisation. Hence, universities were asked to analyse their situation and their activities and to define their plans for the next

14   A first in-depth study based on some 80 interviews was conducted in 1987. A graduate student conducted interviews and wrote a report on the same topic in 1991 (Sanchez 1991). These two research works were presented in the book E. Friedberg and I published in 1993. In 1994 and 1995, I held other interviews with the main actors of the contractual policy and analysed many internal documents in order to reconstruct the emergence of this policy (Musselin 1995). With S. Lipiansky, I also studied the effects of funding through negotiation in three universities (Lipiansky and Musselin 1995).

15   Every four years, the research teams within a university write a scientific project for the next four years. Scientific experts in the central administration examine them and decide whether to allocate them specific resources or not. Until 1989, a global amount was attributed to the president of the university concerned who could then redistribute the money among the research teams. As from 1989, the amount of resources was decided at the central level (Paris) so that the university level could not modify the distribution of resources among the research teams.

four years. Then, the Ministry had to decide which of the priorities defined by the university would also be its priority, and to negotiate the resources it would allocate to enable the university to attain them. So, the Ministry came to distinguish between the four-year project of the university (that is, the perspectives of the university, its priorities and the action it would develop) and the contract itself (the perspectives, priorities and actions recognised by the Ministry and for which it earmarked resources that would be allocated in the next four years). This 'contract' was signed by the university president and by the Ministry. Obviously, these contracts had no legal value and, as such, should be called 'reciprocal commitments' rather than contracts. There was no sanction if they were not respected because there was no contingent liability to enforce them. Furthermore, in the legal and economic definition of contracts, they were to be concluded between parties that were free and equal; neither of these terms are respected in the present case. Universities were in a way subordinated to the state bodies, and even if they could refuse to fund through negotiation, it would have been a difficult decision to take. So it was, in a way, more of a symbolic contract.

The changes contained in funding through negotiation

We shall describe the kind of changes foreseen and the new practices which had to be implemented to achieve these changes.[16] Thus, we shall develop four dimensions of funding through negotiation that clearly show an evolution of the modes of intervention we described previously for France.

Contracts meant, above all, going from the thematic[17] to the global. To us, this does not mean that the intentions behind funding through negotiation were not targeted towards specific goals, and that they included all types of considerations, that is, economic, social, financial, pedagogical, scientific, and so forth. It refers to the fact that the various activities within a university are considered with respect to

16   For the presentation of the objectives of the contractual policy and a discussion on their effects on the central administration and on the pattern of French state intervention see Berrivin and Musselin (1996).
17   Under 'thematic', we include every policy centred on one discipline, or on one cycle of study or on one problem area. 'Global' means that many aspects must be taken into account, especially the different components of a university and their interrelations.

one another, rather than in themselves: what is sought is consistency and setting priorities among activities. In other words, global consistency prevails over the juxtaposition of activities or disciplines. That is why, for the central administration, a 'good' contract should rely on a project that is more than a sum of projects: choices have to be made and priorities set in order to launch strategic actions. Thus, for instance, in an internal document in 1989, a first assessment of the projects sent by 19 universities made a distinction between the universities that had 'an evaluation and a university project integrating all components and linked to their environment'; those that made a 'global synthesis of all the sectors of university life but with no critical analysis or no internal policy or prospective'; those that presented a 'compilation of colleges'; and those that submitted 'slapdash work, quick sketches or no answers at all'.

Generally speaking, the people we interviewed were in favour of the emergence of a prospective, aggregated view of the university rather than a fragmented image.

> Some issues were to be found in the project. And we wanted more relationships among the colleges so that the project would not be a juxtaposition of colleges. The first time I went in this university, it was funny because all the deans were there. They were extremely polite and presented to me a project that was totally compartmentalized. The president was weak but the deans strong. The project was actually 6 projects! I sent it back. I said we wanted a common project. (A university adviser[18])

Another consequence of the prevalence of the global over the thematic was the broadening of the spectrum of actions for policy incentives. The latter did not disappear[19], but they offered greater possibilities and were less centred on targeted thematic issues. The state bodies still set priority themes, but they were broader, more numerous, and less narrowly defined. A university was not asked to

18   These are a small number of faculty members working for the DPDU, who have generally been presidents or vice-presidents before. They are responsible for a small number of universities in a geographical sector and must give them methodological assistance in the elaboration of the project and the negotiation of the contract. We do not have the space to go into details about their role, but they have been very important in the whole process.

19   In a way, funding through negotiation means 'contractualise and you will get more positions'.

respond to each incentive but to select those it preferred, those it would react to, according to its specific situation and the objectives it pursued. However, this orientation towards a more open and more diversified incentive funding was not radical. During the same period, other policies were launched (such as the reform of the first cycle of studies or the creation of IUPs (Vocational University Institutes) that were closer to the previous model and were sometimes even in contradiction with the contractual policy, as some people told us.

> The pedagogical renewal for instance ... It swept the contracts away: we told the universities 'you have to do that'! (DPDU)

> The idea was to strengthen the president. C. Allègre said 'no more going up to the counters (*guichets*) with an outstretched hand, there is only one partner, the president'. There was a strong consensus on this, even if sometimes some practices remained directive. But, when the cabinet ignored the 'no counter policy', it went wrong. See what happened with the pedagogical reform. (DPDU)

Funding through negotiation meant reinforcing the powers of the university presidency. If a university is no longer a juxtaposition of activities, then the person responsible for the whole institution becomes the privileged partner at the expense of the deans. The latter can no longer come to Paris to defend themselves, bypassing the president or even acting against him.

> We strengthened the presidents but the deans have been neglected by the central administration. It was all the more the case when the presidents themselves neglected their deans. It is clear. This policy recognizes only the university and the president. (DPDU)

The presidents' duty is to give consistency to their university, to help it to define a line of action, in other words, to be a little more managerial[20], to be able not only to represent their universities, but

---

20 One should not conclude from this that the Ministry wanted to transform the universities into firms and their presidents into executives. There is never any question of this in the internal documents or in the interviews. But if the presidents had to acquire new skills, it raised once more the question of the professionalisation of this function and of the transmisson of experience between them (they are elected for a five-year mandate which is not renewable).

also to negotiate compromises, to integrate different constraints, to set priorities.

Governing through contracts and seeking integration thus modified the relational habits of the central administration. It reduced the number of relevant partners and prevented (at least a little) one from playing on the internal disputes within universities and setting power on the discrete allocation of resources by office managers.

Funding through negotiation also meant modifying the process of resource allocation. One can see these new practices as a consequence of the search for the global. If universities are more than the simple sum of their activities, then their budget can no longer be the simple sum of the resources allocated to each activity. The policy of funding through negotiation thus led to a reconsideration of the way positions and budgets were attributed, at the time when the Rocard government made education a priority and when the number of students, as from 1988, increased so suddenly that the state was obliged to take specific measures in favour of higher education. The question then was how to allocate extra resources, while rebalancing the situation among the universities. (This increase in resources is generally presented as a *sine qua non* condition for the success of the contractual policy. Yet, in some other public sectors, contracts have been accepted and negotiated on retrenchments.)

Two decisions were taken at the time. The first concerned the composition of the university budget: one part was allocated automatically on criteria, but the other was the result of the contractual negotiation. On average, for all of France, the contractual budget represented only 5 per cent of the total budget[21], but one should bear in mind that this did not include salaries and that the creation of new positions was another important element of the negotiation until 1994. The second innovation concerned lump-sum budgets. The universities received resources (and no longer a budget for each curriculum) that they could then use as they wished.

21   According to those we interviewed, this percentage was not decided *a priori* but
     a posteriori. A few years later, the agents in charge of funding through
     negotiation in the Ministry asked to contract 10 per cent of the budget, but did
     not obtain satisfaction.

Last, funding through negotiation meant less opacity and more confidence. The practices we just described induced a change in the content and quality of the relations between the central administration and the universities. The contracts[22] contradicted the relational pattern that M. Crozier (1964) and later F. Dupuy and J-C. Thoenig (1983) presented as characteristic of the French administration. In order to fund through negotiation, it was less relevant than before to let problems be dealt with by an isolated state agency or to conceal local arrangements. On the contrary, universities had a new interest in giving more information about their situation, in bringing to light their specificities. It was better for them to become more transparent. Thus, for instance, in the three universities in which we studied the effects of funding through negotiation (Lipiansky and Musselin 1995), the faculty members we interviewed explained that, as a consequence of the contracts, it made sense to ask for 20,000 francs in order to obtain 10,000, either from their university or from the Ministry.

> The contractual mode is more credible. As we know how much the university will receive in the next four years, we have no reason to ask for unnecessary positions. We have reduced our requirements; we rationalized our requests for new positions. Next year for instance, as I know what we can have, I will only ask for two positions (...) We adapt ourselves. We will examine the needs and the university council and the scientific body, we will decide where the priority is (...) As a matter of fact, we are ourselves doing the regulation. I think it was one of the goals of the Ministry. (A dean)

Thus, even if globality gives more autonomy of choice to the universities, it also paradoxically strengthens the influence of the central administration, which thus has a better knowledge of what happens in the units. All those who worked in the state agencies before 1988 stressed this aspect.

---

22   In the case of higher education, we showed that the contracts were a new means of intervention. Yet, contracts are not a solution in themselves. The way they are implemented, their content, the areas they cover, etc. have an impact on the success of such a policy and may lead to very different results. Comparing contractual policies at the Equipement and in EDF-GDF, R. Berrivin (1995) concluded that contracts were an issue that had to be managed and not a solution in themselves.

It was an innovation. We went into the universities. Before the presidents called the rue Dutot[23] 'the crying office' and 'the counters (*guichets*)'. They went to the counter to get a few francs. Some of them came every week, others were never there. It has been an innovation for the agents of the rue Dutot to see the universities from inside. They were electrified because what they saw before from far away had another aspect in the reality. They discovered another way of acting. The same holds true for the universities: they saw State agents coming not as a delegation but as colleagues! (DPDU)

In order to contractualise, the universities had to accept to shed light on their situation and the state bodies had to take greater account of this. On this basis, more trustful relationships developed: the good will of the centre was not only written in the documents, it also appeared in practices that convinced enough people in the universities to accept the new rules of the game imposed by the central administration. This trust[24] was reinforced by the fact that the contracts were generally respected. Even if the new positions foreseen in the contract were not always created in the grades or in the categories wished for by the university, the central administration generally kept its promises (at least until 1993[25]). Thus, relations with the Ministry generally improved. The day-to-day contacts remained the same, but the academics and the administrators who participated in the preparation of the contracts spoke of the Ministry in terms that were unheard of before. Relations with the DPDU agents were described in warm terms and

23   Most of the directorates responsible for higher education are located in this
      street in Paris.
24   Many people were sceptical about the contractual policy and saw it as a
      demagogic attempt to enforce the large rise in student numbers. But this
      scepticism did not provoke opposition or debates. It can even be said that it did
      not give rise to controversy.
25   The weakness of this policy appeared with the political change of 1993: budget
      retrenchments led to the failure to respect the creation of positions and the new
      Minister, Fillon, decided that there would be no further mention of the
      positions in the next contracts. During the studies we led in three universities in
      1994 (Lipiansky and Musselin 1995), many academics spoke of betrayal. They
      felt 'they had been tricked', as they accepted growth in student numbers in
      'exchange' for more resources ... which they did not receive.

expressions such as 'collaboration', 'capacity to listen', or 'comprehension'. The universities greatly appreciated that the Paris staff came to them and witnessed *de visu* the problems they faced. The disappearance of habits that favoured the academics who were able to impose themselves or to go to Paris was also appreciated.

> I do think it is a very good tool. It is better than going to Paris –
> presidents were obliged to knock at the different doors – and to be
> in the favour of a Mr X or Y! It was a struggle for resources. It was
> clientelism. One would knock on one door then another. The contract allows us to develop our own project and helps the
> universities that have a project. (A dean)

It seems to us that this description of the concrete objectives of funding through negotiation and the new practices that supported it shows that what we presented as the main characteristics of state intervention in higher education in France must be revised. In fact, funding through negotiation affected the two dimensions we defined as change: the nature and content of the relations between the state and the universities on the one side and the logic of actions on the other. In a way, the intervention of the French state bodies came closer to the actions of their German counterparts, even if it was still centralised: they paid more attention to the universities than to the disciplines than before, they took decisions more on a case-by-case basis (each university being a specific case), they promoted more integrated priorities. All this leads us to say that funding through negotiation was not so much another public policy on higher education as a redefinition of what universities are (or should be) and of the place of state regulation in the higher education system. The role of the central agencies also evolved: less importance was given to the definition of national rules that were to be implemented everywhere than to possibilities for differentiation among the universities within a national framework.

The limits met by funding through negotiation

In the previous section, we tried to show that funding through negotiation had introduced new dynamics. We must now put this hypothesis into perspective and try to analyse the limits of this policy. At the moment (1996), the general diagnosis is that funding through negotiation has been frozen since the second cohabitation in 1993. But this explanation that reduces the problems to political factors seems too simplistic to us. Of course, we shall not deny that the political changes that occurred in 1993 had an effect. But problems were also to be found in the learning process that such a new orientation implied and in the emergence of new issues. So we shall first describe some of the difficulties caused by the contracts in the universities and some of the unforeseen effects they had on the central agencies before coming back to political factors.

It is easier to prepare university projects than to implement them

In 1994, we carried out a comparative study (Lipiansky and Musselin 1995) on the effects of funding through negotiation in three universities. In each university we conducted some 30 interviews with those who prepared and implemented the contracts, as well as with deans, members of university bodies, administrators and faculty members. It is not possible to present all the results of this work which focused on the preparation and implementation of the contracts, so we shall concentrate on the aspects that show the difficulty of learning to act collectively.

The problem of collective action first appeared in the preparation of the contracts and we have stressed great differences among the universities in this phase. The role of the president, but also of the deans and of the administrative staff, was crucial here. Most of them saw that the contracts could mean more resources and accepted the need to play the game. But they rarely foresaw that funding through negotiation could also be a way of mobilising reflection, redefining the missions and setting priorities among them; in other words, of managing differently. In the three universities we studied, the more the presidency had an instrumental understanding of the contract, the less a vast, long-term and iterative negotiation within their university was engaged. The collective project was sometimes the result of very isolated reflection.

The internal *rapport de force* at the time when funding through negotiation was introduced was also difficult to manage. The contract never succceded in bypassing the existing cleavages: it was not able to modify the attitudes of the colleges; in fact, it suffered from them. For instance, strong colleges[26] resisted the wish of their president to include them in a university project, arguing that they were too specific to join in a common project.

Yet, working together on the preparation of a collective project, even if not easy, generally succeeded in introducing, or at least in launching, a global dynamic within the university. But even then, the movement engaged during the preparation phase and the needs it revealed slowed down during the implementation phase. Implementing a collective project was not spontaneous. Let us give a few examples.

When they prepared the project, the universities became aware that they did not know themselves and that data were lacking on elementary aspects (about the evolution of the student population, for instance) needed to analyse the situation and to decide on future projects. But after the signature of the contract, they often did not succeed in implementing mechanisms that would enable them to continue to collect and update data.

The collecting of data on the university for the preparation phase also made the faculty members aware of the imbalance within their university and the need to rebalance. In fact, such data were subsequently used to reject certain requests from relatively rich colleges or departments that had a hard time to legitimate their needs. But, if this affected the allocation of new resources, it only rarely led to the redistribution of existing means.

We reach the same conclusion if we consider operations scheduled in the contract that required cooperation among different colleges, departments or groups: they were also very difficult to implement. It was difficult to transform the enthusiasm and the good will that prevailed during the preparation of the contract into concrete action. Hence, the contracts and their implementation often showed the incapacity of universities to act more collectively and develop internal synergies.

26   In France, many universities are not pluridisciplinary and consist of two large colleges (e.g. one of law and the other of medicine) that each develops its autonomy *vis-á-vis* the other and *vis-á-vis* the president.

Funding through negotiation also had feedback on the central administration

The contractual policy also suffered from the problems the central administration had in managing the process. In fact, the authors of the contractual policy did not seem very aware of the consequences it could have on the central administration. They did not see that the change in the relations between Paris and the universities would also change the relations between the universities and Paris.

Two different levels of consequences can be distinguished. The first concerns internal issues: the redistribution of power within the central agencies[27] on the one hand, and the need for new skills[28] on the other. The second level concerns the regulation of the whole system. So long as nobody took into account the specificity of each university, it was possible to seek national harmony, to use theoretically the same criteria, and to implement the same rules. This kind of regulation relied on the pronouncement of norms that were the same for the whole country and that were supposed to respond to the general interest. Adjustments obviously occurred at the margin: everybody knows that it is virtually impossible to apply equal treatment, but everybody deals with this issue.

Funding through negotiation breaks this down. The central administration faces a new problem: how far are the general principles and rules compatible with the recognition of specificities? In theory, the boundaries are clear: state agencies define the goals, make choices and set the rules with which, and in the limit of which, universities may deal with situations that are more diverse than before. In practice, it seems much more difficult. First, universities react to the given framework, either by bypassing or extending it. The

27 As long as the central administration acted thematically, the quasi-absence of relationships between the directorates (Musselin and Brisset 1989) was not a real problem. But this does not fit in at all with a policy which seeks integration. The creation of a directorate which is able to integrate different aspects and to coordinate different actions did not occur 'naturally'. The conflict that arose between the DESUP and the DPDU handicapped the process.

28 Until then, it principally needed agents who could produce and interpret rules. This continued but other skills were also required to lead, coordinate, give assistance for mediation and dissemination, as well as to manage the new process, integrate the different aspects of a contract, develop new relations with the universities, support them, and provide information about recent innovations in some universities.

framework itself can never be defined clearly enough and therefore it is also subject to interpretations, negotiations and adjustments. Moreover, it can be in contradiction with local specificities. Furthermore, the framework may be modified by political change, by the bargaining between the directorates themselves and, of course, by the interplay between the central administration and the universities.

More political factors

We shall now analyse political aspects that also opposed the whole process. It seems to us that the second cohabitation was another threat to funding through negotiation for two reasons.

First, the new government decided to reduce the growth of the budgets when the number of students was still increasing. In November 1993, the new Ministry announced that the agreement on faculty positions included in the contracts would not be respected. This doubly endangered the contracts. It revealed their fragility and their reversibility, as well as the absence of contingent liabilities to enforce the respect of the terms. At the same time, it destroyed the basis on which funding through negotiation had been developed that, in the case of higher education, linked the contracts to the allocation of more resources and not to the negotiation of restrictions.

The second reason concerns what the Ministry included in the term 'contract'. We tried to show above that the objectives embodied in funding through negotiation were manifold: to allocate resources better; to develop a new kind of relation between the state and the universities; and to create an internal dynamic within universities. What seems[29] to have happened after 1993 is a change in the meaning of funding through negotiation. The contract became a management tool: the information required was much more formalised, its content was restricted. In a sense, the contracts were diverted.

29   Based on informal talks with university or central agencies administrators, presidents and faculty members.

Some conclusions on changing the relation between the state and the universities

In the second part of this chapter, we have tried to explain why we consider that the funding through negotiation policy introduced some changes in the French national pattern of higher education and to present some of its limits. To conclude, we shall present some reflections on what we learned from this about changing the relations between the state and the universities.

First, we can say that this policy did not avoid the traditional problems met by the change process: the perennial nature of change and the risk of bureaucratisation through institutionalisation. A characteristic of the French higher education system was that actors had a high turnover. This is true for the political actors. Lionel Jospin was in office for four years: not long to manage a long-term process (even if four years is a long time in this position, compared to his predecessors). His successor (Jack Lang) remained for one year and François Fillon, two. It is also true for the staff of the central agencies[30] (Friedberg and Musselin, 1993), for the university presidents (they are elected for five years and only one mandate) and for the university bodies. This turnover is all the more a problem in that, as we explained above, the personal involvement of the actors is very important in the process. The transmission of experience between presidents is usually not organised and in two of the three universities which had a new president, he was less active, less enterprising than his predecessor: maybe the electors wanted a break after a period of internal moves.

The thinning (in resources and in meaning) of the contracts as from 1993 can be seen as a consequence of the will to perennialise the contracts through more formalisation. The transformation of the contract into a management tool was the consequence of an attempt to harmonise the forms sent to the universities to prepare their next contracts. Formalisation is generally a difficult step for innovation because it limits the possible options: and so it was in this case too. But this case also contains more specific aspects. For instance, it raises the question about who can provoke change in the public higher education system. In the case of France, it seems that universities can

---

30   For instance, the DPDU had three directors between 1989 and 1993.

become more autonomous only if the state decides/ allows this. As we have tried to show, funding through negotiation changed the logic of intervention of the state in France, but it did not weaken the influence of the state on them. This is the ambiguity of such contracts: they can allow greater differentiation but they are also a kind of recentral-isation from the centre: the latter defines (at least at the beginning of such a process) how far differentiation can go, what content it can have, and so forth.

So, control over the universities remained strong and when the state agencies changed the rules of the game, as from 1993, they were not able to resist. Changing the relationships with the state seemed so very dependent on the good will of the state. In a recent book, a French philosopher (Renaut 1995) explains the situation of French universities by the fact that, if they succeeded in a first modernisation in the Middle Ages when they became free from clerical control, they did not achieve the second modernisation that would have meant becoming free from the state. Our case study clearly confirmed this dependence, even if funding through negotiation could represent a step away from it in the longterm.

The last point we would like to mention about changing the relations between the state and the universities is that it has to do with the university's capacity for change. The limits met by funding through negotiation also concerned the organisation of the universities: the fact that, within them, interactions are loosely coupled and that the autonomy of faculty members is great can explain why transforming the contracts into acts has been so difficult. Everybody thought that the dynamic of the contract would transform itself into a dynamic for collective action. But changing the relations between the state and the universities involved learning processes that should not be neglected, especially in such specific organisations.

References

Allain, G. (1986) 'Les enseignements supérieurs en France: contraintes, ambïguités et privilèges.' *Politiques et Management Public*, 4, 15–26.

Allegre, C. (1993) *L'âge des savoirs – Pour une renaissance de l'université*. Paris: Gallimard.

Berrivin, R. (1995) *Les contrats centre-périphérie comme leviers de modernisation du management public. Analyse comparée des stratégies de changement et du pilotage de deux grands réseaux de services publics, Ministère de l'Equipement, EDF-GDF Services*. Doctoral thesis, Institut d'Etudes Politiques de Paris, Paris.

Berrivin, R. and Musselin, C. (1996) 'Les politiques de contractualisation entre centralisation et décentralisation: les cas de l'équipement et de l'enseignement supérieur.' *Sociologie du travail*, 38, 575–596.

Crozier, M. (1964) *The Bureaucratic Phenomenon*. Chicago: University of Chicago Press.

Dupuy, F. and Thoenig, J.-C. (1983) *Sociologie de l'administration française*. Paris: Armand Colin.

Filatre, D. (1993) *Les politiques universitaires des collectivités locales*. Rapport de recherche pour le Plan urbain, Contrat de recherche Ville-Universités et Conseil Régional Midi-Pyrénées.

Freville, Y. (commissioned headed by) (1981) *Rapport au Premier Ministre* de la commission d'étude de la réforme du financement des universités (Paris, La Documentation Française).

Friedberg, E. and Musselin C. (1989a) *En quête d'universités*. Paris: L'Harmattan.

Friedberg E. and Musselin C. (1989b) 'L'université des professeurs.' *Sociologie du Travail 31*, 455–476.

Friedberg, E. and Musselin, C. (eds) (1992) *Le gouvernement des universités – Perspectives comparatives*. Paris: L'Harmattan.

Friedberg, E. and Musselin C. (1993) *L'Etat face aux universités en France et en Allemagne*. Paris: Anthropos.

Lipainsky, S. and Musselin, C. (1995) *La démarche de contractualisation dans trois universités françaises: les effets de la politique contractuelle sur le fonctionnement des établissements universitaires*. Rapport d'enquête. Paris; CSO.

Maurice, M., Sellier, F. and Sylvestre, J.-J. (1982) *Politique d'éducation et organisation industrielle en France et en Allemagne*. Paris: PUF.

Musselin, C. (1987) *Système de gouvernement ou cohésion universitaire: les capacitésd'action collective de deux universités allemandes et de deux universités françaises*, Doctoral thesis, Institut d'Etudes Politiques de Paris, Paris.

Musselin, C. (1992) 'Steering higher education in France, 1980–1990.' *Higher Education in Europe*, CEPES, 17, 59–77.

Musselin, C. (1994) 'L'état et la profession universitaire en France et en Allemagne.' *Poliques et management public*, 12, 151–173.

Musselin, C. (1995) *La politique de contrats d'établissement dans l'enseignement supérieur*. 1988–1993. Rapport d'enquête. Paris: CSO.

Musselin, C. (1996) 'Les marchés du travail universitaire comme économie de la qualité.' *La Revue Française de Sociologie*, 37, 189–207.

Musselin, C. (1997) 'Les universités … l'épreuve du changement: préparation et mise en ouvre des contrats d'établissement.' *Sociétés contemporaines*, 28, October, 79–101.

Musselin, C. and Brisset, C. (1989) *Rapport sur les administrations de tutelle des universités en France et en RFA*, Rapport final dans le cadre de l'aide accordée par le FRT pour la réalisation du programme sur les systèmes de gouvernement des universités. Paris: CSO-MRES.

Musselin, C., Brisset, C. and Friedberg, E. (1992) 'State and Market: are they contradictory?' EAIR Colloquium. Brussels.

Renaut, A. (1995) *Les révolutions de l'université. Essai sur la modernisation de la culture*. Paris: Calmann-Lévy.

Sanchez, P. (1991) *Le centre et le système: analyse sociologique des quatre directions de l'enseignement supérieur*, Mémoire de DEA de l'Institut d'Etudes Politiques de Paris.

CHAPTER 4

Higher Education and Changing Job Requirements

A Comparative View

Ulrich Teichler

Increased interest in the relationships between higher education and the world of work

Recent debates

The relationships between higher education and the world of work are again one of the key issues frequently debated in the 1990s. We note, for example, that UNESCO considers this as one of the core themes (see UNESCO 1995) and addresses it prominently in its conference series on higher education in 1997 and 1998 (see Teichler 1997). The World Bank emphasized this thematic area as well in its 'Lessons of Experience' (World Bank 1994). The OECD addressed the transition from higher education to employment in one of its largest projects in the early 1990s (OECD 1992, 1993). The OECD Institutional Management Programme in Higher Education focused one of its recent annual conferences on 'students and employment' and chose the relationships between higher education and employment as one of the major themes in a retrospect on the occasion of its 25th anniversary (see Teichler 1994, 1996). Or to take an example from developing countries, the Association of African Universities, in setting up a training programme for higher education researchers, noted that two themes elicited strongest interest at African universities: financing of higher education and the relationships between higher education and employment.

Changing debates

In the 1960s, faith spread in many countries that growing investment in higher education would contribute significantly to economic wealth. In some countries educational markets were expected to serve the wealth of an economy driven by market forces. In other countries educational and manpower planning was closely linked to serve a planned economy, while in others again targeted educational planning was expected to serve a market economy. In the 1970s, pessimism grew that higher education expansion had gone too far and the competences of the graduates no longer matched the needs of the employment system. When, finally, expectations adjusted to a somewhat fuzzy state of affairs, which neither supported the high hopes of the 1960s nor reinforced the deep sense of crisis of the 1970s, interest in the theme as such lost momentum.

Major questions to be raised

Now, the theme is back on the agenda. And we might ask: what is the context which reinforces the interest in the relationships between higher education and the world of work? What job requirements do we observe these days? What is higher education expected to 'deliver'? Should higher education really respond to those expectations affirmatively, and how should higher education define its societal role today?

Before addressing these questions, however, a note of caution is in place. We should bear in mind that our knowledge basis of the relationships between higher education and work is more limited than vocal claims in this area suggest.

Some methodological observations

The relationships between higher education and the world of work are among the most discussed issues of higher education. Unfortunately, our systematic knowledge of these relationships is relatively poor. We observe firm claims about shortages of skills, over-supplies, expected qualifications, mismatches between the competences of graduates and the needs of the employment systems etc. which are not well based on systematic empirical evidence. This does not mean that little information is available. On the contrary, overviews of available knowledge provide evidence of a rich body of knowledge (see

Psacharopoulos 1987; Carnoy 1994; Sanyal 1991; Teichler 1992; Higher Education and Employment 1995a, 1995b; Brennan, Kogan and Teichler 1996). Rather, the available information is often lopsided, biased or not scrutinised.

- One of the weaknesses is an imbalance between quantitative-structural and qualitative data (see the critique by Brennan and Kogan 1993). We can identify a wealth of studies on the whereabouts of graduates and their income, whereas the information is often poor regarding the kind of work tasks undertaken and the extent to which knowledge acquired during the course of study is eventually utilised on the job. As a consequence, data on income and occupational categories of graduates are often over-interpreted as valid indicators of the utilisation of knowledge.

- Employers' statements as regards expected qualifications are too easily taken as objective information. As will be pointed out below, we know that employers over-emphasise needs for skills short in supply, general competences as well as competences directly assessed in an elaborate manner in the process of selection and recruitment. Besides, employers' statements about expectations regarding the education system are often not consistent with their recruitment and personnel policies.

- Many researchers expect the practitioners surveyed, for example graduates, their supervisors, heads of personnel offices, and so forth to be the most knowledgeable experts of the links between competences and work tasks. In reality, however, most people surveyed cannot be expected to provide valid information about the 'qualification issue', the match between job tasks, 'requirements', 'competences', and finally the processes and substance of learning.

- Research findings collected in individual countries are often over-interpreted as universal findings. National differences in appreciating or deploring large proportions of graduates and in putting emphasis on specific knowledge or general competences etc. are often not sufficiently taken into account.

- In-depth analyses of work tasks and requirements tend to be costly and time-consuming. Therefore, most of these address such small sectors of the employment system that it is possible to draw few general conclusions about job requirements and competences of graduates.

Therefore, the following analysis will remain more cautious than readers might wish. Even so, some of the following statements are less firmly based on convincing research evidence than they seem on first glance. One might hope that the pressing problems in the relationships between higher education and the world of work might stimulate further substantial research in this area.

The changing context

In trying to explain the current dynamics of the changing relationships between higher education and the world of work, experts choose different starting points for their arguments: some point at the current state of the graduate labour market, some at general trends in the development of higher education, others at the changing utilisation of knowledge on the job. A closer look reveals that the phenomena discussed are highly interrelated, and we often cannot disentangle what are the causes and what are the consequences. The following issues are named most frequently.

Bleak job prospects

In the majority of leading regions of the world, bleak job prospects for graduates are one of the main reasons for concern. Substantial graduate unemployment is reported in many relatively rich, and in many developing, countries. In addition, employment problems are visible in terms of the transition from higher education to employment as a complicated and protracted period, in a frequent perception of mismatch between graduates' competences and work assignments, and in a spread of shaky employment conditions.

We have to bear in mind, though, that employment prospects vary substantially in different countries and regions of the world. For some time they seemed to be better on average across the countries of the South East Asian Pacific Rim these days than in Europe, as a consequence of rapid economic growth in South East Asia. But within

Western Europe where overall unemployment quotas vary between countries from about 5 to about 20 per cent, the employment opportunities for graduates are bound to differ as well.

We also have to take into account that job prospects of graduates from institutions of higher education in any given country tend to be assessed by young people not in comparison to graduates in other countries, but rather predominantly in comparison to fellow countrymen and women without a degree. In this respect we note, at least in almost all relatively rich countries, an advantage in the labour market for the better educated and trained persons (see OECD 1993).

Massification of higher education

Second, the impact of the massification of higher education on graduate employment is one of the major issues of debate in this context. Growing demand for complex cognitive competences might have contributed in many countries to increasing enrolment in higher education in certain periods, but most experts agree that expansion trends were not similarly halted or slowed down when the supply of graduates seemed to surpass job provisions considered appropriate for them. Notably, we mark a new wave of expansion of higher education in many industrialised societies since the mid or late 1980s which cannot be convincingly explained as a consequence of rising demand in the employment system.

At times, the debate about the consequences of massification is intertwined with that on bleak job prospects for graduates. But even when visible pressures on the labour market due to substantially rising proportions of graduates are minimal, the consequences of the massification of higher education are often deplored. Educated people tend to be disappointed because the most obvious outcome of higher education expansion is the loss of the exclusiveness of higher education degrees. And these complaints are reinforced by the academic profession feeling a loss of exclusiveness as far as the generation and dissemination of systematic knowledge is concerned.

Crisis of the work society

Third, many experts from industrial countries have indicated, notably in the 1980s and again in the 1990s, that we face a crisis of the work society in general. Due to a mix of technological, socio-economic and organisational factors, the work-time for gainful employment is tending to shrink. Or viewed the other way round: in the past, that part of the labour force freed from work annually through rationalisation found new jobs through a professionalisation of work serving new needs which had not existed or were at most latent before. The present crisis of the work society is due to the fact that this mechanism of professionalisation through new needs has come almost to a halt or no longer copes with the speed of rationalisation.

Knowledge society or highly educated society

Fourth, we seem to be heading for what is sometimes called by experts a knowledge society or a highly educated society (Teichler 1991). More and more jobs require substantial cognitive competences, and new systematic knowledge is the key force of rapid innovation. This, among other factors, makes employers more aware of the need to secure qualified labour, and thus has stimulated comprehensive personnel policies, called human resource development, which try to coordinate recruitment and dismissal, employment and work conditions, incentives and training in a systematic and consistent manner.

The move in the direction of a knowledge society does not necessarily mean that more of the high level cognitive education is needed of the kind 'delivered' by higher education in the past. Views vary, however, as regards the changes of requirements. Some experts point to the need for new interdisciplinary knowledge, some emphasise a trend towards flattening of organisational hierarchies and decentralisation of responsibilities, whereas others see the knowledge society driven by innovative high-level expertise.

Rapid technological change

Fifth, we observe rapid technological change, certainly more rapid than in the past. The names of key technologies and key industries turn over more quickly than ever before. This has substantial consequences not only for the structure of industry and services but also for the competences required and for the careers of the individuals. Obsolescence of knowledge is quick, and more highly qualified persons have to reckon with substantial shifts and uncertainties within their careers. Thus, paradoxically, both bleak employment prospects and booming employment might contribute to the phenomenon of a 'risk society' (Beck 1986).

International interdependence of economies and societies

Sixth, the international interdependence of economies and societies is obviously growing. National policies, as well as strategies of individual firms and other organisations, constantly have to be based on a look across borders. Whereas migration of unskilled labour was already common in the past, more highly qualified persons have to be versatile enough to act in an international arena.

Some experts prefer to talk about globalisation, thus notably underscoring the gradual disappearance of national borders of the economy and the labour market. Other experts refer to internationalisation, thus pointing out the growing cooperation across borders, the need to use foreign languages and to understand other cultures, which, in contrast to globalisation, continue to be seen as entities of their own. Other experts again stress the trend towards regionalisation, that is, a deliberate cooperation between neighbouring countries, for example in Europe, in Latin America, in Asia and the Pacific Rim, and so forth.

Domination of the neo-liberal economic and political doctrine

Seventh, we note a domination of the neo-liberal economic and political doctrine in the 1990s. Offsetting international trade regulations, deregulating as far as governmental steering is concerned, reducing job security and social welfare provisions are viewed as the optimal policies for stimulating economic growth and eventually ensuring highest wealth for all.

This domination of the neo-liberal doctrine tends to be attributed in part to the economic collapse of communism and thus to a disappearance of global competition between socio-political systems. Other experts emphasise that economic globalisation undermines the welfare policies of the richer countries through transfer of capital and production sites to cheap labour countries. Other experts point to the strong interventionist policies of the World Bank *vis-à-vis* developing countries. Whatever the main causes are, and whatever the hopes are of the advocates of this doctrine, the current major impacts of the neo-liberal policies are a polarisation within countries in terms of a growing gap between the rich and the poor, as well as growth of shaky employment conditions across all levels of competence within the labour force.

Of course, the socio-economic context for employment and education is so varied across countries that any depiction of general socio-economic trends has to be viewed with some caution. In addition, as already pointed out, we can start off by describing the scene from different angles. By and large, however, there is a relatively high consensus in the descriptions of the general socio-economic scene in this decade, and the millennium according to the Christian calendar seems to stimulate grand scenario descriptions of the current state of affairs.

Developments of job requirements

Emphasis placed on general competences and flexibility

Given the complexity of the context, the methodological problems of identifying job requirements, the increasing diversity of graduate work as a consequence of expansion of higher education, the uncertainties of the labour market for graduates, and the variety of traditions in various countries, we should not be surprised if we observed a bewildering variety of views as regards changes in the job requirements relevant for higher education. But we note on the contrary, at least at first glance, an amazing degree of consensus in this respect. Clearly, the most vocal claim that graduates should acquire general competences, cultivate social and communicative skills, and be flexible (see also Kivinen and Rinne 1993).

If we look in detail at the wealth of proposals made in various countries by employers and committees considering the future of higher education, as well as by the majority of researchers analysing the relationships between higher education and work, graduates are expected to:

- be flexible
- be able and willing to contribute to innovation and be creative
- be able to cope with uncertainties
- be interested in and prepared for lifelong learning
- have acquired social sensitivity and communicative skills
- be able to work in teams

- be willing to take over responsibilities

- prepare themselves for an internationalisation of the labour market through understanding of varied cultures

- be versatile in generic skills which cut across different disciplines, and be literate in areas of knowledge which form the basis for various professional skills, for example in new technologies.

On the 'generalist versus specialist' dimension, the former seems to be more popular these days. There are some obvious reasons for such a preference.

First, it is generally assumed that specialised professional knowledge becomes obsolete more quickly than in the past. This is one of the major reasons why lifelong learning and lifelong professional education is generally viewed as gaining importance.

Second, a growing number of professions, and positions within enterprises and public agencies, are not clearly demarcated and based on knowledge deriving from different disciplines. It seems to be more difficult for higher education to prepare for these positions in a targeted way.

Third, the massification of higher education, the general employment problems as well as the dynamic changes of the economy are likely to lead to mismatches between the skills of the graduates and the demands of the employment system. Flexible and generally educated persons are expected to be less disappointed about those mismatches and adapt more easily to job tasks not anticipated in advance.

There are reasons, however, for caution. I am not certain whether there is a clear trend towards rising demand for general knowledge.

A methodological and practical bias

We know that surveys on criteria employed in the recruitment of graduates tend to underestimate the weight specific skills have, and to overestimate the role of general skills. That is partly due to the fact that most surveys address staff of personnel offices, not the specialists of the various other departments who are involved in the selection process as well. In addition, persons involved in recruitment tend to overestimate the role of general competences, because they themselves spend more time on assessing the general competences than the specific skills that are often measured only on the basis of credentials and frequently play a strong role in the initial stages of selection processes (see Teichler, Buttgereit and Holtkamp 1984). Finally, specific skills show up at the end of lists of skills needed simply due to the fact that they vary between different jobs, whereas general competences are likely to be similar or identical across various jobs. Therefore, the strong emphasis on general skills is in part a methodological artefact.

We also have to bear in mind that statements by representatives of enterprises about job requirements often do not describe the full spectrum of expected competences, but rather put a strong emphasis on those skills in short supply or in danger of being lost. This might explain, for example, why representatives of European employers, when considering joint recommendations about the future of competences needed on the part of graduates from higher education, could agree on a strong emphasis on general cognitive competences as well as social and communicative skills (see, for example, European Round Table of Industrialists 1989). It is unlikely that they would reach such an agreement if they looked at the full spectrum of job requirements and took into account their different national traditions of training and job assignment.

International variety

It is obvious that some statements about global trends in the development of the economy, job requirements and expectations of higher education tend to neglect the variety of national preoccupations concerning job assignments, skills and education. Of course, we have international cooperation and a certain degree of global standardisation in some fields, most prominently in the medical field. And by and large we can agree that training of natural scientists and engineers tends to be more specific than in the humanities and social sciences. But we already note a substantial divergence as regards the occupational fields which are considered 'professional' in the various countries.

Most experts agree that specialists were held in high esteem traditionally in France and to a certain extent in Germany as well. On the other hand, British universities and British enterprises favoured the generally trained mind, and at Japanese enterprises, the typical careers for university graduates rewarded the persons willing to change tasks regularly, whereas the specialist was merely tolerated as a rare exception. In recent years, research has shown that the actual job profiles might differ between countries to a lesser extent than is usually claimed. We also note signs of counterbalance: while in recent years French and German companies put a strong emphasis on general competences and social skills (see Falk and Weiss 1993), Japanese employers obviously have upgraded and expanded specialist positions and are likely to do so even more in the future (see Nihon Keieisha Dantai Renmei 1995).

This notwithstanding, different traditions concerning job assignments and training persist to a remarkable extent. For some years, the European Commission explored the possibilities of formulating certain common core curricula in higher education in select professionally-oriented disciplines. This was not successful even in fields such as mechanical engineering which certainly has far more universal components than, for example, social sciences. Some multi-national firms conceive this international variety as advantage: they are more likely to recruit, for example, French engineers for certain job roles, British engineers for other job roles, and German engineers for yet other job roles. The European Community finally agreed in December 1988 on a very loose regulation of European recognition of professional skills. According to that regulation, graduates from recognised institutions of higher education should be accepted in other European countries after three years of successful study. If, however, a country requires additional qualifications for professional practice, it should offer supplementary study, training and examination schemes for graduates from other European countries.

Major industrial societies differ strikingly in the extent of specialisation at different stages of higher education or different types of higher education institutions. In the USA, we have observed for more than two decades that about 10 per cent of the respective population complete higher education with a doctoral, master's or professional degree which are based on study beyond a bachelor's degree and are conceived to be highly specialised. About 15 per cent complete study with a bachelor's which is based on four-year course programmes often understood as fairly general. In many European countries, the first university degree, usually understood as equivalent to a master's, is viewed as theoretical in emphasis and not as being 'applied' in terms of immediate professional preparation. In various of these countries, we note a second type of higher education providing shorter programmes which are more 'applied' than university programmes. The German *Fachhochschulen* and the Dutch *hogescholen* are notable examples. Even in England, where the sequence of a 'bachelor's' and 'master's' exists, the former polytechnics were more 'applied' than the universities (see Brennan *et al.* 1995) and still, after having been upgraded to 'new' universities in the early 1990s, are conceived as more vocational both by students and employers (see Purcell and Pitcher 1996).

Targeted general competences

It would be misleading, though, to argue that most of the debates on relationships between knowledge acquisition and job requirements focus on the old questions of breadth versus depth of study. A close look reveals that employers in many countries seem to put emphasis on types of competences which do not fit the generalist versus specialist dimension. We note a second set of stated requirements, which could be called targeted general competences, such as:

- problem solving abilities

- key qualifications or key skills.

Of course, these skills are also general in one respect: they are not specific to any single field or professional area. What is different, though, is the concern that general knowledge and general competences are not necessarily applicable to the world of work. Graduates have to find ways of transferring these competences from the world of learning to the world of work (see, for example, Harvey, Moon and Geall 1997).

Orientation toward practice

This is close to a third dimension in the debate about job requirements and the competences expected from the graduates, that is, the ability to employ specific knowledge. Also in the domain of more or less specialised areas of expertise, the transfer of knowledge from the world of learning and science to the world of professional work poses a problem. Higher education is often suggested to be more

- applied
  or
- practice oriented.

Whereas the former argument is calling for knowledge which is immediately useful for work, the latter describes a more complex relationship between learning and work in the area of high-level knowledge and cognitively complex tasks. In a summary of such debates observed in Germany, my colleagues and I argued that university teachers are expected to present a systematic confrontation between the ways of thinking and problem-solving within academic disciplines on the one hand, and the modes of professional thinking and problem-solving on the other (Kluge, Neusel and Teichler 1981).

Again, we note substantial differences between countries. For example, German university students in various fields of study are expected to acquire occupational experience in areas related to their field of study prior to, or during, the period of study. Even where it is not required, many employers state that they prefer recruiting graduates who have acquired prior relevant professional experience. On the other hand, we note that Japanese employers prefer to recruit graduates as 'raw material'; students might be active during the course of study in earning money, but they are not likely to choose work related to their field of study because employers do not tend to reward this. Also, hardly any Japanese employers offer students opportunities of internships during their course of study.

Specific skills cross-cutting disciplines

Finally, demand seems to be rising for some skills which apparently cut across the various disciplines, but in some respect are quite specific. One example which has drawn much attention in recent years in many parts of the world is that of international competences. There seems to be a clearly increasing demand for graduates from institutions of higher education versatile in handling an international environment.

This is a typical example of a functional definition of requirements, i.e. by the purpose of its utilisation, rather than by the type of competences actually needed. In looking at the competences or the areas of knowledge, 'international' teaching and learning in higher education comprise quite heterogeneous elements (see Van der Wende 1996), for example:

- 'area studies'

- foreign language proficiency

- comparative methods

- international sub-disciplines, such as international law or international trade

- sensitivity to different cultures, customs, modes of thinking, coping with the unexpected, etc.

The interest in this area of competence is clearly on the rise. For example, in Europe almost 100,000 students annually study in another European country for about half a year or one year in the framework of the ERASMUS programme, recently embedded in a wider educational support programme called SOCRATES. A survey of former ERASMUS students showed that 18 per cent lived abroad five years later. More than half had considerable international functions on the job, and an even larger proportion considered the learning useful for their job assignments. The majority believed that temporary study abroad turned out to be helpful for first employment. Only a minority, however, believed that the study abroad phase facilitated access to higher positions (Maiworm and Teichler 1996).

This growing interest in study abroad is not only due to the fact that an increasing number of graduates work in an international environment. Also, intercultural competence tends to be considered beneficial for professional work in a national context, for example for coping with varied persons and unexpected situations.

Implications for higher education

Diversification

By and large, we note that recommendations as to how universities should prepare their students for the world of work are often phrased in very general terms. Over the last decades, we clearly note a shift of emphasis in this respect. Some decades ago, we observed widespread claims as regards the competences an engineer, a lawyer, a sales person etc. should have acquired. Since about 1970, however, institutional diversity is a major issue. One institution might favour a different profile of an engineer from that of another institution.

Enormously high hopes are held for the diversification of higher education. The growing diversity of students in terms of their motives, competences and job prospects is considered to be best met by a corresponding diversification of higher education. National systems of higher education vary substantially according to the modes of diversification (see the overviews in Teichler 1988; Meek *et al.* 1996). For example:

- In the US and Japan, a steep hierarchy of quality differences between higher education institutions of the same type is acceptable, whereas higher education policies in the majority of European countries aim to keep those quality differences within bounds

- Countries vary substantially in the extent to which they accept a horizontal diversity, that is, a diversity of curricular approaches in the various fields of study, or in the extent to which curricula are standardised nationally

- In some countries, different types of higher education institutions are viewed as the major mechanism of diversification whereas in others intra-type diversification is dominant (see Scott 1996)

- In some countries, stages of courses and degrees are major means of diversification.

In the meantime, we note that almost all institutions continue to deal with an increasingly diverse student population. In most countries, only students graduating from very prestigious institutions of higher education can be certain that the prestige of their credential will ensure a good career, whereas graduates from other institutions have to rely on themselves to a larger extent than in the past. One could even argue that we are talking now of inter-individual diversity rather than of inter-institutional diversity as means of improving job prospects.

Cooperation between higher education and the world of work

Institutions of higher education are advised in recent years more than in the past to seek cooperation with the world of work. The more higher education expands, the more knowledge becomes a key factor of productivity, the more global competition intensifies, the more institutions of higher education are expected not to understand themselves as 'ivory towers', but rather to see communication and co-operation with the world of work as a means of improving the education and also the employment opportunities of their students.

The following means of communication and cooperation are most frequently advocated:

- involvement of practitioners in curriculum development (see Skilbeck and Connell 1996)

- participation of industry in decision-making processes, for example through memberships in boards or advisory councils

- mobility between academic and professional careers as well as part-time teaching of practitioners

- internship of students prior to, or during, the course of study

- involvement of students in research projects sponsored by industry

- cooperation in professional counselling of students and placement of graduates.

In observing the various arguments in favour of cooperation between higher education and the world of work, we note not only a plea for professional relevance of study as such. In addition, two other arguments come into play.

First, cooperation with the world of work is often advocated, because it is so difficult to identify the future tasks of the graduates and the competences expected. Rather than setting up a blueprint of qualification requirements, constant communication is expected to ensure the right signals, even if they are diverse, contradictory or vaguely expressed.

Second, various means of cooperation are advocated because representatives of higher education admit that they cannot prepare students well for the world of work in the framework of class instruction, even if they would like to do so. 'Experiential learning' in a comprehensive way is viewed as a powerful instrument supplementing cognitive processes of learning clearly separated from work. It is obvious that temporary study abroad is highly appreciated for the same reason: it provides insights and fosters inter-cultural learning beyond what can be achieved within classroom instruction and learning.

Lifelong education

If higher education is confronted at all with clear, targeted and consistent advice as regards improvements of the links between study and professional work, it is expected to be more strongly engaged in lifelong learning. In this framework, there are eight functions of higher education besides initial education and training for young students (see the overview in Teichler 1990):

- advanced academic study

- advanced professional programmes

- short updating professional training courses

- public lectures and other forms of general knowledge dissemination to adults

- part-time, evening and distance degree programmes suiting persons who are employed while studying

- remedial and second-chance provisions

- short study provisions for adults (sub-degree level programmes)

- in-service training of staff at institutions of higher education.

Continuing professional education for graduates, addressed notably as the second and third points in the above stated list, are certainly the areas in which most growth is expected (see Cochinaux and de Woot 1995; OECD 1995; Hunt 1992). Many experts claim that pre-career education ought to be reduced, and parts of its functions should be transferred to continuing education; this model is often called 'recurrent education'. Even if this is not advocated, many experts see the need for moves towards an integration of pre-career and continuous education. Some experts even claim that institutions of higher education might provide more courses of continuing education in the future than courses serving pre-career education.

Relationships to the world of work and academic responsibility

It is difficult for higher education to strike a balance of appropriate links to, and distance from, the world of work. According to the

Humboldtian ideal, for example, a significant distance might be most productive for society, but a relatively strong and concurrently self-restrictive state is needed as a guardian angel, ensuring an appropriate balance. A recent international comparative survey on the academic profession (Boyer, Altbach and Whitelaw 1994) shows that most academics accept a strong societal responsibility, but are also convinced that the social forces upon them could be too instrumental.

Currently, the pressures are certainly stronger in the direction of providing evidence that higher education is becoming more useful for the world of work. In the process of the massification of higher education, an increasing number of graduates end up in positions in which 'applied' knowledge is expected. The more knowledge becomes a productive force, the more higher education is expected to be evidently productive. Governments often stress 'accountability' and mean instrumentalism. All this is reflected in widespread concern in many societies these days that institutions of higher education have become too far segmented from the world of work and that academics do not sufficiently strive for an appropriate balance.

This, in turn, is likely to increase concern about undue instrumentalist pressures. There is widespread anxiety that intellectual enhancement for all and equality of opportunity are sacrificed for presumed industrial demands (see, for example, Taylor 1997) and that teaching and learning in higher education might be so much geared to immediate needs that higher education might lose its functions of fostering critical thinking, of preparing students for future indeterminate professional tasks and of contributing to innovation in society.

On the other hand, we hear claims that the world of work nowadays requires the whole personality (see Council for Industry and Higher Education 1996). The 'human resource development approach' in industry seems to reduce the conflict between coaching the most useful worker and full enhancement of personality.

Controversies on those matters are likely to persist within institutions of higher education. This should not be deplored. On the contrary, the shaky balance of a creative distance to society is likely to collapse in favour of the 'ivory tower' or in favour of narrow instrumentalism, if the controversy does not persist. What is obviously more needed than in the past, however, is an in-depth knowledge of the needs of society on the part of all in higher education, responsible for administration as well as for teaching and learning.

Higher education cannot afford to bury its head in the sand like an ostrich when it faces the world of work.

References

Beck, U. (1986) *Risikogesellschaft*. Frankfurt a.M.: Suhrkamp.

Boyer, E.L., Altbach, P.G. and Whitelaw, M.J. (1994) *The Academic Profession: An International Perspective*. Princeton, NJ: Carnegie Foundation for the Advancement of Teaching.

Brennan, J. and Kogan, M. (1993) 'Higher education and the world of work: an overview.' *Higher Education in Europe 18*, 2, 2–23.

Brennan, J., Kogan, M. and Teichler, U. (eds) (1995) *Higher Education and Work*. London: Jessica Kingsley Publishers.

Carnoy, M. (ed) (1994) *Economics of Education: Research and Studies*. Oxford: Pergamon.

Cochinaux, P. and de Woot, P. (1995) *Moving Towards a Learning Society: A CRE-ERT Forum Report on European Education*. Geneva and Brussels: Association of European Universities and European Round Table.

Council for Industry and Higher Education (1996) *A Learning Nation*. London: CIHE.

De Weert, E. (1994) 'Translating employment needs into curriculum strategies.' *Higher Education Management 6*, 3, 305–320.

European Round Table of Industrialists (1989) *Education and the European Competence*. Brussels: ERT.

Falk, R. and Weiss, R. (1993) *Zukunft der Akademiker*. Köln: Deutscher Instituts-Verlag.

Harvey, L., Moon, S. and Geall, V. (1997) *Graduates' Work: Organisational Change and Students' Attributes*. Birmingham: University of Central England, Centre for Research into Quality.

Higher education and employment (1995a) *European Journal of Education, 30*, 1.

Higher education and employment (1995b) *European Journal of Education, 30*, 2.

Hunt, E.S. (ed) (1992) *Professional Workers as Learners: The Scope, Problems and Accountability of Continuing Professional Education in the 1990s*. Washington, D.C.: U.S. Department of Education, Office of Educational Research and Improvement.

Kivinen, O. and Rinne, R. (1993) 'Educational qualifications and the labour market: a Scandinavian perspective.' *Higher Education & Industry 7*, 2, 111–118.

Maiworm, F. and Teichler, U. (1996) *Study Abroad and Early Career: Experiences of Former ERASMUS Students*. London: Jessica Kingsley Publishers.

Meek, V.L. *et al.* (eds) (1996) *The Mockers and Mocked: Comparative Perspective of Differentiation, Convergence and Diversity in Higher Education.* Oxford: IAU Press and Pergamon.

Nihon Keieisha Dantai Renmei (1995) *Shinjidai no 'Nihonteki keiei' – chôsen subeki hôkô to sono gutaisaki.* Tokyo: Nikkeiren.

OECD (1992) *From Higher Education to Employment.* 4 vols. Paris: OECD.

OECD (1993) *From Higher Education to Employment: Synthesis Report.* Paris: OECD.

OECD (1995) *Continuing Professional Education of Highly Qualified Personnel.* Paris: OECD.

Psacharopoulos, G. (ed) (1987) *Economics of Education: Research and Studies.* Oxford: Pergamon.

Purcell, K. and Pitcher, J. (1996) *Great Expectations: The New Diversity of Graduate Skills and Aspirations.* Coventry and Manchester: Higher Education Careers Services Unit, Careers Services Trust, Institute of Employment Research.

Sanyal, Bikas C. (1991) 'Higher education and the labor market.' In P.G. Altbach (ed) *International Higher Education: An Encyclopedia.* New York and London: Garland.

Scott, P. (1996) 'Unified and binary systems of higher education in Europe.' In A. Burgen (ed) *Goals and Purposes of Higher Education in the 21st Century.* London: Jessica Kingsley Publishers.

Skilbeck, M. and Connell, H. (1996) 'Industry–university partnerships in the curriculum.' *Industry and Higher Education 10*, 2, 9–22.

Taylor, A. (1997) 'Education for industrial and "Postindustrial" purposes.' *Educational Policy 11*, 1, 3–40.

Teichler, U. (1988) *Changing Patterns of the Higher Education System.* London: Jessica Kingsley Publishers.

Teichler, U. (1990) 'The challenge of lifelong learning for the university.' *CRE-action, 92*, 53–68.

Teichler, U. (1991) 'Towards a highly educated society.' *Higher Education Policy 4*, 4, 11–20.

Teichler, U. (1992) 'Occupational structures and higher education.' In B.R. Clark and G.R. Neave (eds) *The Encyclopedia of Higher Education.* Oxford: Pergamon.

Teichler, U. (1994) 'Students and employment: the issues for university management.' *Higher Education Management 6*, 2, 217–225.

Teichler, U. (1996) 'Higher education and employment – twenty-five years of changing debates and realities.' *Higher Education Management 8*, 3, 25–37.

Teichler, U. (1997) 'Graduate employment – challenges for higher education in the 21st century.' *Higher Education in Europe 22*, 1.

Teichler, U., Buttgereit, M. and Holtkamp, R. (1984) *Hochschulzertifikate in der betrieblichen Einstellungspraxis.* Bad Honnef: Bock.

UNESCO (1995) *Policy Paper for Change and Development in Higher Education.* Paris: UNESCO.

University Competence and Industry (1990) *CRE-action, 92.*

Van der Wende, M. (1996) *Internationalizing the Curriculum in Dutch Higher Education: An International Comparative Perspective.* Utrecht: unpublished doctoral dissertation.

World Bank (1994) *Higher Education: the Lessons of Experience.* Washington, D.C.: The World Bank.

CHAPTER 5

Different Graduates, Different Labour Market
Is There a Mismatch in Supply–Demand?

Helen Connor

Much has happened in the graduate labour market in recent years as a consequence of both supply and demand side changes. There are considerably more, but different kinds of, graduates being produced, entering a wider range of jobs and employing organisations, and experiencing more varied employment outcomes and career paths. The graduate labour market has expanded considerably but at the same time has become more differentiated and fragmented, thus making it increasingly difficult to make broad generalisations about graduate jobs, the graduate labour market or specifically the extent of mismatch between graduate supply and employer demand. While the market evidence indicates an improving supply–demand situation overall, the variation in outcomes between different kinds of graduates, and particularly in the 'quality' of initial jobs they get, suggests something different.

This paper describes the main features of the changing graduate labour market. Its focus is on the impact of supply changes on employment, in particular the rapid expansion of graduate output and increased higher education participation rates, both of which have been strongly influenced by government policy. It raises questions about the extent and nature of any graduate supply–demand imbalance, especially qualitative mismatches between the skills and attributes of the graduates being produced and the requirements of employers. It sets some of the context for the following chapter which focuses on an important aspect of mismatch, that of being overeducated for the job being done.

The previous decade

Higher education in the UK has trebled in size over the last twenty five years but it experienced a particularly rapid period of growth and change between 1989 and 1994. This was fuelled by two government aims in the late 1980s: to increase participation rates, especially among young people, and to make universities more cost efficient by subjecting them more to market forces. Together, they provided a strong incentive to many universities to expand and widen their provision and access. Overall, higher education student numbers grew by over 50 per cent in the 1989–94 period (by more at some of the universities established after 1992) and various internal reforms were introduced including: more flexibility in mode of study; choice of degree subjects and assessment systems; more emphasis on the development of personal skills and vocational studies; and wider access and admission policies to attract more students without the traditional A level/Highers entry qualifications. (See Connor *et al.* 1996 for more details of student trends and higher education developments.)

The overall expansion strategy proved to be so successful that by 1993 a capping policy was introduced to rein back expansion in full-time first degree student numbers in order to stay within government public sector spending targets. The participation index for young people (API) had increased dramatically from 15 per cent in 1988/89 to 30 per cent by 1993/94 (well ahead of the government's long term target figure of one in three by 2000), and most students achieving two A levels or more were going on to higher education (Smithers and Robinson 1995). Participation on full-time degree courses by older people had also grown during this expansionary phase, though from a much lower base than for young entrants, as had participation by women, students from ethnic minority backgrounds and with vocational qualifications, making the higher education student population broader in terms of personal characteristics and more heterogeneous. Full-time degree courses became less dominated by the conventional type of student, A level or Higher school leavers going away from home to study at a university, though they continued to be the main student group at many universities, especially pre-1992 ones.

Looking back, the pushing up of the participation rates and the rapid growth at many universities was less about the need to meet an identified growing demand for graduates in the economy but seems to have been driven more by a government belief in the market economy and that Britain required more better-educated people for reasons of a general 'international competitiveness' nature. The economic arguments for expansion were not well developed, as Murphy (1993) showed in his detailed review of the economic benefits of the expansion of higher education. Rather, expanding higher education was seen to be 'in everybody's interests' (HMSO, 1990 Intergovernmental Review), and there was an increasing demand for university places from school leavers and their parents, and from older people, some of whom were seeking career changes.

This is not to say that labour market signals played no part at all in expansion plans. By 1987/88, there were growing shortages of graduates, in particular in information technology (IT) (see Connor and Pearson 1986), graduate unemployment was falling (down to 6 per cent by 1988) and the 'demographic timebomb' (falling numbers of young people) was beginning to be a concern to some large employers. Demand for graduates was expected to continue upwards during the 1990s, though (even then) graduates were expected to enter a wider range of occupations in the future (see IER 1989). However, these shortages were coexisting with some underemployment: in 1986 almost one in three 1980 graduates were in jobs where a degree was neither required nor useful (Creigh and Rees 1989), and other studies showed that a significant minority felt 'overqualified' (see, for example, Brennan and McGeevor 1988; Boys and Kirkland 1989).

At the end of the 1980s, the emphasis in government policy was on increasing overall supply and taking selective action on the supply side to avoid possible future shortages in certain areas, especially related to new technology. Rather less attention appears to have been given to the likelihood that the higher education system, if expanded significantly, would be catering for a wider segment of the population and providing (at least some of) them with a different learning experience from their predecessors. How would the labour market adapt to this change? An Institute for Employment Studies report for the Council for Industry in Higher Education in 1989 on graduate supply and demand trends gave a warning, which now seems rather familiar:

> Much of this (future) demand will be focused on traditional young graduates with a reasonable class of degree and broad basic com-

petencies. Any increase in supply is going to include an increasing proportion of non-traditional graduates who, while they may not be 'worse', will be 'different'. A challenge ... will be to ensure the attributes of the new supply and the nature of demand will coincide, otherwise there will be a significant number of graduates who will find it difficult to enter what they regard as suitable employment in the 1990s. (Pearson *et al.* 1989)

The graduate labour market of the 1990s

It was only when the economy went into recession in 1990 and the boom years turned into gloom years for graduates, when graduate unemployment shot up to double figures and the traditional graduate recruiters slashed their intakes, that people began to realise that the optimism of just a few years previously had possibly been misplaced. The depressed labour market situation for graduates was made rather worse by the unfortunate timing of expansion of higher education just when the economy started to go into recession, so the first output from the expansionary phase (students who started studying in 1989 with high expectations about jobs) met rather different circumstances on graduation just a few years later in 1992. By then, there were a lot more graduates competing for fewer jobs and shortages had virtually disappeared, even in areas like IT where recruitment problems had been significant.

With the economic recovery has come a steady improvement in the graduate market. Unemployment levels have been slowly coming down since 1992, from a high of 13 per cent of newly qualified graduates, to 8 per cent in 1996. Graduate vacancy levels are increasing once again. This recovery has been more noticeable over the last year or so, and a recent survey of mainly large graduate recruiters (members of the Association of Graduate Recruiters, AGR) showed a 6 per cent growth in graduate recruitment between 1995 and 1996, and a further increase of 12 per cent forecast for 1997 intakes. Signs of a tightening in parts of the labour market are starting to emerge: graduate salaries grew faster last year than average salaries, and over a third of firms reported unfilled vacancies for graduates in 1996 (compared with 28 per cent in 1995, AGR 1996). Graduates have also benefited from the current job growth overall in the UK economy and the increasing emphasis on higher skills and education levels in the workforce (DfEE 1996).

Longer term trends

It is hard to disentangle the effects of the recession from the longer term changes in the graduate market, but there are a number of ways in which the graduate labour market is changing:

- it is more broadly based, both in terms of employers who recruit graduates and the jobs which graduates fill

- there is greater variation in output, in students' backgrounds, personal characteristics and their university experiences

- it is more segmented in terms of employers' demands and approach to getting the graduates they want

- there is increased emphasis being placed by the majority of employers on work-relevant skills

- there are increasing concerns about standards in higher education and quality of output.

These are discussed further below.

Variations in employer demand

There is now a much wider range of employment opportunities available to graduates, away from the traditional focus on large blue chip companies towards smaller firms and the services sector. Graduates have been encouraged by various government initiatives to look more for jobs in small firms, partly because there are fewer vacancies in large firms but also because small firms are seen to be major engines for growth in the economy. A recent estimate suggested that about one in three of small and medium sized enterprises (under 250 employees) had recruited a graduate in the last five years (Williams and Owen 1997).

There are also fewer formal graduate entry schemes and more direct entry of graduates to jobs with more individualised training programmes. Many of the large graduate recruiters have undergone internal restructuring which has reduced their demand for graduates to fill future management posts. Where graduate entry management schemes have been retained, they tend to be smaller in size, shorter in length and with a more functional emphasis. A significant proportion of graduates, however, are taking up non-graduate jobs. (This is discussed further in the next chapter.) Because of the difficulties in defining a 'graduate job' and measuring under-utilisation in relation to qualification, it is impossible to judge whether underemployment is greater today than ten years ago. Certainly many employers took advantage of the slack in the graduate market to employ graduates in jobs which were previously undertaken by non-graduates. Whether this will continue in the current tighter labour market is unclear.

Student diversity

The second significant change is that it is no longer possible to talk of a 'typical graduate' or to generalise in the way people did in the past about graduates and graduate demand. As outlined above, the expansion in graduate output has brought with it much greater diversity, for example, by:

- Type of university attended: There are now 124 universities (compared with 25 in 1960) plus 75 other colleges providing higher education. Although the binary divide has disappeared, each university has its own distinctive mission, individual strengths and student profile. This diversity is likely to increase in the future.

- Age profile: 25 per cent of all first degree students are over 25 years old, but at some universities this proportion is well over half, while at others it is 10 per cent at most. It is also higher in certain subjects (e.g. social studies).

- Ethnicity: Participation by ethnic minorities has been growing and currently around one in eight (UK) entrants to full-time degree courses are from an ethnic minority group. But ethnic minority (UK) students are concentrated at only a dozen or so universities (mainly the new universities in London and other cities). There is also variation in participation rates by ethnic group and by gender.

- Entry qualifications: Almost 30 per cent of entrants to full-time degree courses now have non-traditional qualifications (i.e. not A levels or Highers but BTECs, GNVQs, professional or access qualifications). Access students are concentrated in subjects like social studies and 'subjects allied to medicine', while vocational qualifications are more common in business and administration and computer science. Quality of intake, as measured by A level points, varies considerably by course and institution.

- Subject choice: There has been a growth of multi-disciplinary degrees and a removal of some of the traditional boundaries between disciplines and departments. Most universities now offer modular degree systems which aim to offer students greater choice and flexibility in what they study.

Different labour market outcomes and recruitment patterns

These graduates with more varied backgrounds and personal characteristics as well as varied university experiences, have, not surprisingly, different expectations about jobs and careers (see for example Purcell and Pitcher 1996) and end up taking different career paths. The initial employment experiences of graduates vary, for example:

- only 27 per cent of graduates go into full-time paid permanent jobs, and slightly more, 30 per cent, take up other employment (e.g. temporary, voluntary, part-time)

- overall, 21 per cent take further study after getting their first degree. This proportion rises to over 30 per cent among scientists but falls to 8 per cent among business studies graduates

- unemployment is higher for men than for women; it is also higher than the average in some of the recently expanded subjects like media/communication studies

- of the graduates entering full-time employment, only half take up professional or managerial occupations. Male graduates are more likely than females to be in professional occupations; while female graduates are more likely than males to be in secretarial/clerical occupations.

Some of this variation in graduate employment outcomes is clearly supply side induced. But because there is a wider range of employers and job opportunities for graduates, there is growing diversity in the employment market. Employers seek to recruit graduates for different purposes and the importance they attach to different factors, such as academic ability (especially class of degree, university, A level and GCSE grades), transferable skills (e.g. communication, inter-personal skills, problem solving), degree subjects, specific job relevant skills and work experience, varies also. Priorities differ, for example between many small and large firms, where the former may be recruiting a graduate to fill a specific immediate need and looking for relevant job skills and work experience, while the latter are more likely to be recruiting graduates with longer term needs in mind, for future managers, and to put more emphasis on good personal skills and academic abilities. This in turn leads to different approaches to graduate recruitment. Although many have recruitment programmes which are open to any graduates who wish to apply, targeting a small number of universities in recruitment campaigns or campus visits is increasingly common among large recruiters, either at an institutional or subject/department level. So, too, is developing links with undergraduates, by offering vacation work, sponsorship or industrial placements, and then using this as a recruitment mechanism. Developing corporate degree programmes is also on the increase. The extent to which students' initial choice of university and degree course affects their labour market outcomes is unknown, but if employers continue to be more selective in their recruitment approaches it stands to reason that students at the universities which are less popular with employers, on the basis of judgements they make about its academic reputation, 'quality' of students or relevance of their courses, will do less well in the labour market, at least initially.

Work-relevant skills

The importance employers give to the development of skills in graduates has been highlighted by many reports recently, especially the value of work experience (see Dearing 1997; Harvey *et al.* 1997; AGR 1996). There is a general expectation from employers that higher education should be providing more in the way of 'skills for work' and giving more emphasis to 'employability' in undergraduate studies. A number of initiatives have been taken to help develop this area (see for example Enterprise in Higher Education, work-based learning development programmes funded by the DfEE). However, there are two main issues which are hampering progress: one is the lack of consensus among employers on what the key skills should be and where priorities lie, and the second is the piecemeal approach to skills development within higher education to date and the lack of whole-hearted staff support in some subjects, especially the non-vocational areas of degree study.

Standards and quality

There are increasing concerns coming from employers about the overall 'quality' of today's graduates and standards across higher education. As higher education has expanded, its boundaries have changed in several important ways: more higher education is being undertaken in further education colleges, in the workplace or in partnership with employers and at different stages of life; and there are more cross-disciplinary studies and a wider participation, new kinds of students with different needs and abilities from the traditional kind. The combination of more and different students within a tighter public funding environment has obviously led to a greater range and more variation in the 'quality' of graduates emerging from the system, especially between what is regarded as the most and least able (and the universities and courses producing them). For some employers, it is difficult to keep up with all the changes and many have not made sufficient adjustments to their recruitment policies to take more account of the changes within higher education: for example a smaller proportion of graduates with traditional entry qualifications (e.g. high A level scores). Some continue to use selection criteria which are not as relevant to today's output and restrict their recruitment mainly to the pre-1992 universities. These tend to disadvantage the older students, or those from less conventional backgrounds, and can also give employers relatively poor returns to their recruitment efforts (too many recruiters fishing in the same pool). As a consequence, despite the increased supply of graduates, they experience difficulties in finding sufficient numbers of 'suitable' applicants and vacancies are left unfilled. Some perceive this as due to a drop in quality but this may not be justified.

Current mismatch?

Although the improving economic conditions have led to a more buoyant labour market for graduates, and initial unemployment has been steadily falling in recent years, there is a question mark over whether current supply is adequately meeting demand. The aggregate statistics clearly show that the supply of graduates has been expanding at a faster rate than demand for degree qualified people in the UK. There are now some 50 per cent more graduates being produced annually than ten years ago, while the overall growth rate for 'traditional' graduate demand (i.e. employees in professional or managerial occupations, those traditionally taking graduate entrants) has risen by 20 to 30 per cent at most overall. The economy has been able to absorb some of the growth in graduate supply through graduates going to a wider range of jobs and displacing less qualified people.

Despite recent growth in reported vacancies, many new graduates experience difficulties on entry to the labour market, typically found in prolonged job search, taking temporary filler jobs, especially to pay off debts, and intense competition for the most attractive jobs. (For example, 3000 plus applications for some corporate graduate entry schemes; an average of around 90 applications per vacancy (see AGR 1995). Further evidence of imbalance comes from a number of other sources: 7 per cent of students who graduated in 1996/97 were unemployed at the six month stage – down from 10 percent three years before but still higher than the graduate boom years of the late 1980s; a widening range of salaries are being taken up – a relatively small number of 'highflyers' can achieve high initial annual salaries (£20,000 plus) but substantial numbers of graduates earn much lower salaries (under £14,000); and there is evidence of widespread graduate 'under-utilisation' or underemployment, particularly in the growing services sector and initial graduate jobs (see Mason 1995; Connor and Pollard 1995).

Future scenarios

It is likely that, barring a sudden economic downturn, graduate unemployment levels will continue at current levels or possibly decline slightly in the next few years, but by the early 2000s it is expected that there will still be an excess of graduate supply over demand (IER, 1996). As at present, this 'excess' is expected to confirm a continuing underemployment pattern and substitution between graduates and those with lower qualifications. Overall, output of first degree graduates is still expected to grow but more slowly as a result of the 'capping' by government of university full-time degree intakes since 1994. Any removal of this cap in the next year or two will not have any major impact on supply until 2003 at least. A major influence on graduate supply is drop-out rates. If they increase, as they are expected to do, then the fully qualified output may be lower than forecast. On the demand side, there is likely to be overall job growth in the next few years, both in the traditional types of graduate recruiters and in the newer employers of graduates but it is impossible to obtain any numerical forecasts from employers about their likely future demand.

A supply–demand imbalance?

But does the UK really need to produce more graduates? To some, who believe that investment in education is a necessity for sustained economic development, this is not seen as even a sensible question to be asking (see, for example, CBI 1994; CIHE 1995). More recently, the Committee of Vice-Chancellors and Principals put forward a strong belief, which is supported by others, that under-supply is far more dangerous than over-supply (see its submission to Dearing). Several projections have highlighted a continued upward demand for places in higher education, both for the traditional type of degree study and new types of lifelong learning (IES, DfEE).

But if we look at the strict economic case for further expansion it is still fairly weak. International comparisons show that the UK produces similar numbers of graduates per capita as its main competitors (see Jagger, Morris and Pearson 1996), and while the evidence on financial rates of return from taking a degree show that it is still a good individual investment, the doubling of higher education participation rates among young people and the considerably increased supply of graduates may dampen the graduate 'pay premium' in the future (Lissenburgh and Bryson 1996). With the pick-up in the economy has come an improved job market which is already being seen in decisions about whether or not to enter higher education in the first place, and in time is likely to affect any graduate premium.

But 'the economic argument' has never been the main driver of expansion of higher education. Many people would argue that the wider educational and social benefits of having a 'mass' higher education system with more open access and greater diversity are equally, if not more, important (especially if the funding of higher education shifts more towards individuals making a greater contribution, as the Dearing Report recommends).

It has never been easy to match accurately higher education output numbers and employment demand, except possibly in some very specialist areas where there is a direct relationship between education and professional training and employment (e.g. medicine). But it should be possible to meet more modest aims, namely to supply a high level of education in an efficient and equitable way to as many people as possible, maintain degree standards and produce graduates who are adaptable and have a range of skills which are relevant to employers.

This then leads to a second question: are we producing the right kind of graduates, that is an output from higher education which is broadly in line with employers' needs, or should we be altering the mix? The current evidence suggests that the student profile is going to become broader over time, which will have further implications for the extent to which a qualitative match between the attributes of the graduates being produced and requirements of employers (see for example Harvey *et al.* 1997) can be achieved. Essential work-relevant skills are seen to be deficient in the majority of graduates, and there are concerns about maintaining the 'quality' of the graduate output. Experiences of individual graduates in finding suitable work vary considerably.

Conclusion

It may be that the full impact on the labour market of the rapid expansion of higher education during the early 1990s, producing a new graduate product, is only now being fully recognised. The economic recession of the 1990s had a substantial effect on graduate demand but it was short-term and, from a research perspective, a diversion, confusing the analysis of the more important longer term trends, in particular the changing structure of the graduate labour market. As the evidence in the next chapter confirms, underemployment is not a short-term phenomenon, not just a consequence of the recession and the oversupply of graduates at that time. It is likely to be a lasting feature of the graduate labour market here and in other countries in Europe and the USA.

There are two other trends in the USA graduate market which may be lessons for the UK. The first is the importance given by employers to work experience when recruiting, a view that is gaining ground here (see the Dearing Report). The second, and more significant, is that despite the expansion, higher education is greatly valued in the USA. It remains a major avenue through which individuals can improve their job prospects and income data show a strong relationship between earnings and educational levels (Court and Connor 1995).

If students here in the UK are to continue to see higher education participation as of value, as they still do on the whole (see Connor 1996), with the economic case for participation probably being given more attention in the future, as fees become more of an issue, then they need to have realistic expectations of jobs and the labour market they are likely to enter. They need to appreciate, too, the range of skills and abilities which meet the needs of employers, in particular good personal as well as academic skills, adaptability and flexibility. They need to be made more aware of the graduate labour market trends at an early stage so that they can make their choices from an informed base. Choices made before and during degree study, especially those relating to choice of university and the opportunity they then get to improve their skills and 'employability' (e.g. through relevant and quality work experience), can have significant implications for their subsequent success in the labour market and the ability to obtain their preferred kind of job or employer.

On the employer side, they need to do more in practice to back up their assertions that they 'value graduates' and graduates having 'work experience' (see Harvey *et al.* 1997) and look to how they can utilise and help to develop graduates better. The expansion in higher education has meant a graduate output which is different and more varied, not necessarily worse, and further expansion is likely to make it more different. Recruitment approaches and selection methods will need to be adjusted accordingly.

In conclusion, the realities of the changes in our higher education system need to be grasped better by all, so that the employment and career expectations of the wider body of graduates coming on to the labour market in the twenty-first century are realistic and can be fulfilled, and so that the economy and individuals benefit as fully as possible from the investment.

References

Association of Graduate Recruiters (AGR) (1996) *Graduate Salaries and Vacancies Surveys* (annual surveys undertaken by the Institute for Employment Studies (IES) for AGR).

Association of Graduate Recruiters (AGR) (1995) *Skills for Graduates in the 21st Century*, produced by Whiteway Research for the AGR.

Brennan, J. and McGeevor, P. (1988) *Graduates at Work*. London: Jessica Kingsley Publishers.

Boys, C. and Kirkland, J. (1989) *Degrees of Success*. London: Jessica Kingsley Publishers.

Connor, H. and Pearson, R. (1986) *Information Technology Manpower into the 1990s*. Brighton: Institute for Employment Studies.

Connor, H., Pearson, R., Court, G. and Jagger, N. (1996) *University Challenge: Student Choices in the 21st Century*, IES Report 306, Institute for Employment Studies: Brighton.

Connor, H. and Pollard, E. (1996) *What do Graduates Really Do?* IES Report 308, Institute for Employment Studies: Brighton.

Connor, H. (1996) *What's the Point of a Degree?* Observer, 18 August 1996.

CBI (1994) *Thinking Ahead: Ensuring the Expansion of Higher Education*. London: Confederation of British Industry.

CIHE (1995) *A Wider Spectrum of Opportunity*. London: Council for Industry and Higher Education.

Court, G. and Connor, H. (1994) *The US Labour Market for Graduates*, IES Report 387.

Creigh, S. and Rees, T. (1989) 'Graduates and the labour market in the 1980s.' In *Employment Gazette*, January 1989.

CVCP (1996) *Our Universities, Our Future*, submission to Dearing Inquiry, Committee of Vice-Chancellors and Principals of UK Universities.

Harvey, L., Moon, S. and Geall, V. (1997) *Graduates Work: Organisational Change and Students' Attributes*. Birmingham: Centre for Research into Quality, University of Central England.

HMSO (1990) *Higher Education: Meeting the Challenge*, report of the Interdepartmental review.

IER (1989) *Review of the Economy and Employment*, Institute of Employment Research, Warwick University.

IER (1996) *Review of the Economy and Employment: Future Employment Prospects for the Highly Qualified*, Institute of Employment Research, Warwick University.

Jagger, N., Morris, S. and Pearson, R. (1996) *The Target for High Level Skills in an International Context*, IES Report 307. Brighton: Institute for Employment Studies.

Lissenburgh, S. and Bryson, A. (1996) *The Returns to Graduation*, Research Studies RS15, DfEE.

Mason, G. (1995) 'The new-graduate supply shock: recruitment and utilisation in British industry,' NIESR Report Series, No. 9.

Murphy, J. (1993) 'A degree of waste: the economic benefits of educational expansion.' *Oxford Review of Education 19*, 1.

National Committee of Inquiry into Higher Education (NCIHE) (1997) *Higher Education in the Learning Society (The Dearing Report)*.

Pearson, R., Pike, G., Gordon, A. and Weyman, C. (1989) *How Many Graduates in the 21st Century: The Choice is Yours?* Institute for Employment Studies.

Purcell, K. and Pitcher, J. (1996) *Great Expectations*, a report to AGACS and CSU, IER, University of Warwick.

Smithers, A. and Robinson, P. (1995) *Post-18 Education: Growth, Change and Prospects*. London: CIHE.

Williams, H. and Owen, G. (1997) *Recruitment and Utilisation of graduates by small and medium sized enterprises*, Research Report No. 29, DfEE.

CHAPTER 6

Overeducation
Problem Or Not?

Peter J. Dolton and Anna Vignoles

The previous chapter by Helen Connor outlines some of the more important trends in the market for graduate labour. In particular she highlights the increasing diversity of both graduates and employers and the possibility of mismatch between supply and demand in the market for qualified manpower. Here we focus more narrowly on one specific aspect of the graduate labour market, the problem of so-called 'overeducation'. In particular, we attempt to assess whether graduate 'overeducation' is a significant problem and to address the following questions:

- Do most graduates get graduate level jobs?

- Can we define what is or is not a graduate job?

- Can we quantify the extent of any 'overeducation' problem?

- What are the effects of 'overeducation' on the financial return to a degree?

- Can we explain the causes of 'overeducation'?

Defining overeducation

A graduate in a job requiring only sub-degree level qualifications (or perhaps no qualifications at all) is defined as overeducated. Thus the term *overeducation* has a specific economic meaning, based on the reductionist assumption that the purpose of education is to prepare students for employment commensurate with their qualifications. Implicitly, individuals are assumed to invest in education only to secure higher pay and better jobs. Clearly, in reality, education has much wider benefits, both for the individual and for society as a whole. In fact many educationalists argue that if only we could quantify these wider benefits, it would become apparent that there is no such thing as overeducation. When assessing whether we have too many graduates, these non-monetary benefits of higher education should not be ignored and we return to this important issue later. First, however, we detail the various methods used by economists to measure the incidence of overeducation in the labour market.[1]

Measuring the extent of the overeducation problem has proved to be very difficult, not least because it requires us to determine the appropriate education level for any given job. Commonly researchers have used employee surveys which ask respondents directly about the minimum education level needed to do their jobs (Duncan and Hoffman 1981; Sicherman 1991; Sloane, Battu and Seaman 1995). With this method the workers themselves define whether or not they consider themselves to be overeducated for their job. Other researchers have attempted to use more 'objective' methods, relying on formal job analysis to determine the average required education for a particular occupation. Rumberger (1987), for example, used the *US Dictionary of Occupational Titles* which provides information on the educational requirements of a wide range of occupations. Yet another method has been developed by Verdugo and Verdugo (1989), who calculated the mean education level across a range of occupations and defined an individual as overeducated if he or she had more than one standard deviation above the mean education level for his or her occupation (see also Groot 1993; Groot and Maasen Van Den Brink 1997).

All the methods described above have certain problems and potential biases. Surveys may be biased because they rely on the objectivity of respondents. Individuals who are overeducated, and perhaps more negative about their jobs, may be less likely to complete an employment questionnaire in the first place. If this is the case, surveys will tend to underestimate the incidence of overeducation. Furthermore, workers probably need to compare their own job to other 'benchmark' jobs, in order to assess the educational

---

1   Although in this paper we are interested primarily in graduates, much of the other work in this field has analysed the overall incidence of overeducation in the labour market as a whole.

requirements of their work. This is likely to be easier in larger, more structured firms, where there are clearly defined jobs. Hence public sector employees and workers in large firms are more likely to be able to determine whether or not they are overeducated, again biasing survey results.

Equally, objective measures of overeducation are based on the critical assumption that all workers with the same job or occupation title are doing work of equal difficulty. Yet some job titles are very general, encompassing a wide range of different types of work. For example, a sales manager in one company may be doing a quite different job as compared to someone with the same job title in another organisation. It is likely to be extraordinarily difficult to construct a meaningful list of job titles with appropriate education levels attached. This problem is compounded by the fact that, over time, technology and management structures change and hence jobs also change. Some jobs become more responsible, requiring superior skills, others have become much more routine. Updating the educational requirements of various jobs is therefore a complex and ongoing process, if the information is to be at all valid.

Equally, the method used by the Verdugos may not be appropriate because it is somewhat mechanistic. Their definition of overeducation implies that there will always be some people who are overeducated (or undereducated) because they have more (or less) education than the average person doing that job. If we accept that within any occupation there will be a distribution of easier and more demanding jobs, then it is likely that we will also see a distribution of people with more or less education filling these jobs. One can therefore question whether the Verdugo definition is measuring anything other than the diversity of jobs within a particular occupation.

Finally, all measures of overeducation tend to reflect what employers say they need, not necessarily what is actually required to do the job. Certainly there is evidence of 'qualification inflation', whereby employers upgrade the educational requirements of jobs but do not change their content. This may be in response to an increase in the supply of graduates, which has allowed employers to be more demanding of prospective employees. This problem will lead to underestimates of the incidence of true overeducation. For example, executive officers in the British civil service used to need only A Level qualifications.[2] Today increasingly they need a degree to do this kind of work, although in many instances the actual job has been changed very little. Another complication is that, as the number of graduates increases, employers may perceive that the value of a degree is falling. This kind of 'grade inflation' may not actually be occurring but the important point is that if employers believe that degree standards are less rigorous, they are likely to demand ever higher standards of job applicants (first class degrees or masters qualifications only).

All these methodological difficulties clearly show that the whole notion of an 'overeducated' graduate is problematic. Just as different researchers have used various alternative ways of measuring overeducation, so estimates of the extent of the problem also vary quite widely. There is a growing consensus, however, that many graduates are working in jobs that in some way do not match their skill level. This in itself is cause for concern. Below we review the empirical evidence on the extent and effects of overeducation and attempt to draw some broad conclusions that may help to guide policy makers in the future.

The incidence of overeducation

As we have already discussed, estimates of the incidence of overeducation in the work force differ according to the research method used. Work in the USA suggests that, among white males, the incidence of overeducation in the work force as a whole ranges from 11 per cent (Verdugo and Verdugo 1989) to 40 per cent (Duncan and Hoffman 1981; Sicherman 1991). Oosterbeek (1991) looked at this problem among Dutch workers in the early 1980s and concluded that the incidence of overeducation was around 20 per cent. Sloane, Battu and Seaman (1995) have also confirmed that a significant proportion of the work force in the United Kingdom is overeducated. Using the self-assessment method, they found that approximately 30 per cent of survey respondents in the UK in 1986 were overeducated. However,

2   Executive officers have a largely administrative role and are equivalent to junior managers or team leaders.

more recent work, using the Verdugo measurement technique, has suggested that the incidence of overeducation in the UK may be much lower than this, at around 15 per cent for men (Groot and Van Den Brink 1997). The incidence of overeducation also appears to vary by race, sex, occupation and education level. Duncan and Hoffman, for example, estimated the incidence of overeducation to be approximately 50 per cent for black men, compared to 40 per cent for white men, despite the fact that black men had lower average education levels. In fact, they found that generally the incidence of overeducation was higher (proportionately) among the less educated, particularly the semi-skilled and unskilled. Verdugo and Verdugo (1989) and Rumberger (1987) confirm this.

Estimates of the incidence of overeducation differ according to whether 'subjective' or 'objective' measurement techniques are used. However, it is certainly not the case that 'objective' techniques always generate lower estimates. For instance, McGoldrick and Robst (1996) use three different methods to measure the incidence of overeducation in the USA in 1985: the self-survey technique using data from the Panel Study of Income Dynamics, the external approach using the *US Dictionary of Occupational Titles* (DOT) and the Verdugo method. The survey approach indicated that just under one third were overeducated, whilst the DOT method suggested that approximately half of the sample were overeducated. The Verdugo method implied that just 10 to 16 per cent of the sample were overeducated. Van der Velden and van Smoorenburg (1997) have also compared self-reporting techniques with results based on job analysis and concluded that in their Dutch data sets, job analyst data systematically overestimated the incidence of overeducation.

Graduate overeducation

Here we focus specifically on graduate overeducation in the UK, an issue which has concerned an increasing number of researchers over the last five years. Much of this work has relied on surveys of graduates early on in their careers. A typical example of a study in this area was undertaken by Brennan *et al.* (1993). They surveyed graduates from the early 1980s who were two years into their careers. Only 30 per cent of the sample considered themselves to be in 'traditional' graduate jobs, although nearly 60 per cent claimed that a degree was a requirement for their position. In common with other research in this field, Brennan *et al.* found that the subject of a graduate's degree significantly affected whether he or she ended up in a non-graduate job. For instance, they found that arts, humanities, and combined studies graduates were more likely to end up doing clerical or secretarial work.

More recently, work by the Institute of Employment Studies (Connor and Pollard 1996) indicated that just over half of a sample of Sussex University graduates claimed that a degree was a formal requirement for their job,[3] slightly less than the proportion found by Brennan *et al.* Connor and Pollard's research is also helpful in highlighting the effects of using different definitions of overeducation. Among other questions, graduates were asked whether or not a degree was helpful for their job and whether the previous incumbent had been a graduate. All these questions yielded somewhat different responses. For instance, although half the sample felt they were doing graduate level work, a high proportion (65 per cent) also considered themselves to be underemployed. This illustrates some of the limitations of work based on surveys which simply ask workers whether they are overeducated.

Still more recently, Labour Force Survey data indicate that the incidence of overeducation among UK graduates is between 27 and 28 per cent (Alpin, Shackleton and Walsh 1997). Like Brennan *et al.*, this study found that degree subject was an important determinant of whether or not a graduate was overeducated. Architecture, business and finance, arts, humanities, social science, and combined honours graduates were more likely to be overeducated. Their research also showed that non-whites were more likely to be overeducated, as were younger graduates and those working in the private sector or for small organisations.

In addition to surveying graduates, some researchers have focused on the employer's side of the employer–employee relationship. In particular they have tried to ascertain employers' views on the types of work undertaken by the graduates. For example, Rigg *et al.* (1990) looked for evidence that employers were systematically recruiting graduates into jobs previously considered to be at the non-graduate level. About a quarter of his sample of employers in the late 1980s admitted that they had selected graduates for non-graduate jobs and

3   See Tables 5.6 and 5.7, Connor *et al.*, (1996).

only about one third of this group had changed the content of the job to reflect the higher skills level of the graduate occupant.

Using a similar approach, Geoff Mason (1995) analysed the extent of graduate under-utilisation in certain UK industries. Mason's use of the term under-utilisation is stronger than the concept of overeducation, as defined here. He defined a graduate as under-utilised if: the graduate's predecessor in the job was not a graduate; the job had not been changed as a result of a graduate being appointed; and the graduate was being paid the same as non-graduates doing similar work. Mason found that many, but by no means all, non-graduate jobs had been upgraded once a graduate was appointed. Even more significantly, he found evidence of extensive under-utilisation of graduates in the financial services sector, although the problem was minimal in the steel industry.[4]

Harvey, Moon and Geall (1997) have conducted a more general survey of employers' views of UK graduates. The consensus appears to be that employers need graduates that are 'adaptive', 'adaptable' and 'transformative'. Graduates must fit in with company culture and be flexible enough to deal with change but also be able to initiate change when appropriate. They must add value to an organisation and ideally they would also be immediately effective on joining a firm. This is obviously a lot to ask, and the employers surveyed seemed to agree that at the moment higher education in the UK does not provide graduates with all these skills. However, the report then goes on to say that employers' recruitment strategies are generally 'risk averse'. In the face of rising numbers of graduates and scarce graduate jobs, employers resort to A Level scores, degree classifications and institutional reputations to assess the quality of prospective graduate employees. The implication of this finding is that graduates with fewer or low grade A Levels, those studying at less reputable universities and those with non-honours degrees will miss out on the graduate jobs. Harvey *et al.* (1997) do not comment on whether improving the quality of higher education and better meeting the needs of employers will actually create more graduate jobs. If it does

---

4   For example, he found evidence of graduates in financial services being appointed to unmodified mid-level clerical jobs at salaries of up to one-third less than their graduate peers, and into basic clerical jobs at the going clerical rate.

not, employers will continue to select the best graduates by various criteria, leaving others to take up non-graduate jobs.

Robinson and Manacorda (1997) consider the overeducation question tangentially, using Labour Force Survey data. They study changes in the educational attainment of the UK work force over time, compared to changes in the UK labour market's occupational structure. The authors are primarily interested in whether the overall increase in the educational attainment of the UK work force is the result of foreign competition and technological change which have reduced the demand for unskilled labour. They also seek to determine whether the rising demand for skilled labour, as a result of this structural change, has exceeded the education and training system's ability to provide such labour. Their hypothesis is that, if competition and technological developments are driving changes in the demand for skilled and unskilled labour, this process will be uneven across occupations. In fact, their work suggests that the overall increase in educational attainment has been evenly distributed across occupations. It is not the fast changing industries, facing stiff foreign competition and rapid technological change, that employ the most skilled staff. Instead, the average qualification level of staff in almost all industries has risen. According to these authors, this suggests that employers are simply increasing the educational requirements of jobs in response to changes in the supply of skilled labour. This implies that we will increasingly see better educated people in lower level jobs (i.e. overeducation).

We have also undertaken our own research in this field (Dolton and Vignoles 1996a). We use the 1980 National Survey of Graduates and Diplomates,[5] a one in six random sample postal survey of UK graduates. The survey was undertaken six years after these students graduated (1986) and includes detailed questions about academic qualifications, work history and socio-economic background. We assessed the extent of graduate overeducation from the survey question 'What was the minimum formal qualification required for (entering) this job?'. Respondents had a choice of formal qualifications in response to this question or could opt for the 'other' category.

5   The survey was carried out jointly by Social Community Planning Research (SCPR) and the Department of Employment's Employment Market Research Unit (EMRU).

From these answers we constructed variables measuring not just whether a graduate was overeducated or not, but also the extent of their overeducation. Hence an overeducated graduate could be in a job in any of the following five categories: no qualifications required, O Levels only required, A Levels required, sub-degree vocational qualifications required and other sub-degree qualifications required.

Our research indicates that:

- 38 per cent of all 1980 graduates surveyed were overeducated in their first job

- 30 per cent of graduates were overeducated six years after graduation

- 15 per cent of the sample required no qualifications at all in their first job and even six years on, this figure is only down to 11 per cent

- similar proportions of male and female graduates were overeducated

- graduates with a 'higher quality' education, i.e. those who attended universities (rather than polytechnics) and those with better degree grades, were less likely to be overeducated

- graduates with a postgraduate academic qualification were more likely to be in jobs requiring at least a degree or above

- graduates from the social science, art and language faculties were more likely to be overeducated than individuals with engineering, technical or science degrees. More than half of the arts graduates in our sample were overeducated in their first job and about a third were overeducated six years later.

In addition to these main findings we also found that the incidence of overeducation was similar in both the public and private sectors. However, a higher proportion of those working in government administration, specifically, were overeducated. Overeducation was highest amongst those who worked for small firms (less than 20 people), although generally the incidence of overeducation did not decrease linearly with firm size. Interestingly, more than 70 per cent of the graduates who were overeducated and working in small firms claimed to require no qualifications at all for their job. It may be that the lack of benchmark jobs and formal qualification requirements caused a higher incidence of overeducation to be recorded amongst graduates who work in small firms.

One issue ignored by many studies in this field is that of life-cycle effects. Researchers have used cross-sectional data to look at the overall incidence of overeducation at one point in time. This does not tell us how overeducation affects the individual graduate over his or her life time. Our data allowed us to measure how long graduates spent overeducated and to isolate the factors that could speed up a graduate's transition to a graduate level job (Dolton and Vignoles 1996b). We found that, among male graduates at least, once a graduate was overeducated the probability of getting a graduate job was very low. Most of our sample of graduates who started out overeducated never succeeded in getting a graduate job. One reason for this may be that employers view overeducated graduates as being of lesser quality. This suggestion is supported by the fact that graduates with first or upper second class degrees were most likely to make the transition into a graduate job. Perhaps the high quality of these individuals' degrees offset any negative effect from being in a non-graduate job. We then predicted how much the overeducated graduates would earn if they did manage to secure a graduate job, based on their personal and educational characteristics. Graduates with the highest predicted earnings got a graduate job more quickly, perhaps because they had the greatest motivation to do so.

Overeducation and its effect on earnings

Much of the research in this area has focused on the effects of overeducation on the financial return to a degree. Do overeducated individuals earn less than their peers who find graduate jobs? This question is of interest for two reasons. First, from the perspective of the individual, overeducation may only be a real problem if overeducated workers earn significantly less than their peers in graduate jobs.[6] Second, if overeducated graduates do earn less than those in graduate jobs, this appears to contradict human capital theory, the dominant paradigm in this field. Human capital theory assumes that individuals are paid the value of their marginal product,

---

6   This ignores the psychological effects of working in a job for which you are overqualified.

that is, are paid on the basis of their productivity in the work place. This means their pay will be determined by their human capital (education, training, work experience and so forth), rather than the characteristics of their job *per se*. Firms are assumed to utilise fully their staff and to be able to adapt their production technology in response to changes in the relative supply of skilled labour. Hence if more graduates come onto the labour market, graduate wages will tend to fall and firms will change their way of working to utilise the increased supply of this cheaper and more skilled labour. More high level jobs will be created and graduates will tend not to end up doing sub-degree level work. Theoretically in the long run at least, the supply of graduates will match the demand for graduates and overeducation will not exist.

The consensus from the research in this field is that not only does overeducation exist, but also that overeducated graduates suffer financially relative to their peers in graduate jobs. Certainly overeducated graduates earn more than non-graduates.[7] In economic terminology, this means that 'surplus' education has a positive return. However, overeducated graduates consistently earn less than their peers who secure graduate jobs. This indicates that the return to surplus education is less than the return to required education. For instance, Hartog and Oosterbeek (1988) concluded that the return to a year of overeducation was positive, but 20 per cent less than the return to a year of required education. Duncan and Hoffman (1981), Alba-Ramirez (1993) and Rumberger (1987) found that the return to surplus education was approximately only half the return to required education. So why do students continue to invest in a degree if significant numbers of them end up overeducated and earning a much lower financial return than their peers in graduate jobs? The answer is that graduates do not know, *a priori*, whether or not they will be overeducated and hence make higher education investment decisions based on the average expected return to a degree. Taking into account the risk of ending up overeducated, if the average expected return to a degree is higher than the interest rate on other

---

7   In contrast to most of the literature, Groot (1993) found that the return to a
    year of overeducation was negative and larger than the positive return to a year
    of additional education. This implies that overeducated workers earn less than
    workers who are correctly allocated.

equivalent investments, people will continue to see a degree as a good investment.

Dolton and Vignoles (1996a) looked at the effect of overeducation on graduate earnings in the UK. Graduates who secured graduate jobs earned more than those who ended up in a non-graduate job after they finished their degree. For instance, a graduate in a job requiring no qualifications at all, or just O levels, earned 13 per cent less than someone who managed to secure a graduate level job. We found some differences between men and women, in terms of the impact of overeducation on earnings. Women seemed to incur a greater earnings penalty for being overeducated. For example, women in a first job requiring either no qualifications at all, or simply a vocational qualification of some sort, suffered badly, relative to both their female peers in graduate jobs and as compared to the earnings penalty incurred by similarly overeducated men. These overeducated women earned 12 per cent less than women in graduate jobs. Men in jobs requiring a vocational qualification actually earned the same as their male peers in graduate jobs. Also for overeducated women, generally the higher the level of education required for their job, the greater their earnings. This was not true for men. For instance, men in jobs requiring no qualifications earned the same as those in A level jobs.

The differences between the sexes appear to reflect partly the different types of work undertaken by men and women in the 1980s. As we have already argued, typically occupational classification systems are not sophisticated enough to identify precisely what kind of work was done by each graduate. Nonetheless, further analysis of the job titles of various groups of overeducated workers suggested that men in jobs needing no qualifications at all tended to be doing labouring or manual work in industry or catering. They also worked in sales or clerk/cashier jobs. Women in the same overeducation category were largely in secretarial, clerical, welfare, or catering jobs. In general the lower skilled male jobs were relatively better paid than the types of lower skilled jobs that women were doing, particularly women in welfare roles. Also for men the 'no qualifications required' category covered a more diverse range of jobs than for women, including some higher paying semi-skilled industrial processing jobs. This would have tended to boost the average earnings of this category, particularly as compared to those in lower grade clerical work requiring O levels. Hence we conclude that the incidence of overeducation, and the financial penalty for overeducation appear to vary by type of job, sector and sex.

We also analysed these graduates' earnings six years after they had left higher education. Overeducated graduates in certain types of non-graduate job were still earning less than their counterparts in graduate jobs. If a job required O Level qualifications, the earnings loss was almost 11 per cent; for jobs requiring A Levels, the loss was about 9 per cent. Again there were differences between men and women.

The evidence therefore suggests that graduates who are overeducated earn considerably less than those who secure graduate level jobs. Hence at a personal level, overeducation is a real problem for the individual graduate. By and large, the lower the education level of the job, the greater the loss of earnings. The earnings penalty for being overeducated appears, at least in our data, to be higher for women, especially in unskilled jobs. From an economic perspective we can also reject a pure human capital interpretation of the labour market. Human capital theory suggests that the return to education does not depend at all on the educational requirements of a job, only the human capital of the worker. Yet research on overeducation indicates that individuals' productivity and earnings depend both on the educational level of their job and their own educational achievements (in addition to other human capital they may have).

Explanations for overeducation

Although we have reservations about the methods used to measure the incidence of overeducation, the evidence overwhelmingly suggests that a significant number of UK graduates are overeducated. We do not attempt to develop a complete theory of overeducation here but merely suggest some possible explanations for the phenomenon.

Overeducation can be interpreted as a simple excess supply problem. For a number of reasons, the supply of graduates has increased dramatically over time and it appears that the demand for graduates has not kept pace. This has resulted in significant levels of overeducation, as graduates are forced to take non-graduate jobs rather than remain unemployed. The increase in the number of graduates is attributable to a number of factors. First, the staying-on rate at school has increased dramatically. This may be linked to very high youth unemployment, particularly among those who leave school at 16 with no qualifications. There is also a paucity of A Level jobs. Hence once students remain at school to take A Levels, they also tend to go on to university. The Conservative government also decided to expand higher education in the late 1980s. The large increase in the number of university places was matched by rising, previously unmet, demand. This rise in demand is partly attributable to the fact that, although the variability in the financial return to a degree has risen, the average financial return has remained high. Some of the high return is due to the continued subsidy of university students. This, too, explains the increase in higher education participation in response to an increase in the number of university places. Whatever the cause of the increase in graduate numbers, it is the market's inability to absorb this increase that is causing the problem.

However, human capital theory predicts that overeducation will not be a long-term problem. Eventually the supply of, and demand for, graduates will equalise. Individuals will not continue to invest in a degree if they end up overeducated and earning a very low financial return to their degree. Equally firms will not continue to underutilise graduates and will eventually adapt their technology to make full use of this highly skilled labour. Human capital theory therefore appears to contradict the empirical evidence. How can this be the case?

It may be the case that education is a 'consumption' good and that people continue to want to go to university because they enjoy the education process, irrespective of the financial return to a degree. An alternative explanation for high and persistent overeducation, however, is that firms are unable to alter their way of working in response to an increase in the supply of graduates. Only in the very long term might firms be able to alter their methods radically to accommodate a permanent and large increase in the number of graduates. For example, the motor car industry has invested a considerable amount of money in a particular technology and would not be able to change its production process quickly, even if it became obvious that the average education level of the work force had risen.

It is also possible that overeducation is a cyclical phenomenon. Firms tend to cut back on the number of people they hire during recessions. New graduates are therefore one of the first groups of workers to suffer in an economic downturn. Graduates that come on the market during a recession may be unable to secure graduate jobs and instead take lower level jobs as a preferable alternative to unemployment. Dolton and Vignoles (1996b) found that graduates who start out overeducated tend to remain overeducated for some considerable period of time. Hence overeducation may have cohort effects. Graduates coming on to the labour market in a bad economic period may be overeducated for their first job and remain that way because of the bad start to their career. There is also evidence that certain types of graduates, namely those from the 'new' universities, are less geographically mobile. Hence overeducation may also be a symptom of a regional demand problem. Even in the face of limited demand for graduates in a particular region, certain graduates do not move to secure a graduate job and instead remain in a job for which they are overeducated.

Another possible explanation is based on the assumption that education is used by employers only as a screening device and that it does not necessarily make workers more productive. Hence employers do not need more educated workers, rather they just need to identify the most able workers. As the numbers in higher education increase, this may cause 'grade inflation' and over time a degree will become a less accurate indicator of a person's ability. Employers may then set still higher educational requirements to attract only the most able people. Workers realise this and invest in more and more education in order to set themselves apart from the less able. Even if graduates increasingly end up overeducated this is a logical process if they are able to get jobs that people without degrees cannot secure.

Another less extreme argument is the 'substitution hypothesis', which is based on the assumption that education only increases the productivity of workers when combined with some work experience ('on-the-job' training). Hence, overeducated graduates end up being passed over for graduate jobs because of their lack of work experience. Certainly the empirical evidence does suggest that overeducated workers tend to be younger and less experienced than adequately educated workers (Groot 1996).

Linked to the 'grade inflation' argument is the issue of degree quality. Most commentators believe that a degree is much less of a homogeneous entity than it once was. Hence graduates have had a diverse range of educational experiences and reached very different educational standards. Employers recognise this increasing heterogeneity of degrees and are well aware that not all degrees are worth the same. Hence, graduate jobs tend to be offered only to those with the highest quality degrees, from the 'best' universities. Other graduates take jobs labelled as non-graduate, which may in fact be quite appropriate for their true standard of education. To give an example, a graduate from Cambridge working as a supervisor at B&Q may be overeducated, whereas another graduate from a less prestigious university may not be overeducated in that kind of role. In other words, we may be moving towards the USA system with increased heterogeneity of both universities and degree 'products' and hence graduate outcomes.

Various related explanations have also been put forward. The overeducated may be more upwardly mobile, accepting a period of overeducation in order to achieve higher earnings in the future. An example of this might be when graduates accept shop floor positions in order to gain the experience necessary to progress to store manager level. Sicherman and Galor (1990), Sicherman (1991), Alba-Ramirez (1993) and Sloane *et al.* (1995) found some empirical support for this theory, although it is difficult to find data that is adequate to test this hypothesis.

It is also possible that overeducation is simply one symptom of a bad match between the graduate and his or her job. This might occur because prior to accepting the job, the graduate was unsure as to what the job entailed and indeed whether the job was a graduate level role. However, it would seem likely that these bad matches would end in a quit, as the worker seeks out a more favourable job. This would again suggest that overeducation will not be a long-term problem.

Conclusions and policy implications

This brief survey of the literature suggests that a significant proportion of UK graduates enter non-graduate jobs when they leave higher education. Our research indicates that in the 1980s, around 30 per cent of all graduates were in non-graduate jobs, at least early on in their careers. As higher education has expanded considerably subsequently, it is unlikely that the incidence of overeducation has fallen since that time. Naturally, this assumes that the recent rapid growth in the number of graduates has not stimulated a dramatic increase in employers' demand for this kind of labour.

This evidence seems to support the view that we have too many graduates. Unfortunately, however, there are some fundamental difficulties interpreting the data on this issue. Most of the literature on overeducation has used self-survey methods to determine whether graduates are overeducated or not. We have already indicated that this is not necessarily an accurate measure of whether or not the person is truly overeducated. The previous Prime Minister might argue that he only needed O Levels to do his job. The new PM, Tony Blair, might claim that a degree or, even more specifically a law degree, is an essential requirement. Even the so-called 'objective' measures of overeducation are problematic, as we have seen. Also graduates may 'grow' jobs, bringing additional skills and knowledge to the job and transforming it into a graduate level job over time. If graduates can do a non-graduate job more effectively than a non-graduate, then their overeducation is less of a problem than first thought. We need to identify the skills and qualities that higher education develops in individuals and relate these attributes to activity at work to be able to fully substantiate the claim that we have too many graduates. Currently our data are not sophisticated enough to analyse this problem clearly.

However, our research does confirm that overeducated graduates earn less than those in graduate jobs and that this difference in earnings persists while the graduate remains overeducated. Therefore from the individual's perspective, overeducation clearly is a problem because it reduces the financial return to a degree. Yet since the average financial return to a degree remains high, it continues to make sense for individuals to invest in higher education, as they do not know, *a priori*, whether they will be overeducated. If there is growing variability in the financial return to a degree, as a result of some graduates being overeducated and getting low paid jobs, this is clearly cause for concern, just as increasing inequality of income in the population as a whole is worrying. However, we did find that overeducated graduates still do better financially than those without a degree. Perhaps fears about overeducation continue because we subsidise higher education. This subsidy keeps the private average return to education higher than would be the case in a free market, and widespread overeducation among graduates might suggest that it is not optimal for the state to subsidise a further expansion of higher education. This is not to say that greater numbers of people should not experience higher education, merely that they might pay for more, or all of it, themselves (Dolton, Greenaway and Vignoles 1997). Clearly the introduction of tuition fees has substantially increased the contribution from students for their higher education.

Lastly, and perhaps most importantly, education generates consumption benefits for the individual and externalities for society. These are not taken into account by looking at job titles and earnings (Weale 1993). For instance, there is extremely convincing evidence that education improves parenting skills and makes you less likely to divorce or commit crimes. It also appears to improve your health. When you also consider the positive externalities and cultural benefits of having a more educated population, worries about overeducating people look somewhat exaggerated.

We argue that the current evidence on overeducation is sufficient to make this an issue of great concern to policy makers committed to further expansion of higher education. It is encouraging that the Dearing report on Higher Education in the UK argued that there should be further expansion of higher education but mainly at the sub-degree level. It may be that the UK lacks workers with intermediate skills and that efforts should be directed towards remedying this failure, rather than simply producing more graduates who may end up in jobs that do not fully utilise their superior skills and abilities.

References

Alba-Ramirez, A. (1993) 'Mismatch in the Spanish Labor Market: Overeducation?' *The Journal of Human Resources 27*, 2, 259–278.

Alpin, C., Shackleton, J.R. and Walsh, S. (1997) *Over- and Undereducation in the UK Graduate Labour Market*. Education, Training and the Labour Market Research Group, University of Westminster.

Brennan, J.L., Lyon, E.S., McGeevor, P.A. and Murray, K. (1993) *Students, Courses and Jobs. The Relationship Between Higher Education and the Labour Market*. London: Jessica Kingsley Publishers.

Connor, H. and Pollard, E. (1996) *What Do Graduates Really Do?* Institute of Employment Studies, University of Sussex, Report No.308.

Dolton, P.J., Greenaway, D. and Vignoles, A. (1997) 'Whither higher education? An economic perspective for the Dearing Committee of Inquiry.' *Economic Journal 107*, 442, 710–726.

Dolton, P.J. and Vignoles, A. (1996a) 'The Incidence and Effects of Overeducation in the Graduate Labour Market.' *Economics of Education Review*, forthcoming.

Dolton, P.J. and Vignoles, A. (1996b) *Overeducation Duration: How Long Did Graduates in the 1980s Take to Get a Graduate Level Job?* University of Newcastle.

Duncan, G.J. and Hoffman, S.D. (1981) 'The incidence and wage effects of overeducation.' *Economics of Education Review 1*, 1, 75–86.

Groot, W. (1993) 'Overeducation and the returns to enterprise related schooling.' *Economics of Education Review 12*, 299–309.

Groot, W. (1996) 'The incidence of, and returns to overeducation in the UK.' *Applied Economics 28*, 1345–1359.

Groot, W. and Maasen Van Den Brink, H. (1997) 'Allocation and the returns to over-education in the UK.' *Education Economics 5*, 2, 169–183.

Hartog, J. and Oosterbeek, H. (1988) 'Education, allocation and earnings in the Netherlands: overschooling.' *Economics of Education Review 7*, 185–194.

Harvey, L. Moon, S. and Geall, V. (1997) *Graduate's Work: Organisational Change and Students' Attributes.* Birmingham: Centre for Research into Quality, University of Central England.

Mason, G. (1995) *The New Graduate Supply-Shock. Recruitment and Utilisation of Graduates in British Industry.* National Institute of Economic and Social Research, Report Series Number 9, London.

McGoldrick, K. and Robst, J. (1996) 'Gender differences in overeducation: a test of the theory of differential overqualification.' *AEA Papers and Proceedings 86*, 2, 280–284.

Oosterbeek, H. (1991) *Essays of Human Capital Theory.* University of Amsterdam PhD dissertation.

Rigg, M., Elias, P., White, M. and Johnson, S. (1990) *An Overview of the Demand for Graduates.* London: HMSO.

Robinson, P. and Manacorda, M. (1997) '*Qualifications and the Labour Market in Britain: 1984–94 Skill Biased Change in the Demand for Labour or Credentialism?*'. London: Centre for Economic Performance, London School of Economics and Political Science.

Rumberger, R.W. (1987) 'The impact of surplus schooling on productivity and earnings.' *Journal of Human Resources 22*, 1, 24–50.

Sicherman, N. and Galor, O. (1990) 'A theory of career mobility.' *Journal of Political Economy 98*, 1, 169–192.

Sicherman, N. (1991) '"Overeducation" in the labor market.' *Journal of Labour Economics 9*, 2, 101–122.

Sloane, P.J., Battu, H. and Seaman, P.T. (1995) '*Overeducation, Undereducation and the British Labour Market*', University of Aberdeen, Department of Economics, Discussion Paper 95–08.

van der Velden, R.K.W. and van Smoorenburg, M.S.M. (1997) '*The Measurement of Overeducation and Undereducation: Self-Report vs. Job-Analyst Method*', 9th annual EALE conference, Aarhus, 25–28 September 1997.

Verdugo, R.R. and Verdugo, N.T. (1989) 'The impact of surplus schooling on earnings: some additional findings.' *The Journal of Human Resources 24*, 4, 629–643.

Weale, M. (1993) 'A critical evaluation of rate of return analysis.' *The Economic Journal 103*, 729–737.

CHAPTER 7

Higher Education Curricula in the UK
The Pushme–Pullyou Effects
Sandra Jones and Brenda Little

Introduction

This paper explores a range of UK government-funded initiatives which have been specifically designed to effect changes in higher education curricula such that there is a closer integration of higher education and work. It will be argued that two particular perspectives can be delineated, namely those of work-based (or 'off-campus') learning and employment-related learning delivered through the ('on-campus') academic curriculum. The context and development of these perspectives and their implications will be outlined. The discussion will point to some significant questions these developments raise about the nature of knowledge, its acquisition and assessment. Ultimately, these are derived from, and highly dependent upon, a more instrumental notion about knowledge, its use and application.

In the last 35 years we have seen significant changes in the size and scope of the higher education sector and its relationship to the rest of society within the UK. In terms of absolute size, higher education in the 1960s comprised some 250,000 students (representing just 6 per cent of the 18 to 21 age group). Entrants to higher education came more or less straight from school and were drawn from the grammar and public schools. In essence, higher education was primarily an élite system (HEQC 1995). The subject range on offer in the 26 universities was relatively limited, and most students were studying full-time for honours degrees. In contrast, by 1996 there were around 100 universities (out of a total of 180 publicly-funded higher education institutions), the student population amounted to more than 1.6 million, of which over 30 per cent were over the age of 30, and 32 per cent were classified as part-time (Brennan and Ramsden 1996). Of the higher education qualifications awarded in 1994/95, 77 per cent were undergraduate (61 per cent first degrees), and almost a quarter were postgraduate (with 12 per cent being higher degrees) (Brennan and Ramsden 1996).

Such considerable expansion of provision, evidenced through increases in both full-time and part-time student numbers, should also be viewed against changes in the nature and purposes of higher education. In the early sixties, the Robbins Report described four objectives essential to the UK higher education system as instruction in skills; promotion of the general powers of the mind; the advancement of learning; and the transmission of a common culture and common standards of citizenship. However, by the 1980s, the rapid pace of scientific, technological and economic change was leading to a reconsideration of these objectives in terms of the need for higher education to become more relevant to employment needs (see, for example, CIHE 1987; Ball/RSA 1990). Studies during the 1980s indicated ways in which higher education curricula might be modified to meet the perceived employment needs in disciplines as diverse as history and engineering (see, for example, Boys *et al.* 1988). The emphasis here was not so much upon filling government-determined quotas within particular disciplines and subject areas, such as in previous attempts at manpower (*sic*) planning, but rather on the nature of the general skills graduates took with them into the workplace. A common theme at that time was the expressed belief by employers that graduates lacked the personal transferable skills which were necessary for rapid effectiveness within the workplace (see, for example, Roizen and Jepson 1985). Here the tension between academic and employer perspectives on the nature of higher education curricula becomes apparent. Thus: 'The spectrum of skills that academics were concerned about promoting includes generic study skills, intellectual skills, experimental and technical skills, and general and specific work skills. Within this range there was increasing interest in identifying and promoting transferable skills' (Kogan and Brennan 1993, p.19).

Since the 1980s, various UK government policy statements have promoted the idea that a continually developing work force possessing high level skills, enterprise and initiative is essential to competing internationally in the global market place. The education system generally has been urged to ensure that people are given an effective foundation for working life and are motivated to achieve their potential and take more responsibility for their continuing development. Employers have been urged to invest in effective action to ensure that people at all levels of the workforce have the necessary skills to operate effectively. However, what may be lacking in such exhortations is a recognition that various studies have shown that the organisation of work itself can facilitate or hinder the continuing skills development of individuals in the workplace (see, for example, Lam 1996).

Most recently a UK government review of higher education, chaired by Sir Ron Dearing, has reformulated the Robbins' purposes and objectives of higher education. The general tenor of Dearing's four main purposes is more instrumental and geared less towards the needs of the individual learner and more towards the demands of an 'adaptable, sustainable, and knowledge-based economy' and 'a democratic, civilised, inclusive society' (Higher Education in the Learning Society; Summary Report 1997). In a sense, the Dearing reformulation of the purposes of higher education has served to formalise the shift, noted above, from the acquisition of knowledge for its own sake to that of knowledge as a commodity to be acquired and used to economic benefit. It brings to the forefront the debate about the role of higher education in preparing people for entry into the world of work, and the continuing relationship between the world of employment and higher education.

Much of the literature about evolving relationships between higher education and work concentrates on higher education's contribution to pre-entry preparation for work. Within this, distinctions are drawn between 'regulatory' and 'training' aspects of these relationships. However, the more traditional sequential pattern of higher education followed by work is becoming blurred by relationships of lifelong education and work, and the need for a continually developing workforce. The irony in this respect is that there are other parallel concerns about the under-utilisation of graduate skills by employers given the move to a mass rather than an élite system of higher education (for fuller discussion see the chapter by Dolton and Vignoles).

These developments are not unique to the UK. A closer integration of learning and work is becoming a central theme of policy debates across Europe about skills formation of the workforce and strategies for economic competitiveness and enterprise renewal (see, for example, Danua and Sommerlad 1996). However, it is against this background that a series of UK government interventions broadly aimed at greater educational responsiveness to the assumed needs of the economy have been developed. In turn these have prompted a reassessment of the nature, assessment and use of knowledge.

Locus of responsibility for government-funded initiatives

In examining specific government-funded initiatives in higher education, it is worth pointing out that in recent times (and prior to the establishment of the Department for Education and Employment (DfEE) in July 1995) it has been the former Employment Department rather than the (former) Department for Education that has played a significant role in funding such developments.

The first toehold was gained through the Enterprise in Higher Education (EHE) initiative which was specifically aimed at changing the 'content, organisation and delivery' of the curriculum in order to better prepare graduates for the world of work. It is interesting to note that it was deliberate ministerial policy to locate responsibility for the implementation of EHE within the Employment Department because of a belief that the Department for Education was too culturally similar to higher education to be effective as an agent for the kind of change implied by the EHE initiative (Jones in Henkel *et al.* (1998) *Academic Identities*, forthcoming). Up until this time, and except where external accreditation by professional bodies was necessary, the form, content and delivery of the curriculum was determined by academe. Indeed, within the traditional university sector of higher education (as compared with the more externally-regulated polytechnic sector) these choices were often left to the professional discretion of individual academics. There were few explicit, externally-driven formal accountability mechanisms for ensuring the quality of courses.

Alongside EHE was a series of government funded projects aimed at particular thematic developments within higher education. Both EHE funding and higher education development funds were administered primarily through the Training, Enterprise and Education Directorate (TEED)/Higher Education Branch of the Employment Department (formerly the Manpower Services Commission, then the Training Agency).

The following discussion first outlines the range of development projects and then briefly reviews some of the key features of, and issues arising from, the EHE initiative. We will argue that taken together, the two perspectives of work-based and employment-related learning necessitate a re-examination of what constitutes academic learning. Further, we will assert that learning within the workplace and learning within the academic setting (and in particular its assessment) are being pulled in non-traditional directions, rather like the 'pushme–pullyou' of Dr Doolittle fame.

Government-funded higher education development activities

From the early 1980s successive waves of development work have covered the broad themes of higher education and employment: accessible higher education, and learning and its assessment. The Employment Department's explicit broad aim in funding such activities was to develop, maintain and support the implementation of effective national policies that would create a higher education system which was high quality, and was flexible and responsive to the changing needs of employers, individuals and the labour market (see, for example, Employment Department 1990). Key elements within the various development initiatives were individual autonomy; academic credits and qualifications relevant and accessible to consumers' needs and those of the discipline; and the learning organisation.

Throughout the period covering the early 1980s through to the present day, a major thrust of funded development work was the question of a 'closer integration of higher education and work' from both the higher education and work, and work and higher education perspectives. Thus, one perspective was that of bringing the learning derived from student work placements/work experience into existing undergraduate programmes. At the same time, another priority was the establishment of a 'new' higher education curriculum based on learning derived from employees' workplace experiences. For example, in the mid 1980s, the (then) Training Agency funded development work aimed at evaluating the potential use of learning contracts to recognise employees' work-based learning in terms of academic credit. This work was quickly followed by a spate of development projects which involved the implementation of learning contracts. For the most part these focused on employees in the workplace rather than students in higher education. This represented a significant step in the process of redefining academic knowledge as contrasted with 'knowledge in use'. Eventually, this was to 'spill' back into academic courses through the development of learning contracts for undergraduate programmes. These were used initially to give formal academic credit for work placement learning and later were applied to 'mainstream' campus-based learning.

During the 1990s successive waves of development work in the area of work-based learning has also been funded by the Employment Department. In general terms, the first wave (1990–92) and second wave (1992–94) covered both the academic recognition of work-based learning of employees, and the work-based learning of (primarily) undergraduate students. The final phase of work-based learning projects (1994–96) was primarily geared to people already in employment. (For further details of the three successive waves, see Brennan and Little 1996, Appendices to Chapter Two.) Overall some eighty-plus higher education institutions were involved in these projects; two were involved in all three phases, and the 'old' universities were more heavily involved in the final phase, rather than the earlier phases.

Also during the early 1990s, the Employment Department was funding activities covering the general area of higher level skills development (covering both further and higher education) – some of which overlapped with more general work-based learning activities.

More recently, the DfEE's Higher Education and Employment Division has funded development work which seems to be focusing on the quasi-training and transition aspects of the relationship between higher education and the labour market. (For example, projects under the theme of Higher Education/Business Partnerships were designed to facilitate ways in which undergraduates can be prepared from employment in small and medium-sized enterprises.) Also, discipline networks have been funded by the DfEE as a means of extending the influence of, and continuing the work begun by, EHE (see below). These had the principal aim of developing common understanding of the training and educational needs of employers and the required responses of higher education (*sic*). At least one such discipline network has turned its attention to work-based learning specifically (Higgins and Simpson 1997).

Most recently (June 1997) the DfEE issued a Prospectus for a Higher Education and Employment Programme inviting employers, employer organisations and higher education institutions in England to submit bids for development work covering a number of themes. Overall, a sum of £9 million may be allocated to successful bids, many of which will cover themes which are particularly relevant to ongoing discussions about the form and shape of higher education curricula in relation to employment. For example, the specific aim of the 'key skills in higher education' theme is to ensure that 'all learners in higher education have the opportunity to develop key skills ... and are able to demonstrate employability': a further theme is 'work experience' with the specific aim of increasing 'substantially the number of students who have the opportunity to improve their "work readiness" through work experience' (Department for Education and Employment 1997). This aim echoes the objectives of the EHE initiative launched ten years earlier.

The Enterprise in Higher Education initiative

The EHE initiative was launched in the mid 1980s with the primary objective of ensuring that all students completing their higher education would be better prepared for the specific requirements of working life. Preparation for work has always been an important function of higher education. In the main this has been through the development of the 'trained mind' which is deemed to be a direct consequence of academic study and/or through the provision of specific vocational courses. What distinguished the EHE initiative was its emphasis upon indirect preparation for work through the development of personal transferable skills, such as communication, presentation, informational technology and problem solving skills. In the mythology which has grown up around EHE, the belief was that this was in direct response to expressed employer requirements and criticisms of the existing output of higher education. This is despite the evidence from studies of the relationship between employment and higher education (Roizen and Jepson 1985) which demonstrate considerable variability amongst employers in their expectations of graduates.

Another distinguishing feature, and one which was to challenge academic authority over what constitutes valid learning, was that the development of these skills was to be achieved through the mainstream academic curriculum rather than specialist 'bolt-on' skills courses. The expectation was that this would be achieved through the greater use of student-centred learning approaches, rather than the more traditional lecture, seminar and tutorial approach to teaching and learning. In other words, opportunities to develop these skills were to be 'embedded' within the curriculum through changes to the content, organisation and delivery of the curriculum with associated consequences for the assessment of student learning. This in turn required that institutional EHE projects included substantial elements of staff development with the explicit aim of changing the culture of teaching and learning within higher education.

A further important feature of the scheme which served to emphasise its relationship with economic imperatives, was that this development of personal transferable skills was to be achieved 'in partnership' with employers, who were also expected to contribute to the financial costs of the scheme either in cash or 'kind'. As part of this partnership, employers were encouraged to provide a range of work experience opportunities for undergraduates. Related to this was the pioneering of forms of assessment, both within the academic curriculum and the work experience elements (such as the use of learning contracts) which resulted in credit being awarded for work-related skills and competencies as part of the academic degree. The introduction of the notion that learning could be negotiated through these learning contracts, and that employers could be involved both in the negotiation of what was to be learnt and in its assessment (and not just for the work based element) was also to provide a challenge to the traditional academic authority over the curriculum.

Implementation of the initiative was through a 'commercial' bidding process. This invited higher education institutions to submit fully-costed proposals for funding which were scrutinised against a defined set of criteria. Successful institutions entered into a detailed contract with the Employment Department's TEED. This contract was subject to annual review and renewal during the five year life of each institution's five year 'enterprise plan'. Nevertheless, despite this commercial emphasis and the voluntary nature of the initiative, a total of 61 higher education institutions applied for EHE funding over the four successive annual rounds of the scheme. The funding per institution was in the order of one million pounds for each five year programme and it is estimated that over the ten years of the initiative the total investment in personal transferable skills development was £100 million.

As the initiative developed during the late 1980s various themes began to emerge. The original entrepreneurial definition of enterprise, which had caused some controversy when the initiative was first introduced, gave way to more 'respectable' reformulations through 'being enterprising' to one of 'enterprise learning'. Indeed, case study material suggests that the initiative went through a series of transformations as it was successively reinterpreted by the various actors involved in its implementation (see Jones 1996). According to this analysis the final transformation of the initiative into the 'enterprise learning' model of EHE was justified as a further response to the changing nature of the labour market and employer expectations. Here the rationale was that employers were now demanding that graduates should be flexible and adaptable in order to meet the (ever) changing needs of a rapidly changing global economy. Accordingly, what employers now needed was not graduates who had a specific combination of discipline/subject-based knowledge and skills plus personal transferable skills. Rather, they required individuals who had also 'learnt how to learn' so that they could continue learning (and if necessary retraining for different and/or new segments of the labour market) throughout their careers. This was also a recognition of the current, and possible future, insecurity in the labour market (with new technologies altering traditional working patterns and practices) and the fact that a first degree was no longer sufficient to guarantee either initial or continuous employment.

What is intriguing about this is that this model of EHE, justified as it was by changing labour market expectations, has its roots in the new orthodoxy of educational development. Thus the specific concrete personal transferable skills became subsumed within the more general (and academically acceptable) notion of 'learning to learn' skills. Part of this process seems to have involved a mapping back of the various elements of EHE (such as personal transferable skills) onto the existing academic value system. Thus, for example, the argument could be sustained that since the most important personal transferable skill was the ability to learn and continue learning in a variety of contexts, key elements of this process were precisely those academic skills which had always been traditionally developed as undergraduates acquired 'trained minds'. In this way the dissonance between EHE and academic conceptions of knowledge and understanding became reduced. At one extreme of the spectrum of values, traditional academics could hold on to the supremacy of discipline-based knowledge and the associated belief that undergraduates should be initiated into the discipline (Scott 1995), secure in the belief that their traditional methods of knowledge transference would produce employable graduates. At the other end of the spectrum, and even within the same discipline or field, academics were able to legitimise their discipline-independent enthusiasm for the approaches to curriculum development, and teaching and learning advocated by the newly respectable educational developmentalists. Nevertheless, one result of this process of transforming EHE is that even those more traditional approaches to teaching and learning (the holy trinity of lecture, tutorial and seminar) have become explicit to academics. Likewise, they have been more willing to explore innovative teaching and learning approaches, including those involving work-based learning. Whether this is a merging of academic values with the more instrumental values implicit in EHE or a colonisation of EHE by traditional academic values is debatable (see Jones in Henkel *et al.* 1999 forthcoming). What is clear is that such shift as there may have been (as evidenced by the acceptance of the legitimacy of the needs of the labour market and in related changing patterns in teaching and learning) cannot be attributed to EHE alone. During the life of the EHE initiative other reforms in UK higher education were to have a more direct impact upon the working practices and values of academics, though there is evidence to suggest that in relation to Teaching Quality Assessment (TQA), EHE was an important forerunner and catalyst (see Henkel *et al.* 1999 forthcoming). As such, EHE was a significant milestone as, for the first time, government policy was to have a direct impact upon what had always been regarded as the relatively sacrosanct academic curriculum. Indeed, part of the Employment Department's strategy was to link EHE developments with other national policies on teaching and learning and to seek to influence the training of TQA assessors such that the development of personal transferable skills became an explicit part of the TQA agenda (HEFCE 1995).

The parallels between EHE and work-based learning development projects become evident since, as discussed above, a corollary of this revitalised 'learning to learn' purpose of higher education is that it produces graduates who are life long learners with a vested interest in continuous professional development in the workplace. Work-based learning curriculum developments tend to give prominence to processes of learning *per se*. Moreover, work-based learning developments have been used by individuals already in employment as a vehicle for their own continuing personal and professional development in ways that meet the higher education institution's criteria for academic awards, and (to some extent) their employing organisation's needs.

Impact of work-based learning development activities on higher education curricula

Developments in work-based learning in higher education raise questions about whose authority determines the validity of learning derived from the workplace. Similar questions are also raised by employment-related changes to the higher education curricula made explicit by the EHE initiative, particularly when learning objectives are negotiated and joint employer-academic modes of assessment are involved. In recent times, much has been written about changing conceptions of knowledge: for example, distinctions between Mode 1 and Mode 2 knowledge production (Gibbons *et al.* 1994; Scott 1995); and, in the professional education area, between propositional and process knowledge (Eraut 1994).

The authority of the university over Mode 1 knowledge. is not in question. However the characteristics identified for Mode 2 knowledge production, viz. it is multivariate and unsystematic; it operates in an open system where users are the 'creative agents' not passive beneficiaries; it is synoptic, transcending individual disciplines; and it does not require a 'privileged' or 'protected' arena for its development, mean that the university does not automatically have sole authority over Mode 2 knowledge. So in the absence of a clear 'authority' over knowledge, questions are raised about who is to determine just what counts as 'valid' knowledge and by whom it should be assessed.

Furthermore, in the context of professional education in the UK, Eraut has drawn distinctions between propositional and process knowledge – in some ways similar to Mode 1 and Mode 2 knowledge distinctions. However, whilst the latter may raise questions about the control and authority of knowledge, in the case of professional preparation, it is the professional body or organisation that acts as a source of authority over what should 'count' as knowledge within the profession's particular sphere of influence. Reviewing these various debates about forms of knowledge in the context of work-based learning, Brennan and Little noted that current changes in higher education and the crisis of authority which they represent, 'provide an opening for the wider development and recognition of work based learning in higher education than has existed hitherto' (Brennan and Little 1996, p.37).

Their review of work-based learning in higher education identified key variables in current practice as the focus of the overall programme of study and the place of work-based learning within that programme (i.e. is it at the heart of the overall programme or a discrete, but integrated, part of the programme). These variables may answer, in part, the question of 'whose authority'. For example, Brennan and Little identified broad categories of curricular frameworks for work-based learning, reflecting the control and design of the curriculum and the status of the learner. The categories were:

- type A – framework controlled by the higher education institution, content designed with employers, learner primarily a full-time student

- type B – framework controlled by the higher education institution and professional body, and content designed with employers, learner primarily a full-time student

- type C – framework controlled by higher education institution, content designed with employer, learner primarily a full-time employee

- type D – framework controlled by higher education institution, focus and content designed primarily by the learner, and learner primarily a full-time employee.

In most cases, the establishment of a curriculum framework for work-based learning raises issues about agreed definitions of cognitive and affective skills such that comparisons about the validity of work-based learning (in academic terms) can be made with learning derived from other sources. It is possible to conceive of EHE in a similar way except that the question becomes refocused upon the validity of the campus-based learning (in employment related terms). The process of developing such curriculum frameworks (and related assessment strategies) frequently led to proponents of work-based learning having to challenge long held (and often implicit) assumptions and beliefs about what should 'count' as higher education. Work-based learning is seen as a vehicle for developing both high level generic skills and subject-based knowledge, skills and understanding; curriculum frameworks are couched in terms which accommodate both these aspects. Moreover, the processes of learning are often given particular prominence in work-based learning. All of these arguments have resonance for the debates surrounding the legitimacy of the original, instrumental aims of EHE.

Approaches to devising curriculum frameworks vary considerably, primarily reflecting whether the higher education institution is setting out to devise a framework which accommodates alternative routes to the 'same' knowledge and skills or providing the opportunity for learners to seek alternative routes to different, but equally valid, knowledge and skills. For example, the University of Leeds' generic work-based learning programme was viewed as matching the problem-centred nature of most work-based learning. Students would address the interrelated problems of managing their own educational and professional development and specific problems related to their work. Accordingly, the overarching framework developed by Leeds to accommodate such programmes was based on the University's general level criteria mapped onto a number of fields reflecting a problem-based focus: formulating problems; devising problems; implementing solutions; evaluating outcomes; presenting findings and information. In this way, the university sought to ensure comparability of standards with its other academic assessments.

A further feature shared by work-based learning and EHE is the extent to which negotiation between the individual learner, the employer, and the higher education institution plays a part in the design of the curriculum. Such negotiation (which can be seen as an example of the push-me, pull-you analogy) comes into play in identifying achievable learning outcomes which are meaningful and challenging to the individual, are relevant to the employer and have academic credibility. Negotiation is important in establishing appropriate methods of, and criteria for, assessment and in establishing and maintaining a supportive learning environment (based primarily in the workplace for work-based learning, but within the higher education institution for EHE).

Impacts and issues

Any consideration of the impacts of government-funded curriculum development work referred to above must be viewed in the light of the more general changing context in which higher education now finds itself. Much has recently been written about the meanings of mass higher education within the changing relationships between higher education and society, higher education and work, developing notions of learning organisations and flexible systems of manufacturing and production. For example, Scott notes that many current developments in higher education appear to question traditional academic assumptions, relating to the need to initiate the learner into particular disciplinary and/or professional cultures (Scott 1995). We have also noted that many of the developments referred to in the foregoing had elements in common, were happening about the same time, and inevitably there would have been effects from one development strand having an influence on other strands. Thus, it is not possible to look at the impact of any one particular development in isolation from other specific developments that were happening at the same time, nor to disassociate these from the wider context of changes in higher education.

However, we can say that both the government-funded EHE initiative and the work-based learning developments have brought about much greater explicitness about teaching and learning methods (and flexibility within these methods). They have been a part of the shifts towards knowledge in the use and processes of learning, rather than the pursuit of knowledge *per se* (and such shifts are reflected in assessment practices). Academics involved in these developments now have much greater appreciation of the links between higher education and the economy, and are better informed about the workplace market.

Higher education institutions are now much more likely to build in elements of work-based learning into existing undergraduate programmes in areas where previously there were none. New higher education programmes, designed at the outset in partnership with major employers within particular industrial sectors and organised around the integration of on-campus learning and work-based learning continue to emerge. For those individuals primarily in employment, work-based learning provides the opportunity for continuing educational and professional development activities to be undertaken within an overarching framework which leads to public recognition in the form of an academic award. All these work-based or employment-related learning developments can lead to situations where the control of the curriculum does not rest solely in the hands of the academics – rather individual learners have more control over the work-based learning curriculum, which itself is often the result of negotiation between the learner, the employer and the higher education institution.

As noted above, within the EHE initiative we have seen specific personal transferable skills becoming subsumed within more general (and academically more acceptable) notions of 'learning to learn' skills. We have also seen how work-related competencies have been pulled back into notions of general intellectual capacities by academic culture.

Also, in the context of undergraduate provision, the question remains about the extent to which these curriculum developments have been related to issues of graduate employability. Thus, the initial purpose of EHE was concerned with preparation for employment such that graduates entering the labour market become an effective and productive part of the employing organisation in a short space of time. However, for higher education the key issue (fuelled by the first destination employment statistics) is how to facilitate the transition from higher education into employment in times when ever greater numbers of graduates are trying to enter the labour market and there are some concerns being voiced about graduate under-utilisation. At least some of the DfEE funded development due to commence in 1998 (and referred to above) seems to cover both these aspects.

The fundamental paradox raised by these developments is that whilst learning in the workplace is being pulled towards academic values, and codified and assessed in academic terms such that workplace learning gains academic credibility and recognition as evidenced by the award of academic qualifications, at the same time academic developments within higher education are being pushed in the direction of relevance and credibility in employment terms.

What we can safely say is that whatever the ultimate impact of these developments, their very nature has raised a number of (sometimes uncomfortable) issues for higher education which are of central concern, and revolve around fundamental questions about the production, distribution and recognition of knowledge in society.

References

Ball, C. (1990) *More Means Different: Widening Access to Higher Education.* London: Royal Society of Arts.

Boys, C., Brennan, J., Henkel, M., Kirkland, J., Kogan, M. and Youll, P. (1988) *Higher Education and the Preparation for Work.* London: Jessica Kingsley Publishers.

Brennan, J. and Little, B. (1996) *A Review of Work Based Learning in Higher Education.* London: Quality Support Centre for the DfEE.

Brennan, J. and Ramsden, B. (1996) *Diversity in UK Higher Education: A Statistical View.* London: Quality Support Centre Special Digest Report.

Council for Industry and Higher Education (1987) *Towards a Partnership – HE Government–Industry.* London: CIHE.

Danau, D. and Sommerlad, E. (eds.) (1996) *Work Based Learning: Findings, Policy Issues and an Agenda for Future Actions.* Maastricht: European Centre for Work and Society.

Department for Education and Employment (1997) Higher Education and Employment Development Programme, Prospectus June 1997. Sheffield.

Employment Department (1990) *The Skills Link.* Sheffield: Employment Department.

Eraut, M. (1994) *Developing Professional Knowledge and Competence.* London: Falmer Press.

Gibbons, M., Limoges, C., Nowtny, H., Schwartzman, S., Scott, P. and Trow, M. (1994) *The New Production of Knowledge: The Dynamics of Science and Research in Contemporary Societies.* London: Sage.

Government Green Paper The Development of Higher Education into the 1990s. Cmnd 9524. London: HMSO.

Henkel, M. (1999) (ed) *Academic Identities.* London: Jessica Kingsley Publishers.

Higgins, M. and Simpson, F. (1997) *Work-based Learning Within Planning Education: A Good Practice Guide.* University of Westminster Press (on behalf of the DfEE Discipline Network in Town Planning).

Higher Education Funding Council for England (1995) *HEFCE Quality Handbook. Assessors' Handbook April 1995 – September 1996.* Bristol: HEFCE.

Higher Education Quality Council (1995) *Graduate Standards Programme Interim Report.* London: HEQC.

Jones, S. (1996) 'Transforming the Academic Enterprise.' Paper presented to the Swedish Council of Higher Education, April, 1996.

Kogan, M. and Brennan, J. (1993) 'Higher Education and the World of Work: an overview.' *Higher Education in Europe,* Vol XVIII, No2.

Lam, A. (1996) 'Work organisation, skills development and utilisation of engineers, a British-Japanese comparison.' In R. Crompton, D. Gallie and K. Purcell (eds) *Changing forms of Employment – Organisations, Skills and Gender.* London: Routledge.

The National Committee of Inquiry into Higher Education (1997) *Higher Education in the Learning Society, Summary Report*. London: HMSO.

The Robbins Report (1996) *Report of the Committee on Higher Education under the Chairmanship of Lord Robbins*. Cmnd 2154. London: HMSO.

Roizen, J. and Jepson, M. (1985) *Degrees for Jobs: Employer Expectations of Higher Education*. Guildford: SRHE/Nelson.

Scott, P. (1995) *The Meanings of Mass Higher Education*. Buckingham: Open University Press.

CHAPTER 8

State Finance of Higher Education
An Overview of Theoretical and Empirical Issues

Gareth Williams

Preamble

In most of western Europe it has been taken for granted since Napoleonic times, when the State replaced the Church as the main source of moral and intellectual authority, that the State is a senior partner in the provision of higher education. Just as previously the Church had controlled education, partly for the benefit of individual souls but also to ensure that each generation was brought up in the ways of the Church, so in the nineteenth century the State took over the responsibility of ensuring both individual development and that each generation grew up to be good French men and women or good Prussians or good Italians (see, for example, Green 1990). Universities merely carried this ideology to the highest levels.

It is not logically necessary that state control of education means state funding but in liberal minded societies it makes the control easier if it does.[1] Hence, state funding in publicly administered universities has been the predominant mode of higher education provision since the nineteenth century. Britain joined the rest of Europe much later. Although the Local Taxation (Customs and Excise) Act 1890 made it possible for local authorities to offer technical education beyond school, the amount of publicly provided education of higher education level was a trickle before the end of the

---

1   In many of the Asian Pacific rim countries, Japan, Korea, Philippines, Taiwan, for example, but also increasingly the People's Republic of China, most students are in universities that are predominantly privately funded, but this does not prevent the state from exercising quite tight control over many aspects of their work.

Second World War (Burgess and Pratt 1970). It was not until the 1950s that there was any significant public provision of advanced further education. Meanwhile the universities were, and remain to this day, private foundations and only after the Second World War did central government funding account for more than half of their income.

The purpose of this preamble is to demonstrate that Britain long differed from most other European countries[2] in its assumptions about the role of the state in the provision of higher education and that public funding of higher education in this country does not have a very long historical tradition.

An examination of the economic basis of the case for government finance of higher education

There are five main reasons (see Eicher and Chevallier 1993) usually given to justify government involvement in financing higher education:

- equity
- avoiding waste of talent
- risk-sharing
- external economies
- pursuit of national interest.

However, none of them is clear cut.

Equity

The equity case is usually made on the basis that young people from less affluent families would be unable to meet the costs of tertiary education and, therefore, would not achieve their full educational potential unless public funding were available.

---

2   Also the USA which, although seen by many as the country where the market has always ruled in higher education, has a tradition of state provided and funded higher education since the middle of the nineteenth century, and by the end of that century the majority of students were in public universities and colleges.

However, once some groups have their educational expenses supported, it becomes difficult to devise schemes of subsidy that do not discriminate against others. In the USA, for example, both rich and poor students are able to attend major private universities but it is difficult for members of middle-income families to do so (see McPherson and Schapiro 1993).

In Britain it is widely claimed that the system of subsidy discriminates in favour of full-time students on first-degree courses who are drawn disproportionately from relatively affluent families. In fact this is not absolutely clear cut. Student maintenance grants are severely means tested, with about one third receiving the full grant, one third no grant and one third a partial grant. It is easy to demonstrate that on this basis about 83 per cent of grants goes to the poorest 30 per cent of students. There is little doubt that abolition of maintenance grants would further discriminate against students from less affluent families.[3]

Loss of talent

There are potential economic, as well as welfare, losses if some people are deprived of educational opportunities from which they could potentially benefit. This was one of the claims of the Robbins Report in the early 1960s and underlies several of the recommendations of the Dearing Committee Report 30 years later (NCIHE 1997). In the future, even more than it is argued, Britain must depend on the brains and skills of its people for its economic well being. In a recent inaugural lecture at the University of Bath, Hugh Lauder claimed that economies with a relatively equal distribution of education, and the economic benefits that derive from it, are more likely to be economically successful than those where it is spread unequally.

However, this is not self evident. The precept that everybody should achieve his or her full potential needs to be used with care as an efficiency criterion. If education and training are treated as national investments, they need, like any other public or private investment, to be evaluated in terms of costs and benefits. It may well be the case that

---

3   Since this was written, the decision by the UK government to replace grants by loans and to introduce means tested fees at least maintains some of the advantages of means testing.

for any individual person the costs of extra education exceed the benefits before all potential achievements are realised.

However, the implications of this kind of reasoning are more counter-intuitive than this. Johnson (1983) in a rigorous econometric analysis has shown that

> it may not be such a bad thing to tax relatively poor people to pay part of the educational expenses of that part of the population that, because of superior innate ability, is relatively rich in a permanent income sense. The reason for this is that, because of the likely complementarity between labor with low and high skills, the relatively poor realise a portion of the gains from increasing the average skill level of those more able than themselves to benefit from higher education. Indeed, under some institutional arrangements (specifically, where the number of university places is controlled by central government) the brighter segment of the population has an incentive to restrict the supply of university places. This can be overcome by a financing arrangement in which the poor pay part of the educational expenses of the rich – to the mutual advantage of both (Johnson 1983, p.317).

There are suggestions here of the reported behaviour of extended families in some developing countries, where all members of the family contribute to funding the family member deemed most able to benefit from study in Europe or North America, in the expectation that the whole family will benefit from the advanced skills of one of its members. More interesting still, it may offer an explanation of the economic success of many Asian Pacific Rim countries in which well funded 'National Universities' cater for a minority of students whose education is heavily subsidised from public funds. The system of relatively well funded *grandes ecoles* in France also has some affinity with this model.

There may be other reasons for continuing the education of any individual beyond the point where the costs to taxpayers of additional learning exceed the likely economic benefits that will be obtained from it (for example in the case of students with disabilities) but it is important to appreciate that those reasons imply normative judgements about the distribution of welfare, not about economic efficiency. Efficiency suggests that it may be in the national economic interest to invest more heavily in individuals who learn easily, and cheaply, than in those who require more resources to reach their full potential.

These reservations are particularly important when tertiary education becomes a mass system with open access. If it is offered to individuals free of charge, there is an incentive for some of them at least to pursue it, so long as there are some individual economic benefits. However, since the community as a whole is incurring costs, it may be economically efficient for society as a whole to stop spending before that point is reached.[4] In the past A (or H) level grades were the traditional means of restricting access to the most able students.

This is not to say that the precept of 'tertiary-education-for-all-who-can-benefit-from-it' has no relevance as an efficiency criterion. Obviously there is an economic loss if individuals who potentially have much to contribute to society are prevented from doing so by their family circumstances. However, it is not necessarily efficient to extend the same financial support from public funds to all individuals regardless of the amount of benefits obtained from it.[5]

This type of analysis has led some to propose that any transfer of the costs of higher education to the private sector should be accompanied by state scholarships for the very able, even if this does mean more subsidy for those from relatively affluent families.

Risk sharing

Although, in general, tertiary education in the UK has private rates of return as high and as secure as many blue chip commercial investments, it is long term and very risky for individuals. Returns for some individuals are very high; for others they are low, or even negative.

Employers who invest in tertiary education through student sponsorship face further risks. As well as the danger that their faith in a particular student may be unjustified, there is the problem in a free labour market that graduates whose degrees have been paid for by one employer may take their skills elsewhere. These risks mean that total reliance on private funds would result in less than optimal levels of expenditure on universities and colleges when it is seen as a national

4   This is another way of making the point that private rates of return are almost always higher than social rates in a publicly funded tertiary education system.
5   This analysis may have some relevance to the debate about whether students at Oxford and Cambridge should receive a greater subsidy than those at other universities.

investment. The state, so the argument goes, is in a position to offer what is, in effect, collective insurance for all individuals and all employers against the failure of the investment in any particular case.

This is the economic basis of the case for an 'income-contingent loan scheme'. Under such a scheme, students repay loans only if their income actually does exceed some specified limit, usually linked to national average income levels. This means that someone else, usually the taxpayer, must bear the risk associated with graduates unable to make repayments that meet the costs of their higher education. This leads to growing interest in the question of how a student loan scheme can be financed which leads to a range of technical problems which are outlined below.

However, income-contingent loans are not the only way of sharing risks. An alternative is to share the risks amongst those who have benefited from higher education, which means something like a graduate tax. It is a pity that the undoubted problems of implementing a graduate tax[6] preclude it from serious political consideration. In many ways it is the alternative that most nearly meets both equity and efficiency criteria and has the incidental potential advantage of bringing extra money into higher education very quickly (London Economics 1993).

External benefits

External benefits are another reason often given for public funding. They arise because some of the benefits of tertiary education accrue to third parties. The article by Johnson (1983) referred to above may be interpreted in terms of the external benefits of higher education. The highly educated, able people create employment and income for those who are less able to benefit from higher education. This argument was widely used to justify publicly funded expansion of higher education in the 1960s and 1970s. For example, it is claimed that qualified doctors bring benefits to patients which go beyond the earnings they receive. Levin (1991) has assembled evidence which shows that, in the USA at least, public investment in education, particularly of disadvantaged groups, helps reduce crime, lowers the costs of social welfare, and increases the attractiveness of cities as

---

6   It is important to appreciate that there is a sharp distinction between a graduate tax and the repayment of loans through the tax or national insurance system.

places to live. Unfortunately he does not go on to examine the question of whether it is more cost effective to invest in policing or education as a means of reducing crime.

Again, however, a strict economic analysis suggests some reservations. The modern world both identifies and rewards high ability. Some writers claim that the shoe may now be on the other foot. The 'Diploma Disease' (see Dore 1976) and the 'screening hypothesis' (e.g. Arrow 1970; Whitehead 1981) suggest that, in a modern economy, graduates are often employed in preference to secondary school leavers, even though the latter could do the particular job just as well. To the extent that this is so, higher education may benefit the individuals who receive it, while penalising their neighbours who leave school earlier. In other words, there may be negative external benefits. A careful review for the Dearing Report (1997) was unable to find convincing evidence of external economies of higher education in stimulating economic growth.

There is a substantial literature in the USA, which will almost certainly be replicated in Britain following the massive expansion of higher education in the early 1990s, on the effect of 'overeducation' on the job satisfaction of individuals themselves. Tsang, Rumberger and Levin (1990), for example, report empirical research, again from the USA, which shows that 'surplus schooling has a negative effect on job satisfaction' and that 'the negative influence of surplus schooling on job satisfaction is more significant for workers with a higher level of surplus education' (p.209).

National interest

Finally there is the 'national interest' that transcends individual interests. National governments inevitably have a concern with education and training that goes beyond the market. In tertiary education this is most apparent in some quality issues and in matters related to the national priority given to certain subjects. It is now widely realised also that financial incentives are an effective 'steering mechanism' (e.g.Goedegebuure *et al.* 1993; Neave and van Vught 1994) and in order to use it the state must be making a significant financial contribution.

However, the 'national interest' case goes far beyond this. In addition, it is now generally recognised that all markets require some regulation by the state, if only to ensure that all participants play by the rules. Beyond this, however, higher education has special features which make heavy reliance on the market a doubtful proposition. If markets are to operate properly, consumers must be well informed about the likely outcomes of their purchases, and they must have the opportunity of learning from experience in making subsequent purchases. Most decisions about post-18 education, on the other hand, are irreversible and are made on very few occasions. The ultimate outcomes of a particular choice are not apparent for a long time, are usually mingled with the effects of other decisions and are influenced by decisions taken at the same time by other students. Thus the essential information feedback loops of efficient markets are absent.

Higher education provision determined solely by the wishes of large numbers of individual students would be unlikely to meet their real long-term needs, or those of society as a whole, as effectively as a system in which significant resource allocation authority is held by a democratic government, advised by expert agencies that can interpret the economic and social processes with which tertiary education interacts.

The uncertainties of private funding

One case which has sometimes been made in this country for public funding is the need for some stability in an activity that is inevitably long term. Until 1980 it was widely believed that public funding through an intermediate or 'buffer' agency protected higher education from the vagaries of the market. However, in the mid 1990s, sharp changes in public policy make it hard to claim that as an advantage. The two biggest jolts were the Education Reform Act of 1988 and the Further and Higher Education Act of 1992, but there have been many other changes of policy, strategy and administrative regulation, as well as big variations in the amount of funds available. Manipulation of the funding formulae in both further and higher education have resulted in very large, purely arbitrary gains and losses in individual institutions and subjects.

Radical changes in all three constituents of tertiary education (universities, polytechnics and colleges, and Further Education colleges) were imposed on a system that, before 1980, had become accustomed to considerable stability in its funding arrangements. Private sector critics claimed that universities expected too much certainty in an uncertain world. The fact is, however, that in recent years policy and management changes have created environmental turbulence as severe as any faced by free market organisations of equivalent size. Excessive security has given way to unreasonable uncertainty.

Incentives to expansion, for example, were sharply increased and then suddenly withdrawn. After the 1988 Education Reform Act, funding arrangements powerfully encouraged universities to recruit 'extra' students for their 'fees only' (i.e. without additional block-grant subsidy). That policy pushed down average costs per student and penalised universities that did not take part in the expansion. Institutions found that their financial health depended on their capacity to recruit additional students.

Headlong expansion followed. The effect was to reduce public expenditure per student by 25 per cent, but also to increase total public expenditure on higher education by 25 per cent. Government concern about excessive demands on public funds led to its 1993 decision that there should be no further publicly funded growth in higher education until 1997, a restraint since extended to 1999. Undergraduate fees were reduced to about 20 per cent of costs, and severe financial penalties introduced for universities and colleges that recruited 'fees only' students. Some found themselves trapped by financial commitments undertaken on the assumption of continued expansion.

It is quite clear now that a system of finance and regulation appropriate for a relatively small élite higher education system cannot simply be diluted to meet the needs of such extended tertiary education.

Some writers have interpreted these fluctuations and the damage arising from them as the result of the operation of quasi-markets (see, for example, Le Grand *et al.* 1991, 1992) rather than real markets. In real markets, buyers and sellers of goods and services confront each other directly. Suppliers are rewarded for providing the services that buyers want and buyers can use their purchasing power to obtain what they really want. They are subjected to the basic economic discipline of opportunity costs. If they spend resources on higher education they lose the opportunity of buying something else. The state may intervene to increase the purchasing power of those it considers worthy, and to ensure that trading standards are maintained, but otherwise there is a constant balance between what consumers want and what suppliers provide. Certainly this equilibrium fluctuates over time but, so its proponents claim, experience will soon tell providers how much fluctuation they need to allow for in their strategic planning.

There is no mechanism to ensure that quasi-markets, at least in the form in which they operate in British higher education, in which a monopsonistic buyer acts as a proxy for final consumers and purchases higher education services on behalf of students, result in economically rational outcomes. The resources available to such a purchaser are determined by many influences other than the demand for higher education by potential students. Thus, they may be confronted with big reductions in income or, more rarely, increases in income, for which it is virtually impossible to plan. Institutional managers are more concerned to meet the requirements of the proxy buyer than the real consumer. If the proxy buyer is a monopsonist, then all suppliers will have an incentive to act in much the same way to maximise their incomes.

Some writers, for example Tooley (1996), use such arguments to argue for real markets in education with students paying for their own higher education and any subsidy being paid directly to students and not to a quango (see also Barnes, Chapter 9). It is generally acknowledged that any such scheme must involve another feature of real markets, a financial market in which those who wish to invest (in themselves in this case) can have the opportunity of borrowing to invest now and repay at a commercial rate of interest when the benefits of the investment are realised.

The economics of student finance

This has been a continuing theme in the literature of the economics of education since the 1960s when the subject as a serious sub-discipline was born. The basic issues are simple. It is easy to show that, on average, men and women with more education have higher lifetime earnings. There are opportunities for much debate about the reasons for these differentials which are crystallised in the human capital versus screening hypothesis. Human capital theorists believe that education creates the capacity to be more productive and hence earn higher income, while to screening theorists education merely identifies the individuals with the innate ability to succeed in employment. However, from one point of view the reason is not important. If, for individuals, there are higher earnings following graduation, then from the point of view of that individual, higher education has many of the characteristics of an investment. However, mass higher education reduces the effectiveness of higher education as a screen or selection mechanism.

Tertiary education differs from that of younger age groups in two fundamental ways. One is that its students are adults who have a much greater responsibility for their own learning than younger people. The second is that there must be great diversity of provision. Those features have far reaching implications for policy and funding.

The most important is that there is now widespread agreement in most parts of the political spectrum that the share of costs borne by students themselves should be increased and that they should have the opportunity of paying these costs out of their higher income after they have graduated.[7] There appear to be two distinct theoretical rationales for these proposals. They may be labelled the funding gap and the equity deficit.

There is, however, a flaw in the concept of a simple funding gap. Universities and colleges are not permitted to show a continuing deficit in their budgets. Impending shortfalls must be covered by reductions in expenditure. Thus, a funding gap is in reality a quality gap where available resources are insufficient to maintain higher education of acceptable quality. This is more insidious than a funding gap because there are few unambiguous indicators of quality of the sort that will carry weight with Treasury ministers. Indeed, universities have been assiduous in denying that quality in their own institutions has suffered as a result of funding cuts, and most of the evidence to the Dearing Committee, broadly accepted by the Committee, claims that there is a serious threat of quality deterioration but it has not happened so far. Most teaching quality assessments (and certainly the recent Research Assessment Exercise) appear to bear this out. It is therefore hard to make an absolutely convincing case that a failure to obtain additional funds (from students if from nowhere else) will have disastrous consequences for universities.

---

7   This evaluation has now been 'legitimated' both by the Dearing Committee and by the government. They differ in the details of implementation but agree absolutely on the principles. (See NCIHE 1997 and DfEE 1997)

Of more quantitative substance is the equity case which was prominent in the reports of the National Commission on Education (1993) and the Commission on Social Justice (1994). They lay stress on disparities in the financial support available to different categories of students. Equity gaps are the more pronounced if the students who benefit most from public subsidy are from relatively more affluent households, or tend to pursue courses likely to lead to above average incomes in the future. This argument also seems to have carried some conviction with the Dearing Committee.

Different forms of course attract different levels of financial support. That creates incentives for institutions to offer, and for students to attend, courses in the most financially favourable form, even if they could be more effectively offered otherwise. That is certainly the reason why some courses have been redesignated as full-time degree programmes which attract mandatory student grants. There are indications of similar redesignations in the further education colleges, too, as they try to exploit funding disparities. Thus the inequities may actually promote inefficiencies.

At the level of institutional funding, different categories of students attract different financial treatment. There are differences in average costs in the different sectors of tertiary education but also wide variations within each sector. Typically the most expensive department in each subject area spends more than twice as much per student as the least expensive. Some of these differences are undoubtedly the result of historical accidents at the time when the funding formula was frozen in its present form. However, some are the result of what the HEFCE in its consultants' report on the evaluation of the funding method for teaching describes as 'different specifications'. In other words, some programmes of a higher specification course than others in the same subject. On the ground this means smaller classes, closer contacts with teachers, and better libraries and laboratories.

There are other disparities in the educational experiences of students. Teaching Quality Assessments of the first 14 subject groups assessed showed that of the 313 departments assessed in England, 126 were deemed to be excellent, 182 satisfactory and 5 unsatisfactory. Students in the 'excellent' departments are, presumably, being better taught and so getting a better bargain than their contemporaries in departments rated merely 'satisfactory.'[8]

There are also wide differences in the salaries earned by graduates of different subjects. Rate-of-return calculations based on what graduates earn and what they and the state pay for their higher education show it to be a much better investment for some than for others. Table 8.1 below shows some estimates made for the Dearing Committee of social rates of return in the late 1980s to different subjects. The private rates are not given by subject but overall they are about 60 per cent higher with the difference for social scientists less because they are less expensive than engineers and physical scientists to teach. A rough estimate of the private rates of return is given in the final column of the table.

Table 8.1 Rates of return to higher education

Subject	Social Rate of Return	Approximate Private Rate of Return*
Social Sciences	11%–11.5%	16%
Engineering	5%–6.5%	10%
Science	4.5%–5.5%	8.5%
Arts	<0	2%

Source: Dearing Report (1997) Report No.7 Paragraph 2.28
* Estimates by present author based on relative costs of teaching different subjects

Significantly there appear to be no more recent estimates of rates of return to different subjects following the huge expansion of the early 1990s. However, it is quite clear that students of some subjects obtain a more valuable investment than others from the public subsidy they receive, both in the costs of their education and the returns they receive in later life. If the figures were available, it is likely that they

---

8   In Scotland by October 1994, there were 29 Departments deemed 'excellent', 40 'highly satisfactory', 29 'satisfactory' and one 'unsatisfactory'.

would also show that some universities offer their students a better financial return to their studies.

Present systems of institutional and student support intensify the disparities. Most favourably treated are the 800,000 UK students on full-time first degree courses. All receive free tuition, regardless of actual costs, are eligible for a loan that is (in real terms) interest-free and may receive a grant towards their living costs, the level of which depends on family income. About 30 per cent of them receive a full maintenance grant (in 1997 of about £1900) because of low family income, slightly fewer than 30 per cent receive no maintenance grant because of high family income and the remainder are somewhere in between. All are eligible for loans up to about £1500 per year. Much of the debate about student finance concentrates on this favoured group of students.

For other students, the opportunities for financial support are more varied and usually much less generous. About 75,000 full-time students above the age of 18, mainly in colleges, receive discretionary grants from their local authorities. Only about 10,000 receive grants at the full rate; the others receive less for maintenance, and often less for tuition as well. Since 1980 discretionary awards have become smaller and fewer.

For postgraduate students the picture is very varied. Research Councils are the commonest source of support; they financed about 15,000 full-time and 1000 part-time postgraduates in 1992. Another 4000 receive awards directly from the government, mostly through the British Academy awards scheme. These students are entitled to full payment of fees and an allowance (£5050 in 1995/96) supposed to cover basic living expenses. About 20,000 find funds from other public and private sources ranging from generous grants to small contributions towards fees. The remaining 25,000 full-time and 100,000 part-time postgraduates pay their own fees and expenses, though employers probably subsidise some of them.

Few part-time students have any of their living costs met from public funds. British and other European Union students benefit from the universities' subsidy from the Funding Councils, but must pay course fees and other expenses themselves. There are about 260,000 part-time undergraduates in higher education institutions and a further 300,000 part-time 'tertiary' students in the colleges.

Students on different courses, therefore, and those at different institutions pay very different 'prices', and receive very different 'products' when they 'buy' tertiary education. These differences ought to be taken into account in developing efficient and equitable programmes of financial support for students.

The general case for students' contributing to the costs of tertiary education is that 'he or she who benefits should pay'. Students receive most of the benefits: they, or their families, should contribute to the costs. The principle is now generally agreed. There is less consensus about which students should pay, when they should pay, how they should pay, and how much they should pay. What is fair, what is efficient, what is politically acceptable, and what is practicable?

Students can contribute to the cost of their tertiary education in three main ways.[9]

1   They can pay fees while they are studying.

2   Their studies can be free but their subsequent taxes higher to help pay for their successors' education.

3   They can borrow while they study and repay when they are earning.

The first option is plainly the simplest but it has the obvious disadvantage of excluding those unable to raise the capital needed to buy a higher education course.

The second option is the Welfare State model in operation between 1945 and 1980. People received benefits according to their needs and paid according to their means. Not only has there been a general reaction against this principle since 1980, but it fits tertiary education rather badly: although most students come from the more affluent families and enter better paid jobs, the extra tax payments from the higher income associated with tertiary education are probably

---

9   In each case a distinction can be made between *tuition* costs and *maintenance* costs: the former might be further subdivided into *essential* costs for an acceptable course of study in a particular subject and *supplementary* costs to cover quality-enhancing extras.

insufficient to repay the debt to the rest of society.[10]

The current policy debate in Britain is largely concentrated, therefore, on the third model.

The political acceptability of any change in student contributions depends ultimately on perceived costs and benefits. From the viewpoint of students in general, any scheme which transfers some costs from general taxation to them or their families is a loss. But the losses will be greater for some groups of students than others and some may actually gain; different schemes distribute the costs differently.

Any proposed redistribution of costs risks short-term political opposition from influential groups of students and their universities. Change will be more acceptable in the longer run, however, if benefits flowing from the additional costs are explicit, if students from less affluent families face no obvious obstacles to following their chosen courses, and if there is a choice of ways to meet the costs. Student contributions are likely to be more easily accepted if they can be deferred and paid in earnings-related instalments.

Recovering some of the costs from students will affect different institutions in different ways. To abolish maintenance grants for full-time students (for example) and transfer the public money saved to general institutional income, as several commentators propose, would especially benefit universities and colleges with large numbers of part-time students. It would also favour the institutions that are particularly attractive to wealthy students, who are already barred from maintenance grants by the means test. Similarly the general introduction of fees, if not supported by income-contingent loans, might particularly damage courses which do not obviously lead to high incomes.

10   The balance obviously shifts as the number of students and graduates changes. If only a few people have publicly funded higher education, it is likely, unless taxation is very progressive, that non-graduates are contributing to the costs through their taxes. Conversely, if everybody has publicly funded higher education obviously graduates as a group are paying for the higher education of their successors. It seems to follow that on this basis, the more people who receive higher education, the stronger is the case for public funding, though there may be a problem of inter-generational transfer of resources while the numbers are building up. That is, first generation graduates might be seen to have moral obligations to ensure that their parents, who had made sacrifices to pay for their education, had adequate pensions. The problem should not arise with second generation graduates.

Forms of public funding and their effects on the management of universities and colleges

There are two ways in which government can subsidise tertiary education. One is to transfer money to universities and colleges; the other is to give it to students. The debate about those two approaches may become almost as important as that on the balance of public and private financing. In the late 1980s, there was a radical shift towards subsidy of students: in effect students were given 'vouchers' to cover about a third of their tuition costs. This policy was reversed in 1994 when tuition fees were reduced by 45 per cent and student numbers for each institution were capped through MASNs (Maximum Aggregate Student Numbers).

Direct government funding of universities and colleges reflects the idea of higher education as a public service. Between 1945 and 1980, the British University Grants Committee (UGC) was often considered to be the ideal model of public funding of universities. Its quinquennial grant system linked funding to institutional plans, but otherwise gave universities almost complete freedom in deciding how to spend their money.

The university autonomy underpinned by the UGC system brought several benefits. Lecturers and professors could concentrate on their academic work and not be distracted by problems of generating income. In general there were high academic standards and professional integrity. Academic criteria determined resource allocation. The internal dynamic of disciplines and subjects, rather than external economic or social pressures, determined what was taught.

But collegial management styles, in which resource allocation decisions are taken by consensus amongst academic staff, can also become corrupt. There can be little doubt that their self-interested responses to the public expenditure cuts of the early 1980s were at least partly responsible for the dramatic shifts in the funding regimes imposed by government (outlined earlier).

One possible way of dealing with pervasive vested interest is detailed regulation. Many governments have adopted the procedure of 'line by line budgets' and detailed administrative regulation. This has long been the situation in most European countries and was the basis of the local authority control of polytechnics and colleges in Britain before 1988.

Such bureaucratic procedures can prevent misapplication of funds but they give academic staff a sense of alienation. The funding agency comes to be seen as a black box accepting some claims for additional resources and rejecting others. Institutional managers have little incentive to take account of the wishes of their direct consumers or of overall resource constraints. Claims for funds are based on expected benefits rather than a comparison of benefits and costs. Heads of institutions and departments learn to use a variety of political and administrative stratagems to secure staff, space and equipment, but careful weighing of alternatives is rarely among them. The indicator of successful performance is to obtain as much as possible of everything from the central administrators.

A reaction against the shortcomings of both collegiality and bureaucracy has led governments around the world to seek to fund higher education by 'buying' the outputs, and channelling public funds via the students, rather than by subsidising the inputs. The traditional model of public funding of higher education was for universities to be subsidised as universities and the principle of academic freedom and the authority of professional expertise allowed the professoriate to determine what was offered to students and users of research. As higher education has become a mass participation activity, this model of provision has proved inadequate.[11] Mass higher education inevitably has to provide for a wide variety of interests, abilities and qualification objectives. It would be surprising if the services provided by suppliers following their own interests corresponded in detail with the wishes and needs of a much wider variety of clients. Governments have come more and more to interpret their relationship with universities as that of customer and contractors. The government pays not for universities but for the outputs of universities.

In his letter to the new Funding Councils, following the passage of the 1988 Education Reform Act, the UK Secretary of State for Education wrote: 'I shall look to the Council to develop funding arrangements which recognise the principle that the public funds

11 It is also probably the case that public perceptions of the abuse of professional privilege, for example lifetime tenure as the standard form of academic employment, rather than the culmination of several years of recognised academic excellence led to a view that self interest rather than public interest was the main influence on resource allocation decisions in higher education.

allocated to the universities are in exchange for the provision of teaching and research and are conditional on their delivery.' Formulae were subsequently developed that made the income of universities and colleges almost entirely dependent on student numbers in each subject.

It is possible to question whether governments are any more likely to be able to interpret the direct wishes of students than the teachers who come into direct contact with them. One answer is that in a democracy governments have the legitimacy that comes from being elected to power every now and then. However, more and more observers are coming to believe that this is not a satisfactory answer to the problem of diversity either. The Dearing Committee (NCIHE 1997) has recommended to the Government that:

> it shifts the balance of funding, in a planned way, away from the block grant towards a system in which funding follows the student, assessing the shift on institutional behaviour and the control of public expenditure, with a target of distributing at least 60 per cent of total funding to institutions according to student choice by 2003. (Recommendation 72)

The Committee's recommendation at least includes the proviso that the effect on institutional behaviour of each successive shift towards channelling funds through the students should be assessed. It is not at all clear that this almost total dependence on the wishes of consumers is an appropriate way of funding activities such as higher education whose outcome is long term and unpredictable (Williams 1996). It would be a pity if the reaction against the inadequacy of donnish dominion (Halsey 1992) led to an even more irrational dependence on ill-informed consumer choice.

References

Arrow, K. (1970) 'Higher Education as a Filter.' *Journal of Public Economics 2*, 3.

Burgess, T. and Pratt, J. (1970) *Policy and Practice*. London: Allen Lane, the Penguin Press.

Commission on Social Justice (1994) *Social Justice: Strategies for National Renewal*. Institute for Public Policy Research.

Dearing (1997) See NCIHE (1997 below).

DES (1990) *Top Up Loans for Students*. HMSO Cm 1541. London: HMSO.

DfEE (1997) *Teaching and Higher Education Bill*. London: HMSO.

Dore, R.P. (1976) *The Diploma Disease: Education, Qualification and Development.* London: Unwin Educational Books.

Eicher, J.C. and Chevallier, T. (1993) 'Rethinking the finance of post compulsory education.' *International Journal of Educational Research 29*, 5.

Goedegebuure L., Kaiser F., Maassen P., Meek L., van Vught F., de Weert E. (1993) *Higher Education Policy: An International Comparative Perspective.* Oxford: Pergamon.

Green, A. (1990) *Education and State Formation: the rise of education systems in England, France and the USA.* London: Macmillan.

Halsey, A.H. (1995 Paperback edition) *Decline of Donnish Dominion: the British Academic Professions in the Twentieth Century.* Oxford: Clarendon.

Johnson, G.E. (1983) 'Subsidies for higher education.' *Journal of Labor Economics 2*, 3.

Levin, H. (1991) 'The economics of educational choice.' *Economics of Education Review 10*, 2.

Le Grand J. and Bartlett W. (eds) (1992) *Quasi-Markets and Social Policy.* London: Macmillan.

Le Grand, J. (1991) 'Quasi-markets and social policy.' *Economic Journal 101*, 1256–1267.

London Economics (1993) *Review of Options for the Additional Funding of Higher Education.* CVCP.

McPherson, M. and Schapiro, M. (1993) *Keeping College Affordable: Government and Educational Opportunity.* Washington, DC: The Brookings Institute.

National Commission on Education (1993) *Learning to Succeed: A Radical Look at Education Today and a Strategy for the Future.* London: Heinemann.

Neave G., and van Vught F. (1994) *Government and Higher Education Relationships across Three Continents: The Winds of Change.* Oxford: Pergamon.

NCIHE, 1997 *Higher Education in the Learning Society* Report of the National Commission on Higher Education (The Dearing Committee).

Tooley, J. (1996) *Education Without the State.* London: Institute of Economic Affairs.

Tsang, M., Rumberger, R. and Levin, H. (1990) 'The impact of surplus schooling on worker productivity.' *Industrial Relations 30*, 2.

Whitehead, A.K. (1981) 'Screening and education: a theoretical and empirical survey.' *British Review of Economic Issues 3*, 8, 20.

Williams, G.L. (1996) 'The many faces of privatisation.' *Higher Education Management 8*, 3.

CHAPTER 9

Funding and University Autonomy

John Barnes

Introduction

Although British governments of both political colours continue to pay lip service to academic freedom and university autonomy, their actions since the mid1980s have run counter to their words – this at a time when the general trend in Europe is in the other direction. Admittedly British universities still enjoy substantially more autonomy than their continental counterparts, but in both the Department for Education and Employment (DfEE) and the funding bodies there appears to be an increasing desire to plan and control the higher education sector. This is far from surprising. The merging of the university and polytechnic sectors and the expansion of the number of university students were certain to call in question the traditional view of the university as a place where research and teaching went hand-in-hand and where, despite a concern with the education of certain professions, a contempt for the purely vocational was paramount. Whatever the immediate origins of the Dearing review of higher education, this was undoubtedly a large part of his agenda.

The new Labour Government has gone further. There was clearly a feeling in Whitehall that it was not for institutions to settle their own fees unless they were prepared to forfeit public subsidy altogether. Although the regulations will detail precisely what is to happen, Section 26 of the 1998 Act gives the Secretary of State power through the Higher Education Funding Council to prescribe fee levels for all home and EU students and so impinge greatly on the autonomy of institutions and the flexibility they had to address their financial problems.

Although the Government has promised that a high proportion of the £1000 annual student contribution to course fees will go back to higher education, the proceeds have not been ring-fenced and are likely to go to both further and higher education. Even if efforts to secure the entire sum for higher education were successful, the CVCP's victory will be undermined as the Treasury takes the sums into account in their pursuit of a continued reduction in the cost of university places. Even on the Government's calculations the comprehensive spending review envisaged an efficiency saving of 'no more than 1 per cent'. On a more realistic calcaulation the £280 million allowed for 1999/2000 is certainly well under half of the sum required to maintain level funding for higher education, even perhaps as little as a fifth.

The blow to university autonomy, obvious if contributions to the payment of fees are directed elsewhere, will not be lessened if the effect is indirect rather than direct. The change will be more cosmetic than real.

The plain truth is that the Act is a further move in the *de facto* nationalisation of what are still, in theory and in law, private sector institutions. Even if amendments are secured, it will not reverse the overall direction of policy. As in other areas of national life, the trend is to see centralisation as the key to the successful modernisation of the system and the modernisation is to be along lines approved by the Government.

Although perfectly understandable in the context of a funding crisis, which peaks short term in 1999/2000 and then involved a funding shortfall over the run up to the millennium of £800 million, it was far from reassuring to find purely utilitarian and short-term arguments used to plead for some relaxation of the Government's funding curbs on the universities. The chairman of the CVCP, for example, stressed that the power of the higher education sector in this context lay in the Government's need for its help in delivering what have been explicitly identified as key goals by the Government in the areas of competitiveness, regional regeneration and lifelong learning. The CVCP's arguments on funding, its chairman wrote, 'will be made in this context of overlapping agendas and mutuality' (Harris 1998). Coercion, it might be observed, does not need to take the form of law and the exercise of power is no less coercive for having some laudable aims.

Even in a free society, it is not possible for any institution, organisation or élite to enjoy complete autonomy, but if any of these is to enjoy any significant degree of autonomy, it must be in the possession of considerable resources which are not, and cannot be, controlled by others. A degree of outside influence on the way in which those resources are deployed is tolerable, even in certain circumstances desirable, but if an organisation is to remain relatively free to go its own way, influence should never be allowed to lead to any significant degree of control.

Autonomy and external influences

Within a society four kinds of resource can be distinguished, although in practice they combine in different ways to secure the autonomy of an institution or an élite. Three require little more than rehearsal. Material resources are the main topic of this chapter and it is abundantly evident that university budgets, capital investment and even salaries are all dependent to a significant, if slightly varying degree, on government *fiat*. The only resources beyond government control, although even they can be subject to government legislation, are endowments and the numbers of overseas students. There are also administrative and organisational resources, which have been subjected to outside scrutiny and recommendation, but which are not under the supervision of outsiders. Academic institutions and the academic élite (they are not necessarily synonymous) may be autonomous also when they are not dependent upon the symbolic resources of outsiders, when they do not have symbols imposed upon them and are in possession of symbolic resources that are not constructed or controlled by others. The fourth resource, coercive powers, may be exercised within the organisation or institution in relation to sub-élites of one kind or another, but are not deployable in pursuit of any degree of autonomy.

However the coercive powers of the state may be deployed not only to limit or destroy autonomy, but also in its defence. Freedom of speech and expression, academic freedom, even (in the past) academic tenure, have been secured by law. Even when largely financed by the state, it was still possible for the university system to operate with a large degree of freedom because of the interpolation of a body between the state and the universities which was designed not to control or influence the practice of higher education, but to secure it against interference. Correspondingly, as was the case perhaps in Germany in the first half of this century, the academic élite may persuade themselves of the virtues of state power, devise doctrines to legitimise it, and therefore not need to be coerced.

As late as the 1980s, it was still possible to think that British universities had retained their 'sovereignty', although they had forfeited their autonomy to a very significant extent. However, in the course of the 1990s, the activities of the Higher Education Funding Councils, the operation of the Research Assessment Exercise, and the incursions of bodies responsible for teaching quality can be said to have diminished the actual sovereignty of the individual institution, certainly in practice if not strictly in theory. Tracing the changing nature of the successive bodies responsible for the funding of higher education reveals a pattern of steadily increasing government intervention, which was not only predictable but predicted when responsibility for the University Grants Committee was transferred from the Treasury to the Department of Education and Science.

It has culminated (at least for the moment) in the constitution of the present pattern of Higher Education Funding Councils making separate grants for teaching and research 'on such terms and conditions as they see fit'. Without an independent flow of funding a university has no way of exercising sovereignty: unless it is a substantial flow, its autonomy will be severely compromised. About the only moves which have run contrary to the general trend of government policy have been the decisions to make overseas students pay economic fees (surely an unintended effect) and John MacGregor's move to shift the balance of fees and grant in the funding of higher education institutions. The latter move was reversed subsequently by John Patten.

The reduction of 45 per cent in the maximum fees reimbursable through the mandatory awards system was avowedly taken to moderate the rapid expansion of student numbers and epitomises the will of the Government to exercise greater control over the system. In large measure, so far as teaching is concerned, that has meant greater financial control and a will to drive down costs, although the implementation by the funding councils of teaching quality assessment suggests also the furthering of certain modes of teaching (and learning) and an increased emphasis on skills, which is endorsed by the Dearing report (NCIHE 1997).

It may seem ironic that a government dedicated to furthering the market philosophy should have given rise to moves to limit university autonomy (although the intention to do so, as always, was denied), to strengthen central direction and to cap student numbers (although the government claimed that they still adhered to the Robbins principle).

Even less attention was paid to the absence from the Dearing Report of any serious thought about the nature of universities and the bearing this might have on the future of higher education in Britain. One perceptive article from the traditionalist camp raised the question and deserves the credit for doing so (Casey 1997) but the necessary corollary, the means of achieving a higher education sector in which a range of institutions with diverse purposes can flourish, is not addressed. Casey is rightly scathing about one sentence in the Dearing Report, which tells us much of what we need to know about that document: 'In our view, the important defining characteristic of a university is the power to award taught and research degrees which then carry the University's name.' But Dearing goes further, doubting whether the spread of academic disciplines offered bears on the question whether or not the institution in question is a university. To Casey, as to Newman, such talk is anathema: 'the range of disciplines is crucial to the notion of a universitas. A "university" which did not include research and teaching in philosophy, pure mathematics, theoretical physics, history and classics would not be a university at all' (Casey 1997, p.17). In the course of the last quarter of a century, however, liberal pieties like 'education for its own sake', 'the pursuit of knowledge' and the 'cultivation of the intellect' have become suspect as élitist and have been displaced by a narrow utilitarianism.

That does not inhibit continued obeisance to notions of academic freedom and institutional autonomy. Dearing is no exception, but the nods in this direction seem increasingly a matter of form, not substance. After all, the Dearing Committee also want to see better value for money; smaller, more effective governing bodies; and performance reviewed against external criteria. Lip service to the idea that education is not purely instrumental sits in uneasy juxtaposition with the report's stress on what employers want from students and the contribution higher education can make to increasing the wealth of the nation.

The question of how far university autonomy matters is not central to this paper, since its main thrust is to suggest that if the right funding regime is established, those who inhabit the system, those who use it and those who make use of its products can all influence it without controlling it. There will be ample room for choice and, if the result is a diverse and multi-valued system, so much the better. We do after all value pluralism.

One can go further. The sociologist, Eva Etzioni-Halevy, has suggested that the existence of a number of relatively powerful and autonomous élites in the liberal democracies did not only guarantee that they remained liberal through countervailing, and therefore limiting, governmental power, but that they were also essential to the dynamics of a system in which democracy was likely to emerge and continue to develop (Etzioni-Halevy 1993). She draws attention to the particular role of those élites, which in their struggle to remain autonomous, not only sustain key features of the democratic system, but supply information to inform and sustain public discourse.

> The academic élite, engages in research about reality, and interpretation of reality (including sociopolitical reality). To the extent that the output of its endeavour filters through to the public through students, textbooks, public lectures, popularisation in the media and the like, this forms a reservoir of information on which the public can draw to form views on social reality in general, and politics in particular.

Even the controversies which rend academe are seen as 'a boost to the adversary public discourse necessary for democracy' (Etzioni-Halevy 1993, p.105).

Part of this argument is akin to a utilitarian defence of higher education which elsewhere I have described as the 'Court Jester' principle (Barnes and Barr 1988). Current fads and fashions need to be tested and exposed. The emperor may well turn out to have no clothes. Institutions wholly in thrall to the state are unlikely to play that role and the state itself will suffer. In this respect, the record of the Soviet Union speaks volumes. But there is also another utilitarian defence which rests on our inability to know precisely what kinds of knowledge are going, over time, to turn out to be useful. The most obvious example this century was the conviction of those who first split the atom that their research would have no practical implications for the world outside Cambridge. But more recently one can point to the study of fuzzy logic, once a purely academic pursuit of university philosophy departments, now an essential tool in the world of information technology.

There has always been a tension between two aspects of the education system, on the one hand its role in servicing the needs and values of society, sometimes very particular needs, and on the other its pursuit of education as a good in itself. The tension is perhaps greater in higher education than at school level since the task of a university is not only to transmit knowledge and engender critical thinking but to generate knowledge. Planners might seek to resolve the tension by creating a hierarchy of institutions; some major research institutions, others putting their prime emphasis on teaching; some covering a broad range of disciplines, others more narrowly focused; some concentrating on making their students pursue a particular discipline in depth, others pursuing interdisciplinary insights and others still using problem-solving techniques to develop learning and research skills. But what should the balance be and who has the knowledge to strike it?

The limits to centralised planning

Quite apart from the substantial arguments which can be deployed against manpower planning (Psacharopoulos 1987), and more general arguments that government failure is at least as likely as market failure and more damaging in its consequences (Wolf 1988), there is very good reason to suppose that the higher education sector is not susceptible to planning. The drive to induce individual institutions to clarify what they are trying to achieve, and bring together the planning of ways to achieve those goals with the necessary consideration of the resources available, may well have been sensible – could indeed be argued to be long overdue (Allen 1988, p.125) – but even in a tight-knit institution like the London School of Economics and Political Science (LSE), the process necessarily takes the aspect of a quasi-judicial activity, not one of synoptic oversight. In practice it looks, and is, inherently political. On a larger scale, the same can be said of the activities of the Research Councils. This should not surprise: organisation theorists and political scientists have identified the ways in which goals can be subverted to serve particular interests, informal power structures coexist with their more formal counterparts and disinterested altruism is at a discount where there are axes to be ground.

While goals are an integral, and desirable, part of decision making, the extent to which any organisation can have a single goal, or even a coherent set of goals, is open to question. In any case they are rarely as precise as theorists suppose. They may have been left ambiguous quite deliberately in order to maximise support. The pursuit of excellence in higher education, for example, would be universally acknowledged, but hard to define: it cannot readily be translated into operational reality. Claims that such a goal is highly ambiguous might be matched with others that the ambiguity allows for diverse ways of achieving a commonly acknowledged goal. However, it may also allow lip service to be paid to the ostensible objective while very different private goals are pursued. The existence of multiple objectives is not in itself disabling, and reflects not only the process of continuity and change in the life of an organisation, but also the differing aspirations of those who are its members for the time being. Public choice theorists, organisation theorists and those micro- economists who have turned their attention to business organisation or to politics, are well aware of the process by which private goals are substituted for publicly professed ones in the policy process, even if they are less adept at teasing them out. Incoherence and conflict may be the result, but it is also possible that subsuming these various goals may enable the successful furthering of the larger purposes of an organisation. Unless goals can be specified and the trade-offs identified, however, it is hard to judge efficiency or effectiveness. Not only is such specificity hard to achieve in higher education, but the trade-offs would be contested not only by practitioners but by its many beneficiaries.

The problem is further compounded because many decisions are made in the face of uncertainty. This is particularly so with higher education. First, the activity itself is exceedingly complex and differentiated. Second, the flow of information about it is likely to be incomplete and processing it into any satisfactory form difficult. Third, the desired future state is highly debatable and cannot be other than uncertain since it operates at the cutting edge of knowledge, and in important respects beyond it, and also because the future state of Britain in common with the rest of the world, is uncertain. Fourth, there remains a lack of consensus about purposes, to say nothing of the means of achieving them. Finally, the results of any policies proposed are likely to be indeterminate, not least because implementation will be in the hands of what is best characterised as a loosely coupled system (Weick 1976). The component elements seldom mesh neatly. Goals, as we have seen, are always pluralistic and can be in competition. There are contradictions, duplications and gaps in what is covered and the whole system is decentralised with the individual teacher and researcher as a key actor (Becher and Kogan 1992). In these circumstances, it is hard to exercise sufficient authority to deliver externally set goals even if, in the first place, they seem persuasive to vice-chancellors, councils and senates. Theorists would agree that, in this context, the working of the system will be characterised by advocacy coalitions, partisan mutual adjustment, and an argumentative approach to agenda setting and problem definition (Sabatier, Lindblom and Hoppe 1993; see also Fischer and Forester 1993). The neutral rationality on which bureaucrats rely will not be present (Thompson and Tuden 1959).

While it is useful to have in mind the idea of a higher education system since it forces us to focus on the interconnectedness of what is going on, we must be careful not to abstract it from the organisations and individuals which are its component parts. It will not react as an entity nor behave in a passive way when faced with shifts in its environment, and analysts will recognise that the outcome is likely to be one which constitutes a fresh bargain between its functional requirements for survival and the personal objectives of its members.

Lawrence and Lorsch (1967) suggest that organisations should have structural characteristics which fit the environments in which they operate. If a complex organisation is to deal successfully with a highly uncertain world, it may be best to leave many parts of its structure incompletely specified. If one conceptualises the relationships within universities and more generally within the system and between the system and the external agents which seek to affect its activities as a set of contracts, it can be argued that the consequence of attempts to specify those contracts in detailed and rigid terms (necessarily contingent on specific states of the world which will happen) will be that such contracts will turn out to be quite inappropriate and in all probability counterproductive in a rapidly changing and uncertain environment. There are ways of dealing with this. Contracts can be specified in such a way that they contain a variety of clauses which become activated only when certain pre-specified states of the world prevail. In such a case a single contract would be equivalent to a set of individually specified contracts. The costs involved in negotiating such contracts, however, would be extremely high. The range, complexity and often unquantifiable nature of the data which central decision makers would need, would make its processing a costly and time consuming business, something of which university teachers and administrators are now all too well aware, during which opportunities will be missed. The outcome is unlikely to be satisfactory and will be unacceptable to many of those who will have to implement what is decided. The process of drawing more people into the decision-making process and establishing agreement with them, would minimise the costs of imposing an unwelcome solution (which would attract covert resistance as well as overt hostility) but would introduce different costs. Finally, coordination and close supervision of contract compliance are costly and inflexible. There are also costs to interpreting contracts and of settling disputes, and a danger of litigation, since funding is involved. At best, there will be considerable diversion of effort and constant interruption of the smooth flow of decision making. Of course, this is preferable to more rigid contracts which would be even more costly and even less successful. But this is to miss the obvious point: even incompletely specified contracts of the kind suggested by Jackson (1982) and other theorists of bureaucracy are best avoided altogether.

Powerful arguments can be deployed in support of hierarchies on the grounds that they minimise transaction costs (Williamson 1975) although it is worth noting in passing that Williamson himself recognised the pitfalls of a purely hierarchical organisation if it grew to any size, hence his emphasis on the creation of quasi-firms accountable to a central body (Williamson 1971). Whatever the merits of his arguments so far as other worlds are concerned, the increasing returns from the acquisition and use of information which, in his eyes, justify central planning and resource allocation are outweighed, so far as higher education is concerned, by the instability of its universe, the imprecision and inadequacy of the measures available, and the need to achieve a bargained outcome in which multiple and often conflicting objectives are respected. Whether operating by contract or in more authoritarian ways, overly hierarchical organisations seem wholly inappropriate to such a world.

The radical decentralisation of higher education (more accurately perhaps the radical decentralisation of its central functions) avoids the major danger which faces even the most flexible of planning apparatuses – that referred to by March and Simon as 'uncertainty absorption' (March and Simon 1958). In processing information, there is an endemic tendency to portray circumstances as less complex and less uncertain than is in fact the case. Information has to be simplified and summarised as it passes upward; estimates and other forms of approximation tend to harden and paradigmatic interpretations become more rigid. Given the increasing pressures on the upper reaches of the organisation, there is little time to question and reflect. Processed information is treated as more definite and more trustworthy than it is. Inputs from another part of the structure will be treated as given: there will be little disposition to question its status, much less its assumptions and the quality of the data and analysis used to compile it. Nothing in Williamson's analysis suggests that hierarchy in higher education will overcome the cumulative distortion and bias, often quite unintentional, built in to the filtering and interpreting of complex information. Nor does the existence of some central planning mechanism obviate the possibility (some would say certainty) that its output will be distorted by lobbies, logrolling and the composition of the central agency.

March and Olsen (1976) demonstrate that the particular structure adopted in complex and ambiguously-defined situations will determine which (perhaps one should say whose) skills, expertise, background, and values are brought to bear on any particular problem. The phenomenon affects not only the definition of a problem, but the structuring of the information upon which a solution will be based, and the suggestions made as to possible solutions. Great power is 'wielded by those at the point where the greatest amount of uncertainty is absorbed, since they can considerably influence the decisions that will finally be made by others' (Brown 1970, p.148). It scarcely needs to be said that such people are not dispassionate: they too have values and backgrounds which influence their interpretation of what comes to them. Where uncertainty is high and there are few uncontested paradigms, let alone criteria for judgement, Pfeffer, Salancik and Leblebici (1976) argue that personal influence and social relationships will have their greatest effect.

In any system activities are by definition non-random. But those operating within a complex system are often unable to grasp all that is going on and those making decisions will not be able to assess the full significance of the line they take, not least because they suffer from what the distinguished economist G.S.Shackle describes as the human predicament:

> In order to secure its ends, choice must apply a knowledge of what will be the consequence of what. But the sequel of an action chosen by one man will be shaped by circumstance, and its circumstances will include the actions chosen now and actions to be chosen in time to come by other men. If, therefore, choice is effective, it is unpredictable and thus defeats, in some degree, the power of choice itself to secure exact ends. (Shackle 1974)

Higher education and the market model

The case against central planning can, however, be put more positively if we take into account another set of arguments, which, while critical of blind adherence to the simple market model, attacked the way in which the concept of efficiency had been narrowed to allocative efficiency only, thus ignoring variations in the internal efficiency of firms. These arguments were first deployed by Leibenstein in 1966. He argued that standard price theory was a theory of markets only and did not deal with intra-organisational behaviour. Managers of firms were assumed to make optimal input decisions. This view of organisational reality was, he suggested in a later (1973) article, simplistic and naive. His concept of X-inefficiency recognises that firms are organisations easily affected by sub-optimisation and goal-displacement. The problem Leibenstein identifies arises because senior managers and shareholders are imperfectly informed about what those in day-to-day control are doing.

One of the most powerful arguments against the central planning of the higher education sector is the way in which it is affected by the four factors identified by Leibenstein as the main reasons for variations in cost between firms: contracts for labour are incompletely specified; the production function (i.e. the technical relationship between inputs and the resulting output) is incompletely specified or unknown; not all inputs are marketed; and, if marketed, they are not available on equal terms to all buyers. Perhaps the most important of these factors are the multiple and incompletely specified nature of university goals, the uncertain and changing environment in which they operate and the fact that part of their output, for example cultural transmission, cannot be measured. Academics, therefore, should have relatively unspecific contracts, which allow them to pursue their own goals.

More generally, as argued above, the full set of activities necessary to achieve the many and varied goals of the university system can never be completely specified, and certainly could not be translated into individual contracts. In terms of the 'APQT bundle' identified by Leibenstein, university lecturers have great discretion over the Activities they will carry out, the Pace at which they will proceed, the Quality of their activities, and the Time they will spend upon them. Close monitoring of tightly specified contracts, even if technically feasible, would be costly in real resources, would arouse hostility, lead to implementation difficulties, and raise questions of academic freedom.

Because of these difficulties, Leibenstein's analysis points to competition between universities as a relatively inexpensive way of reducing X-inefficiency. Reduction in competitive pressure clearly increases the scope for discretionary behaviour in all parts of an organisation: if there is no threat of being driven under by competition, there is no incentive to become more efficient. Leibenstein, in fact, explicitly recognised the parallels with the concept of organisational slack established earlier by Cyert and March (1963).

Higher education can thus be argued to meet the conditions in which a market solution is likely to be efficient. This is because consumers are reasonably well-informed; students can make sensible choices (as indeed they do already); guides to help them exist and can be improved; and regulation is likely to be more dispassionate if the regulator has no direct responsibility for production. Second, those who run universities are necessarily imperfectly informed because of the diverse and often intangible nature of the output of higher education: detailed planning and monitoring, in consequence, are impractical. The conclusion, on both grounds, is that competition between institutions of higher education is not only possible but, in general, desirable.

Strong arguments can be deployed also that, given the number of stakeholders in the system, its structure should be such that it can be influenced by each of them without being under the dominance of any. It should be scarcely necessary to remind those who see government or its nominees as an equally satisfactory way of balancing the various interests that even if none of the arguments sketched above held, it would still be undesirable that it should have dominance.

Universities' role in society

As suggested above, a key role for the universities is to emulate the part played by the court jester in the middle ages and to speak truth to power. The university must be free to question fashion and undermine consensus where this is perceived to be mistaken. It will serve the interests of the country better if it looks not just to relatively short term economic interests but to the medium and long term, and it has a role in the transmission of knowledge and the maintenance of a culture that goes far beyond the present concerns of government.

In that sense universities ought to form part of civil society, defined by Barry as

> a sphere or realm of human activities which stands outside the direct control of the state, although it is fully integrated into its legal structure. It is characterised by no over-all purpose, no grand rational scheme to which all individuals must adjust their activities, but by the recognition of a fundamental pluralism of human values and purposes. (Barry 1994)

Autonomy lies at the heart of a civil society, for if there is to be effective transmission of this culture and a constant need to question ends and purposes in the pursuit of both liberty and truth, autonomous institutions are needed which can stand fast against the influence of the state. Autonomous universities, although not the only such institutions required by a free society, have a key part to play and they need to have the courage to assert their claim to autonomy.[1]

Higher education has sold out its autonomy in a Faustian bargain and is finding that it is now being called upon to subordinate its own interests to those of society, or, more accurately, the presumed interests of society. Arguably, higher education would serve the longer-term interests of society better by remaining at least partially immune from short-term pressures. The best way to do that is to force society to pay an economic price for the services it requires, shrugging off the temptations of continuing to take any direct government

---

1   For a powerful statement of the need for courage in face of the Government's challenge, see J.A. Griffith (1989).

subsidy. In the current fashion for partnership with the private sector, there would be little danger that the state would be tempted to create a public sector to compete. Rather, the major danger is the implication of current legislation for universities wishing to free themselves from the state's tutelage. The state might look to fund the research it requires, as has been the case elsewhere, through dedicated institutes. However, it is more likely, since the higher education sector would continue to make its services available to government at a competitive price, that government would see considerable advantages in avoiding costly duplication.

The effect of economic imperatives

Although it has always been possible for an individual institution to break with the existing system, there has been little or no financial incentive to do so. Even if it did not face a threat from the government that it would forfeit grant, it would face a government subsidy to all its competitors, effectively undercutting the price it would charge for degree courses. There is a patent and perfectly understandable reluctance on the part of the vice-chancellors to break ranks without either overt encouragement from the government ('a pilot scheme') or substantial backing from their peers. The feeling, common among academics, that the values of education and those of the market are antithetical does not encourage support for any such move. Perhaps the latter need reminding that a market is no more than a decentralised co-ordinating device. Neither its presumed associations with capitalism, nor with supermarket values, are in any way inevitable.

It is ironic perhaps that it was less a concern for autonomy than economic necessity which forced higher education institutions into reappraising their future. It is certainly ironic that an earlier action of government, much criticised at the time, has made it possible for some institutions without rich endowments to maintain substantial flows of funding that do not derive from government. Forcing overseas students to pay economic fees has proved a blessing in disguise. It also affords an important lesson. An international institution like LSE has found it possible to create its own fee structure for overseas students and to find support from among the student body for doing so. It has been able to safeguard the less well off while maintaining its overall fee income. The downside has been the extent of the subsidy overseas students, in effect, make to home and EU students. They have some right to feel aggrieved that they do so. It would be interesting to calculate the extent of the subsidy nationwide. At LSE, which is atypical, the opportunity cost of continuing to take a Home/EU student is probably in the region of £4000. Although the marginal cost of teaching such students, currently in groups of up to 18 students, including a 40 per cent contribution to overheads, would probably be quite low, perhaps £2150, even less if postgraduates were trained and employed to teach them, there is little incentive to expand their numbers even if the Higher Education Funding Council for England was prepared to contemplate such a move. Indeed, since government has hitherto been vastly more tolerant of fees charged to postgraduate students, the pressures are the other way, to become a purely postgraduate institution. Only consciousness of the School's 'mission' and a consciousness that it is valued as a British, as well as an international, institution has prevented serious debate about such a step. Instead, LSE has been one of that growing minority of institutions within the CVCP contemplating moves towards a more economic fee for undergraduate students.

Since the number of EU students seeking access to British universities is growing, the consequences for access have been serious. Consciousness of this problem has been slow to emerge. But at the LSE some 42 per cent of home undergraduate students receive no maintenance grants and about 45 per cent in an average year are from the independent sector. Across-the-board fees would, of course, increase those proportions unless conscious action was taken to redress the balance. The introduction of means-tested fees *per contra* might well reverse what seems to be a 20 year trend. Despite trends within the sector as a whole towards the provision of access courses and the increasing proportion of mature students, it is clear that in recent years the present system has increasingly favoured the middle class.

The LSE is far from unique in the financial pressures it faces, and internal debate has centred on whether too much attention has for too long been given to short-term economies in an institution which would ideally wish to maintain the quality both of its staff and its facilities in a highly competitive international setting. But at least it showed the courage not only to address the issue, but to settle on an increase in fees in principle. By the time this paper was given

(February 1997), it was well into the practicalities of its decision. If a genuinely income-contingent loan scheme had been available, it would have found it easier to contemplate the decision, but it was able to identify a cost-effective way of implementing a scheme of means-tested fees: effectively it would have used the Local Education Authority's calculations to drive the scheme.

The position of government

The reaction of the government and other institutions to such a step is now academic, at least so far as undergraduate fees are concerned. The last government showed itself unwilling to impose a top-up fee scheme and the Treasury no doubt will be hostile to any scheme that will remove its power to cap student numbers. The present government acknowledges that there is a funding crisis, but the policy of tuition fees embraced by Dearing and endorsed by the government is not to be allowed to flow direct into university coffers. The Education and Employment Select Committee has urged the Secretary of State to resist any effort by the Treasury to claw the sums back, but while they may be applied to education, it seems certain that the fee monies will be used to contribute to both further and higher education. In the interim the cuts continue and, as might have been predicted, investment to improve the research infrastructure, deal with the backlog in building and equipment, and cope with any additional demand has been promised. Instead the way forward to which the CVCP (or at least a considerable proportion of its members) was edging, namely to increase fee income with some redistribution in favour of those who could not afford to invest more in their own education, has been blocked. If the CVCP is not careful, these new restrictions will apply not just to undergraduates, but to postgraduates as well. Universities seeking to maintain both autonomy and viability will be left with only two choices, either to accept a further decline in standards or to break free from government subsidy altogether. The CVCP has been left to wring its hands, aware that there will be no real help from this Government, but still unwilling to believe that sense will not prevail. Those of us who predicted this take no comfort in the fact that the Seventh Cavalry is not going to arrive.

There are contradictions in the Government's position, not least a desire to involve business in education and to facilitate public/private sector partnerships. But the CVCP shows no signs of backing their 'demands' on the Government with imaginative alternative proposals, let alone a genuine challenge that if the Government does not give ground, the overwhelming majority of institutions will move to full cost fees. Instead, much as in the earlier flirtation with top-up fees, they will find that while they debate the ethics of such a challenge, the quality of British higher education will be damaged beyond repair and the capacity of the system to reverse its decline will have been very substantially diminished. While persuasion is better than challenge, alternative proposals will need to be found which preserve the ability of the system (or at least its major institutions) to act should their demands not be met.

It is possible that universities have become so dependent on subsidies, however inadequate, that they no longer have the will to act and that the teachers within them so favour public provision that they are ready to ignore the lessons of the last quarter of a century. Whatever government has been in power, they have wanted to coerce the universities into doing their bidding, but have not been prepared to finance adequately the policies they have pursued. Even in areas of education that have, in many ways rightly, been given priority (the schools and nursery education) there is no new money, despite the rhetoric, and the Government wishes to devote more to the college sector and to continuing education. If we care about our students, current and future, and about the quality of what we have to offer in the university sector, we must restore our freedom to act and if that means reasserting our independence of government, that squares with the need for academic freedom and institutional autonomy. In its turn, since there is no likelihood of any re-ordering of its educational priorities nor any realistic way of easing the current downward pressures on university funding, the Government might be persuaded to see the sense of concentrating help on students, not least through the provision of a far more sensible loan scheme than to seek to pick off those institutions which had chosen to raise fees to economic levels. It is in any case likely that if all the more prestigious institutions made the move, political pressures would rapidly develop to prevent the Government from doing so. It would be preferable, however, if the Government accepted the proposals set out below and saw them as by far the best way of maximising funds for higher education and far more compatible with the place of the university sector in a free society.

A possible way forward?

Any new system of funding must achieve several things: it should free institutions from the shackles of a planning system which is as ineffective as it is restrictive; it must allow for any rise in student numbers which the economy requires; it must improve access; if the government feels that it must try in some measure to influence the profile of the nation's manpower, the new system should afford them some effective means of doing so (indeed a more effective system than the present one which allows them to influence the kind of places provided, but affords them no guarantee that such places will be taken up by home students); and, in a plural society, it should allow others to influence the system also. In addition there is a powerful case for a greater degree of autonomy even if it is not one that governments are willing to recognise.

The proposals advanced in Strategies for Higher Education (Barnes and Barr 1988) provide the best way to meet these objectives. Higher education institutions should charge economic fees and government should offset these wholly, mainly or in part by student bursaries which would be linked to the offer of a place and to continued satisfactory progress by a student towards a recognised qualification. Recurrent funding other than for research would be abandoned. Phasing of these changes is an option and the initial moves might take the form of a move to standard levels of fee differentiated only between the four groups of subjects identified in previous discussions. Overseas student fees could be used as an initial guide to setting the appropriate level of fees.

It should perhaps be noted that the money provided to institutions already reflects the numbers they teach and that students already make choices between institutions. Therefore the immediate effect of raising university fees to economic levels and offsetting them with government bursaries to students would only be to channel funds for tuition via the student rather than by recurrent grant. The crucial differences between this reform and the current system are to be found first in the absence of government control, but not of government influence, and second, in the provision of government support in the form of consumer subsidies rather than the production subsidies characteristic of the present system. However, the dynamics of the funding system would be very different and the effects over time substantial.

In relation to the main subject of this paper, the essence of the proposal is that higher education institutions would be left largely to conduct their affairs as they wish. They would obtain most of their income direct from those to whom they offer their services in the fields of teaching and research. Subject to certain regulatory safeguards, they would determine their own structure, contractual arrangements with staff, the courses offered, their nature and duration, and the fees charged for them. They would determine also the charges made for research done under contract for industry and the research councils. When he spoke to an LSE conference on higher education in September 1988, Robert Jackson, then the junior minister responsible for higher education, argued that public funding delivered to higher education institutions through students would not in itself increase institutional autonomy, although he saw other benefits in consumer power. If the only source of funding for higher education remained the Government and the only channel student fees, his claim might have some force. Even then, it does not follow that the transmission mechanism is unimportant. The politics of such a funding regime would be very different from and arguably more beneficial to university autonomy than those which affect the setting of the level of recurrent grant. Not only would potential students and their parents have expectations but they would be unlikely to accept lightly restrictions placed on their choice. If the payment of fee bursaries at certain institutions or for certain subjects were made subject to specific conditions, those conditions would become the subject of public debate and would have to be seen as reasonable to survive.

Indeed if a large proportion of the bursaries were tied initially to performance in an overarching certificate embracing A levels, GNVQs and AS levels, it would be difficult for the Government to attach additional restrictive conditions. The result almost certainly would be a substantial increase in the freedom of institutions to control their own destiny, even if further sources of student finance were not available. But of course they would be. An important part of our proposals is that there would be sources of fee funding other than the state. Not only would the private sector be encouraged to provide bursaries covering the totality of fees and generous maintenance, but students who were not eligible for a fee bursary from the state should have access to a limited loan facility to back their judgement of their own abilities. This would be particularly valuable to those who at present have to rely on the very patchy non-mandatory grants system to access courses.

In this context it is possible to envisage the EU becoming a source of bursaries. Given certain problems with the ERASMUS programme in so far as it applies to students, there would be a strong case for an EU programme, extending in the first instance to 10 per cent of the total volume of higher education students, which again would be quite consonant with institutional autonomy, the particular aspirations of national actors and others within the European Community (EC), and which would maximise cost effectiveness within the higher education sector. It is worth noting that the European Council of Ministers have stressed the importance of a number of themes, one of which, the promotion of institutional autonomy, is close to the concerns expressed earlier in this paper. The remaining themes are the need to promote inter-institutional links; the continuing importance of student and teacher mobility; the need, subject to the safeguarding of standards, to work towards improved credit transfer and accreditation; and the need to promote resources for research.

Reasons for EU involvement

Why should the European Union act in this matter? There are four good reasons for addressing the expansion of higher education at community level: first, the contribution it can make to a furthering of European culture and consciousness; second, to assist and promote the kind of mobility required within the single market; third, to ensure that skill shortages are adequately dealt with on a Europe-wide basis and not artificially limited by considerations of domestic economic finances; and last, because it would ensure the most cost effective development of higher education within the Community.

The expansion of higher education in EU countries is widely seen as a prerequisite for their continued economic success in an increasingly knowledge-based economy. Although the pace of development was slowed by recession in the 1990s, there is no reason to question the direction and extent of the changes required when they were identified in the late 1980s. In the face of steadily increasing global competition, the EU will maintain its position only by increasing the quality of its inputs, both labour and capital. In this context it is worth recalling the emphasis on education in recent studies of competitive advantage. In order to increase the flexibility and productivity of their industries, the developed economies of the EU will not only have to improve the skills of their workforce but are likely to require a much higher proportion of graduates. The IT and telecommunications sector is well set to become the most important industrial sector by the turn of the century, and it has been estimated that no less than two out of three people employed will need to make use of its services. It is clear also that the proportion of the workforce employed in the professions is increasing steadily and that a trend towards a well educated and multi-skilled workforce in the service industries as well as in manufacturing can be anticipated. Demographic trends, in particular the sharp decline in the European birth rate since the early 1960s, are of considerable concern to economic policy-makers and the report made to the President of the European Commission by the Round Table of European Industrialists in 1989 noted this decline in the context of the increasing industrial demand for trained manpower and warned that, in the absence of sweeping educational reforms, the Community was in danger of losing its technological edge.

Tables included in the 1991 EC Memorandum on Higher Education showed a marked decline in the number of young people between the ages of 15 and 24 in all countries of the EC between 1988 and 2010, with little evidence to suggest any recovery for at least a decade beyond that. The fact that the extent and incidence of this decline vary from one member state to another, although all are affected, strengthens the case for a Europe-wide solution. These figures suggest both the need and the inevitability of increased cross border flows. The skill shortages already evident within the Community are likely to increase and, with the pace of job destruction and creation increasing, the increasing need for continuing education and retraining in the field of higher education is universally acknowledged.

The process is likely to accelerate if, as seems likely, the European economy's requirement for higher level knowledge and skills requires an extension of the time spent in education and training, and for some time at least the process would seem certain to be self-reinforcing. Indeed, it is likely that industry will press the case for a more unified approach to education and training as the emergence of the single market leads to a clear realisation that, at degree level and above, they are dealing with a single work force. There may well be a need to move towards a common framework for higher education.

The EU not only has a direct concern with securing a sufficient flow of graduates for the needs of the Community as a whole, but there are good arguments why it should look to foster the emergence of comparative advantage within the higher education system. Given the constraint on public resources, there is good reason to reward flexible, innovative and cost effective provision, particularly where this marries continuing education and provision within industry with existing patterns of higher education provision, and there is no reason to let national boundaries stand in the way. If there are disparities between student flows into and out of particular nations, rather than looking for compensatory adjustments, it would be better to have a mechanism in place which would enable the Community to benefit. If we assume for the moment that Britain has a genuine comparative advantage (as the ERASMUS flows and increasing numbers of continental students seeking places in UK universities suggest), expansion of the British system to meet demand from other member states would be to the benefit of the Union by securing cost effective provision, subject only to scrutiny to ensure that quality did not fall. This might stimulate other states to try to match Britain's success.

It could well be argued, therefore, that economic necessity reinforces already powerful arguments for enabling students to take full advantage of their European citizenship and to contribute towards the creation of a sense of European identity by means of student mobility.

Given that labour of this quality and degree of education is likely to be a very scarce resource for the foreseeable future, it is questionable whether the Community can or should tolerate the major variations in the amount of financial help accorded to students and the numbers of students helped. Most countries have some form of grant system, but there are substantial variations in the amount of support given, with Spain and the Netherlands the most generous, France and Ireland giving less than half the sum that they do, and Germany having no grant at all. The way in which grants taper off as parental income rises is a further source of considerable variation. Loan schemes exist in all but France and Ireland, but the balance between loan and grant varies widely. Effectively, therefore, there are three sources of support, the taxpayer, the family and the student him or herself. For low income families the taxpayer share is considerable in all countries, but it falls sharply as family income rises, and is non existent, save in France, for high income families.

What is striking is the extent to which families take the strain in all countries, and it is questionable whether this is either just or efficient. Either parental contributions are voluntary, and therefore patchy, or they are in effect a tax, which is bizarre. There is very little more logic in taxing the parents of bright children than there is for taxing the parents of the ginger-haired! In any case, this degree of reliance on family, effectively parental, contributions is a substantial disincentive to recruitment into higher education, particularly amongst those families who have no experience of it or the benefits it can bring. In view of its importance, the whole question of student support merits a more coherent, systematic and consistent approach from the EU. Given the national variations in tax and welfare structures, there can be no Europe-wide loan scheme for the foreseeable future, but it would be possible to require that effective income-contingent national loan schemes are in place, conforming to criteria approved by the Council of Ministers, but varying in detail to suit national circumstances. However, loans and grants, if they survive in the current economic climate, should be 'portable'. In other words they should be available to the student at whatever higher education institution s/he chooses to attend, subject of course to the student being accepted by the institution and on condition only that the institution is 'recognised' by the Commission as being of sufficient quality.

The suggestion is that in Britain, income-contingent repayments should be made through the National Insurance system. There are two good reasons for this. The first is the upper earnings limit, which effectively makes the scheme neutral between one job and another. The second is that both employer and employee would share the cost of repayment. Persuading industry, other than individual benefactors, to help finance higher education has proved difficult. This scheme would avoid any free-rider problem, channel resources from industry into higher education, and would be a user-charge on graduates to ensure that what may well be a scarce resource is used wisely.

While the gains to the EU from the reformed funding system are evident, it might well be asked what the British government gains. Leaving aside gains from comparative advantage in a single market, although these could prove substantial, the simple answer is that it swaps a highly problematic system of control for rather more effective influence over the system. It may be open to question whether this degree of influence is actually desirable or in the long term interests of society, but if there is a continuing case for public subvention to higher education, democratically elected politicians will settle for nothing less. However, in addition to avoiding the heavy costs of an ineffective planning system, the new funding system will provide incentives to higher education institutions to teach properly, reduce X-inefficiency, and encourage flexibility, innovation and diversity in response to the demands of a diverse market.

Markets, pluralism and university autonomy

One of the major advantages over government which markets enjoy is that, whatever their relative merits in static situations, markets are in general more dynamic. Governments are frightened to disrupt the policy communities which they have been at pains to build and which are essential to the implementation of their policies. They tend to be conservative in action. Whatever the theoretic virtues of the synoptic approach to policy making, mixed scanning seems to be the best that can be achieved; and the norm approximates to Lindblom's twin concepts, disjointed incrementalism and partisan mutual adjustment. In these circumstances, there may well be merit in the market's ability to deliver dynamic efficiency (Schumpeter 1934). Free markets clearly have the capability to promote new technologies, improve product quality, lower costs, and create new and marketable products. There is no reason to think that this would not apply in the field of higher education. The real question is whether this is desirable. In the current state of higher education across the EU and in Britain, there really can be no doubt of the answer. If we are to continue with a massification of the higher education system and to do so in conditions where public resources are severely constrained, creative dynamism will be at a premium.

Although what is proposed is a market-oriented system, it does not preclude government action to deal with 'market failures' of one kind or another. Indeed, if a government feels that it is competent to predict with certainty manpower needs in the public sector, where as potential employer it has some control, or even manpower needs more generally, this system provides it with incentive-based tools to do a more effective job than that accomplished by the creation of dedicated places. Future governments may well wish to offer larger bursaries tied to particular subjects or even deny some subjects bursaries at all: further, if a more effective loan system is in place to fund a large part of student maintenance and some element of student fees as institutions move to full control of their fee structure, forgiveness of part or all of a loan in return for a number of years engaged in a particular type of job or sector of employment is a powerful .tool for influencing individual decisions. It has been accepted already that this could be an inducement to graduates in scarcity subjects to spend some time in teaching. A further example of how influence could be exercised would be an offer of higher bursaries to those who undertake short courses, which in turn would make those students more attractive to institutions. If access were at issue, it would be possible to make more generous bursaries available to poorer students or to those whose parents had not themselves gained degrees.

Nor is the ability to influence the system confined to government or even to the DfEE. It would be open to firms or other bodies to promote themselves by the offer of bursaries and/or forgivable loans, much as the Services do already. In similar vein, a government department concerned with the need to maintain a viable institution for reasons of employment in a particular part of the country might be minded to offer a number of bursaries tenable only at that institution. Since they would have to get the scheme past the Treasury there would be no question of a concealed subsidy: the purpose would be explicit and justified in terms of that department's objectives. Again, departments or local authorities concerned to advance knowledge relevant to them could offer postgraduate bursaries in appropriate subjects. All such actions would be transparent and therefore open to debate in a way which is not true of the present allocation of resources.

A major advantage of this strategy is the power it gives to all stakeholders to shape the system of higher education, not just the institutions and the government, but other sponsors of students and the students themselves. Manpower planning has always been an uncertain science: the market is a classic way for others to hedge the government's bets. Indeed, there is a very good case for making loans available to potential students who are not in receipt of bursaries, and particularly those who are currently eligible only for non-mandatory grants, so long as a genuinely income-contingent loan scheme is in place and the loans are of a size that can be readily repaid out of lifetime earnings.

Such possibilities of intervention by government and others might well make higher education institutions themselves pause, were it not for the growing burden of interference by way of the funding bodies. However, the new system proposed is not only likely to be less oppressive but it will increasingly afford institutions the opportunity to position themselves where they wish to be in the 'market' and to maintain those aspects of their teaching and research which they believe essential to a university even where demand is limited. Nearly everyone gains from the proposal therefore. The government swaps a highly problematic system of control for rather more effective influence over the outputs of the system. The institutions regain control over their own destinies. Both sides are rid of an inefficient and costly bureaucracy. Others will find that this is a system which they can influence, while students are likely to find that their needs, particularly in teaching, are taken far more seriously.

Finally, it should be stressed that the scheme is for a complete system and not a set of particular proposals. The system can be set in different ways and it can be used by governments in a more or less directive manner as the needs of the age, or more probably the relative success (or otherwise) of particular approaches, suggest. There will be no need for any radical changes to the system once it is in place. It is sufficiently flexible to accommodate radical differences of approach, and that is one of its great strengths. But from the point of view of universities, it restores a considerable degree of the autonomy they were fast losing and that can only be to their advantage and that of the society which they serve.

References

Allen, M. (1988) *The Goals of Universities*. Buckingham: SRHE/Open University Press.

Barnes, J. and Barr, N. (1988) *Strategies for Higher Education: The Alternative White Paper*. London: David Hume Institute/STIKERD.

Barry, N. (1994) *The Case for Independent Universities*. Buckingham: University of Buckingham.

Becher, T. and Kogan, M. (1992) *Process and Structure in Higher Education, 2nd edition*. London: Routledge.

Brown, R.G.S. (1970) *The Administrative Process in Great Britain.* London: Methuen.

Casey, J. (1997) 'Rejoice, O Philistines!' *The Spectator* 2 August.

Cyert, R.M. and March, J.G. (1963) *A Behavioural Theory of the Firm.* Oxford: Prentice-Hall.

Etzioni-Halevy, E. (1993) *The Élite Connection. Problems and Potential of Western Democracy.* Cambridge: Polity Press.

Fischer, F.and Forester, J. (eds) (1993) *The Argumentative Turn in Policy Analysis and Planning.* London: UCL Press.

Griffith, J.A (1989) *Universities and the State. The Next Steps.* London: Council for Academic Freedom and Democracy.

Harris, M. (1998) 'Our support has a price' in *Times Higher Education Supplement* 16 January.

Jackson, P.M. (1982) *The Political Economy of Bureaucracy.* Philip Allan.

Lawrence, P.R. and Lorsch, J.W. (1967) *Organisation and Environment.* Cambridge, MA: Harvard.

Leibenstein, H. (1966) 'Allocative efficiency vs. X-efficiency.' *American Economic Review 56,* 392–415.

Leibenstein, H. (1983) 'Competition and X-efficiency: reply.' *Journal of Political Economy 81,* 765–777.

March, J.G. and Olsen, J.P. (1976) *Ambiguity and Choice in Organisations.* Bergen.

March, J.G. and Simon, H.A. (1958) *Organisations.* New York: Wiley.

National Committee of Inquiry into Higher Education (1997) *Higher Education in the Learning Society.* London: NCIHE.

Pfeffer, P., Salancik, G. and Leblebici, H. (1976) 'Personal influence in organisational decision-making.' *Administrative Science Quarterly 19.*

Psacharoupoulos, G. (1987) *Economics of Education: Research and Studies.* Oxford: Pergamon.

Schumpeter, J. (1934) *The Theory of Economic Development.* Cambridge, M.A: Harvard.

Shackle, G.S. (1974) 'Decision: the human predicament' in *Annals of the American Academy of Political and Social Sciences 412,* 1–10.

Thompson, J.D. and Tuden, A. (1959) 'Strategies, structures and processes of administrative decision.' In J.D. Thompson *et al.: Comparative Studies in Administration.* Pittsburgh: University of Pittsburgh.

Weick (1976) 'Educational organisations as loosely coupled systems.' *Administration Science Quarterly 21,* 1–19.

Williamson, O. (1971) 'Managerial Discretion, Organisational Form and the Multi-Division Hypothesis'. In R. Marris and A. Wood (eds) *The Corporate Economy.* London: Macmillan.

Williamson, O. (1975) *Markets and Hierarchies: analysis and anti trust implications.* New York: Free Press.

Wolf Jr, C. (1988) *Markets and Governments. Choosing Between Imperfrect Alternatives.* The Rand Corporation, 1988.

CHAPTER 10

The Paradoxes of Research Assessment and Funding

Ian McNay

Introduction

If we use Trow's thresholds (Trow 1974), during the early 1990s, UK higher education moved decisively to a system of mass participation. Over 30 per cent of young people proceeded into full-time provision; later age entry and part-time participation also increased. After 'consolidation' in the middle of the decade, widening participation further is back on the agenda set by the Dearing and Kennedy reports (NCIHE 1997; Kennedy 1997).

Not so for research. As access by the students to teaching and learning became more inclusive, funding to academic staff to support their research was becoming more selective and exclusive. The instrument for the second policy was a quadrennial evaluation of activity and output – the Research Assessment Exercise (RAE) – conducted by the higher education funding councils in the UK, the results of which were used to inform the distribution of research funds administered by the councils. These had not increased significantly in real terms for several years, so institutions were competing for a larger share in a zero sum game. Funds linked to RAE provided only about 20 per cent of base-line funding of institutions from government and yet the exercise was given much more prominence than evaluation of teaching.

This chapter reports on research on the impact of the 1992 RAE on institutional and individual behaviour in English higher education, with commentary conditioned by participation in, and observation of, the 1996 exercise and its immediate aftermath (McNay 1997a, b).

The policy context

The 1992 exercise was timed to inform decisions by the new councils established to fund newly integrated systems of provision following the 1992 Further and Higher Education Acts. Previously, RAE funding had been available only to institutions under the aegis of the Universities Funding Council, before that, the University Grants Committee. A barely changed quantum now had to be allocated to more than twice the number of institutions.

The designation of over 40 institutions as universities in 1992, with consequent reviews of mission, the near freeze on expansion of student numbers with consequences for income flow from fees that came in 1993, major reviews of research policy nationally and within the European Union, and the introduction of systematic quality assessment of course provision and audit of institutions' arrangements for quality assurance, clustered chronologically to create a new regime for higher education coincident with the 1992 RAE. We attempted to separate out the impact of RAE from the impact of these other diverse policy initiatives. The assessment of quality (the RAE) and the selective allocation of funds were, formally, two separate exercises but nobody outside the funding councils treated them as such: 'RAE' covered both. Our focus groups suggested that money was a great driver in participating in RAE and the money that flows from it was the main means by which it exercised influence for behaviour change.

The conduct of the RAE

Over £600 million (1992 prices) would be distributed annually in England on the basis of judgements within the RAE. The exercise was conducted by the Universities Funding Council (UFC) but all the institutions that would come within the imminent unitary systems were invited to make submissions.

These submissions listed all research active staff with details of their publications and other research output – patents, inventions, productions in performing and visual arts, etc. The best two in each case were marked with an asterisk. Institutional submissions also included, for each academic area, descriptive sections on performance and plans.

Quality was judged by a series of panels covering around 70 units of assessment (academic areas, mainly related to traditional disciplines) on a scale 1 to 5 with 5 as the top grade indicating a body of work of national excellence with a significant part achieving international standards of excellence. In some cases there were separate gradings for basic and applied research. Panels varied in the way they arrived at their judgements.

There was also a letter grade to indicate the percentage of academic staff submitted as being research active, but that was rarely quoted subsequently.

Funds to support research were allocated in a block grant to universities and colleges but aggregated from a series of calculations for each area in which research active staff had been submitted. The main funds in England were allocated on a formula basis: $A = U(Q-1) N$, where A is the total sum allocated to an institution for a particular unit of assessment, Q is the quality rating, N is the number of research-active mainstream academic staff submitted, and U is the basic allocation per point for any particular unit. This last factor varied considerably because the total national quantum for each unit was fixed before other calculations were made. Some units of assessment were more affected by the influx of new institutions than others: there was little, if any, adjustment of first allocation to a subject area to take account of the new profile of participants. There were minor adjustments to the formula to take account of numbers of research students, research assistants, part-time or visiting staff, and research income from some other sources, but the dominant variables are included in that formula. There were variations, too, across the countries: England adopted a straight line gradient parallel to quality ratings; Scotland and Wales diverged from this. Our work was restricted to England.

It is worth noting two major changes from previous practice which are assumed to be responses to the inclusion in the exercise of the major part of the higher education system, the former non-university sector:

1. Student numbers were excluded from the formula whereas they had previously been a significant element serving as a proxy for all academic staff members. The switch to research active staff raised several issues. It posed tactical questions on who to include and exclude in the trade-off between

quality and quantity. For example, if cutting out a tail of, say, six staff from 26 allowed a unit to move up from a grade 2 to a grade 3, and if the basic allocation increase was £1000 per point, the gain was £1000(3–1)20–£1000(2–1)26 = £14,000. It also penalised those with 'efficient' staff: student ratios where there were fewer staff to include than in a unit with a comparable number of students. So, if a department taught 300 students with 30 academics it gained a 50 per cent advantage over one with 300 students and 20 academics, who, with a higher load on teaching and student assessment, might also have less time for research. The grading:funding ratios and the basic units of resource were not known to those preparing submissions.

2. Some units, rated 1, would get no funds for research, whereas, previously, all UFC funded units had received some baseline funds: the funding multiplier went to Q-1 from Q- 0.5. This was, therefore, the first time that research would not be funded for all academic staff in traditional universities as a 'normal' part of their core role.

The project design

The project on the impact of RAE in England (McNay 1997 a, b) was commissioned by Higher Education Funding Council for England (HEFCE) in summer 1995 and finished in summer 1996. It therefore coincided with preparation for the 1996 RAE and, at times, views were expressed about the RAE in general, not just the effect of the 1992 exercise – the main focus of our study.

We approached the topic from several angles:

1. search of HEFCE documents and the increasing journal literature

2. four focus groups of senior staff, which set an agenda for

   • 30 institutional case studies on strategic responses, and

   • two questionnaires within 15 institutions; one to heads of units, the other to academic staff – we had approximately 150 returns for the first and 400 for the second

3. interviews with representatives of other 'stakeholders' –
    funders, industry based researchers, research councils,
    learned societies, professional bodies, as well as an invitation
    to a range of others to submit views.

In this way the project team used public, private and personal
perceptions to develop a picture of impact at four levels: system,
institution, unit, individual (Becher and Kogan 1992).

The next section will highlight key findings at the last three levels
before the final section comments upon system level issues.

Institutional impact

The main effects at institutional level can be summarised as:

*   tighter policy

*   better management and more administration

*   strategic staffing initiatives

*   virement of funds from higher graded to lower graded
    departments

*   some restructuring to cluster research staff organisationally.

All our focus groups highlighted a fuller consciousness of the place of
research and research performance among institutional leaders. This
was particularly so in the modern universities, recently designated. In
them, there were SWOT analyses and similar exercises to help define
investment strategies, often built on two phases: the 1996 exercise
deadlines, and longer term. In established universities, such devices
were more for refinement of policy and strategy and used at
departmental level or in managing the exceptions. Of research staff,
63 per cent supported the statement that 'in my institution, research
is now better managed and supported' (though only 24 per cent
thought their own work was better organised because of RAE
pressures for efficiency!). Of managers, 53 per cent agreed that
'research work is now focused on a smaller number of prioritised
topic areas' – the figure was over 60 per cent in lower rated units – and
62 per cent of heads of unit agreed that 'research administration is
more efficient than five years ago' (77 per cent among those new to
the exercise). These findings support those of Williams (1991) on the

previous exercise, that the main impact is on institutional policy, procedures, and management. Of heads, 75 per cent said the exercise was used as a lever stimulating major strategic review across the institution.

The focus group discussions and related exercises put staffing policy and practices as the main area for expressing this (above the establishment of committees, and of central offices and designation of a senior staff member as leader in the policy area). There was a difference here between older and modern universities. The former set recruitment criteria which excluded those not already proven and designated people in post as 'non-active' in an exclusionary way: the proportion of staff in older universities designated as 'research active' fell between 1992 and 1996. There was also *some* spending on attracting 'stars' but this was marginal. Modern universities retained their greater focus on teaching in recruitment, and used staff development to develop active researchers for inclusion.

In some cases, across the divide, there were structural changes: research centres housed staff freed from teaching responsibilities; graduate schools became the arenas for research, leaving departments to organise undergraduate teaching. Each of these was particular and peculiar but the trend was a gradual separation, structurally, of research from teaching.

I finish this section with a paradox. RAE and its subsequent selective funding was meant to give more money to those judged the better research units. Over half of the heads in our survey saw internal virement of funds to lower rated departments from high rated and, in several of the case study institutions, senior staff articulated that as policy. In part, that was because they disagreed with panel judgements or believed in parity of treatment regardless. In part, however, it was because of a strategic recognition that higher graded departments that preserved their grade gained nothing, whereas lower graded departments that improved their grade increased their income. So, financially, improvers were better than star performers at the funding ceiling. For government, such an internal investment focus may be good: there is some evidence from Australia (Grichting 1996) that middle graded units give better value for money on output indicators. A late change in the funding gradient for 1996, after all submissions were in, caused anger since it contradicted previously stated policy on the basis of which institutional strategies had been developed. There was also internal transfer of teaching funds into research activity especially in lower rated departments (over 55 per cent of heads of units gaining less than a three agreed with that).

Unit level

Heads of unit were divided about the overall impact of RAE. In our total sample 58 per cent said it had been positive, 23 per cent negative, 7 per cent both, and 2 per cent neither. In both of the first two categories, roughly one third put the impact as 'substantial', one third as 'significant', one third as 'moderate'; two people had it as 'negligible'. Those new to the exercise were more positive than those in established universities; those in lower rated units more positive than those in higher rated ones.

The positive side is shown in high agreement ratings for two statements:

- our research work is now more effectively organised than five years ago – 82 per cent

- the quality of our research work is now higher than five years ago – 81 per cent.

For units new to the exercise, those scores exceeded 95 per cent; for those scoring grade 4 or 5, they dropped below 70 per cent. This reflects patterns elsewhere in our results where confident, assured departments are less affected than the anxious ones, or those aspiring to get access to the exercise and its rewards; 59 per cent of heads believed RAE had (re) invigorated some staff with low productivity records.

There is a down side: 70 per cent of heads agree that 'RAE has led to a considerable increase in stress among staff', though this is under 40 per cent for those new to the exercise, who, presumably felt they could only gain. The anxious, grade 3, department heads gave it 90 per cent agreement. There are concerns too: about the inhibition of new research areas (45 per cent), hindrance to interdisciplinary research (46 per cent), encouragement of more conservative approaches (46 per cent) and the rupture between research and teaching (40 per cent). That last is reinforced elsewhere: good researchers spend less time teaching (50 per cent agreement but 67 per cent in low graded departments, 22 per cent in high graded ones); and more undergraduate teaching is done by part-timers and postgraduates (48 per cent). Recent work by Blackman *et al.* (forthcoming) underlines the continued expectation of a research input at this level, but the Dearing enquiry (NCIHE 1997, para 3.69) takes the breach as a *fait accompli*. I return to this later, but conclude this section by breaking down heads' views on RAE impact into its two elements: 71 per cent said there was a positive impact on research; 62 per cent said there was a *negative* impact on teaching.

Two other issues came through at the level of departments. The first was the encouragement to target output articles at prestige journals which were mainly read by other academics, including panel members making RAE judgements, rather than to disseminate results in professional or 'popular' journals which end-users might be more likely to read (84 per cent agreement). The second was the management of staff, first to be more rigorous in designating people as research active (82 per cent) where it was possible to be so: many claimed to have got rid of the inactive for previous exercises. The other aspect of staff management was organisational: teams replacing lone researchers – 64 per cent support, with the dissenters mainly in humanities, defending the 'loners', or where teams had always been the norm, such as chemistry.

Individuals: the researchers themselves

The views of researchers were sought on issues raised in other phases of the work. In contrast to heads' views, most did not feel inhibited about interdisciplinary work (only 20 per cent agreed the statement) nor did they avoid speculative projects (also only 20 per cent) nor new lines of work (25 per cent). Collaboration continued (only 18 per cent agreed it had reduced because of RAE competitiveness). There was little move away from applied research (18 per cent) despite views of its lower esteem; nor were many trying to read the runes and fall in with perceived panel preferences (13 per cent). They believed their own output quality was better than five years previously (64 per cent) but were sceptical about others' – only 34 per cent believed RAE had improved the quality of research. Perhaps it was the causal link they rejected. Those who spent more time on research than five years previously were balanced equally by those who did not; less than half had increased the time spent on teaching, yet 65 per cent believed RAE had increased stress levels. Maybe this was because 79 per cent spent more time on administration – a lot of it on quality assurance processes – which ate away at research time: in consequence, for 70 per cent, higher for women, research work encroached more on their private time.

Most, then, were, despite the pressures, carrying on much as before in an autonomous self-determining manner, though half now worked more in teams. There was some feeling of constraint on choice of topics, conditioned by group or departmental priorities (37 per cent) and, for research activity in general, 58 per cent believed the agenda of programmes and priorities was defined by people other than researchers.

System issues

That last finding is despite the peer review process of RAE and the prominence of academics in committees of research councils, and other funding bodies. However, as with other policy areas such as international collaboration (McNay 1995) what is decided as policy at the top may not be reflected in practice at the bottom.

Some system issues have already been touched upon. The RAE was set up as a technical device to inform funding. Its impact has gone far beyond that in affecting institutional strategies, priorities and use of general resources, not just those flowing from RAE. There was not an overt aim of improving the quality of research, but that is what has happened as average grades achieved have gone up. The number of departments rated 5 went from 348 in 1992 to 573 in 1996, and, in the modern universities, those rated 3 or above went from 96 to 351. So, for little more money, if any, the exercise in itself has been a spur to higher achievements, because of its competitive nature and the search for prestige by institutional leaders. The split between teaching and research may have been anticipated, if not intended, when each was funded separately and separately assessed and accountable, when staff could be deemed 'teaching only' as well as 'research only' and when different organisational forms were increasingly used for the two. The education panel was the only one in 1996 to accept teaching material as output evidence of research.

There are other tensions and separations, many listed by Davies (1997) who does a stakeholder analysis of those with an interest in higher education research. My own concern is over the discreteness of the exercise and the failure to integrate it in to an holistic policy framework or to relate it to other elements in the operation of the system.

There is, then a need for future exercises to recognise that RAE is part of a whole, not entire unto itself, and to connect to:

1. Teaching.

    If, as many claim, research is essential to good teaching in higher education, the link between the two should be a major criterion for judgement. If higher education is now a mass system, this means research is a mass activity as well as teaching. Currently, there is a risk of drifting to separate the two by discrete funding, by staff designation, by establishment of research 'enclaves' structurally separate from teaching units and by possible future plans to fund only a strongly limited sub-set of institutions. The teaching curriculum is being affected as senior staff in universities withdraw support from those with low RAE grades so that taught courses close.

2. Teaching Quality Assessment (TQA).

    The essentiality of the teaching/research link would imply consideration of that link within systems of quality assessment for teaching. This is rarely done, though some Higher Education Quality Council reports did raise the issue.

3. Reward systems.

    Our work showed evidence of teaching funds being raided to finance research and of an increasing dominance of rewards to staff being research driven. If 80 per cent of funding of higher education is for teaching, the rewards for the scholarship of transmission have at least to equal those for the scholarship of discovery in Boyer's classification (Boyer 1994).

4. Practice.

    Even within the research domain, there is a failure to transmit findings to practitioners: a view of all the professional bodies and several employers who contributed. Publishing in professional journals is actively discouraged by some institutional managers. The academic world risks talking only to itself and so sterilising its work. As Gibbons *et al.* (1994) show, this risks also ignoring the emergence of new approaches to knowledge development, the scholarship of discovery, that are grounded in practice.

5. Other research sectors.

Even within the research community, too, there is a divide. The approaches of the funding councils and those of the research councils differ – on discipline/interdiscipline approaches, and on recognition of transfer to practice, to give only two dimensions. Within the dual system this may be healthy, and the top graded departments perform in both. However, there is little consideration of the articulation between the two and, at key thresholds levels, judgements in the one arena, used in the other, may not transfer with validity. There is a cultural difference, crucial to views on, for example, teaching company schemes. The different ministries involved, and their agencies, need to review this together, and reduce the competition, even conflict, that exists between them.

6. Research development and enhancement.

This had not been a prominently stated aim of RAE until Brian Fender, Chief Executive of HEFCE, put it top of his objectives at a conference in Bristol in July 1997 (Fender 1997). Any strategy for such development has been tacit, or emerged piecemeal. People, therefore, created their own view of others' thoughts (if any) and this risked distortion at least and, at the extreme, incipient paranoia because of the intangibility of any coherent policy or strategy. Within some institutions, RAE was a distraction, taking a lot of effort away from other initiatives or from the development of more broadly based strategies for research development. Senior staff managed the RAE; they did less well at managing research.

7. The wider world.

If 'international excellence' is the pinnacle, there are few structures in place to get judgements on it. Staff in the relevant directorates of the European Commission were ignorant of RAE. Few people in other countries knew of it; fewer still understood it or agreed with the approach. Few people from outside the UK sat on RAE panels or informed their judgements.

If the RAE is to be repeated, it needs to find its place in a more integrated approach to the second most important activity of higher education. A more open process, a fuller dialogue with all involved, in contrast to an image of an élitist, protective strategy, may produce few surprises because more are committed to owning implementation in practice, because they have been involved in establishing principles and developing plans for the collective community.

Current indications of policy thinking do not give cause for hope: they are still, like previous efforts by the élite (Harris 1996, NAPAG 1996) aimed at exclusion. The Dearing Committee proposes a 'set-aside' strategy: institutions should be paid £500 per head for staff *not* to submit within the RAE. The consultation paper on the future of the exercise (HEFCE 1997) suggests that departments should lodge 'stake money' with their bid, and make a self-assessed grading. They would lose their money if they were graded two levels below their claim. The money would be forfeited to the funding councils who would be the ones making the decision which triggered the forfeit. That simply emphasises the 'game' element of the whole exercise: a major criticism which has led some to believe that form is more important than substance, presentation more than the essential product. Both those approaches also imply that what is wanted is less research in universities funded by public money. Is that a rational policy for any government on the brink of a knowledge-based new century?

References

Becher, T. and Kogan, M. (1992) *Process and Structure in Higher Education.* London: Routledge.

Boyer, E. (1994) 'Scholarship reconsidered: priorities for a new century.' In *Universities in the Twenty-first Century.* London: National Commission on Education.

Davies, J.K. (1997) 'Universities and research: a failed marriage?'. Paper to EAIR conference. Warwick.

Fender, B. (1997) 'Keynote address' in University of the West of England *Research Assessment: Future Perfect?* Conference Report, 1 July, Bristol: UWE.

Gibbons, M., Limoges, C., Nowotny, H., Schwartzman, S., Scott, P. and Trow, M. (1994) *The New Production of Knowledge: The Dynamics of Science and Research in Contemporary Societies.* London: Sage.

Grichting, W.L. (1996) 'Do our research units give value for money?' *Campus Review of (Australia) 6,* 29.

Harris, M. (1996) *Review of Postgraduate Education.* Bristol: HEFCE.

Higher Education Funding Council for England (1997) 'Research Assessment' (RAE 2/97), Bristol: HEFCE.

Kennedy, H. (1997) *Learning Works: Widening Participation in Further Education.* Coventry: Further Education Funding Council.

McNay, I. (1995) 'Universities going international: choices, cautions and conditions.' In P. Blok (ed) *Policy and Policy Implementation in Internationalisation of Higher Education.* Amsterdam: EAIE.

McNay, I. (1997a) *The Impact of the 1992 RAE on Institutional and Individual Behaviour in English Higher Education: the Evidence from a Research Project.* Bristol: HEFCE.

McNay, I. (1997b) *The Impact of the 1992 RAE on Institutional and Individual Behaviour in English Higher Education: Summary Report and Commentary.* Bristol: HEFCE: summary report and commentary, Chelmsford: CHEM/APU.

National Academies Policy Advisory Group (1996) *Research Capability of the University System.* London: The Royal Society for NAPAG.

National Committee of Inquiry into Higher Education (1997) *Higher Education in the Learning Society.* London: NCIHE.

Trow, M. (1974) 'Problems in the transition from élite to mass higher education.' In OECD (ed) *Policies for Higher Education: General Report.* Paris: OECD.

Williams, Sir Bruce (1991) *University Responses to Research Selectivity.* London: Centre for Higher Education Studies, London Institute of Education.

CHAPTER 11

Strategic Management in Research Funding

Maivor Sjölund

Introduction

This chapter analyses the impact of new funding arrangements for research in Sweden which are intended to cause a shift in emphasis from disciplinary-based research to multidisciplinary and problem-focused research. It focuses on management at the institutional level. It will analyse the tension between the university as a unit for academic freedom and autonomy, and controls exercised by external funding bodies, private or public.

In their book *The New Production of Knowledge. The Dynamics of Science and Research in Contemporary Societies,* Gibbons *et al.* claim that a new way of creating knowledge is being developed in parallel with the traditional way. The authors have named the models Mode 1 and Mode 2 (Gibbons *et al.* 1994). Mode 1 is the traditional, intradisciplinary way of creating new knowledge. The curiosity of scientists and their search for truth are the main driving forces. No direct importance is attached to the *usefulness* of the new knowledge. Critical thinking and testing that the knowledge is, in some sense, true are the central ingredients of this model. The intradisciplinary criteria guarantee the quality of the research. In Mode 1 research matters are formulated and solved within the subject disciplines.

In contrast, Mode 2 is multidisciplinary and problem-based. The questions are posed in the environment in which the knowledge shall be applied. While Mode 1 is characterised by homogeneity and preserving the hierarchic organisation, Mode 2 has the characteristics of heterogeneity and a variable organisation. It includes different parties which work together on a problem which has been defined in a special and local context.

The models are based on different types of quality control. In Mode 1 prevailing intradisciplinary criteria constitute the quality control. The questions posed are intradisciplinary and the new knowledge is tested against earlier experience. The central issue is whether the knowledge is true in some sense of the term. The discussion takes place in a spirit of a *Context of Justification* to use Karl Popper's terminology (Popper 1989). The driving force is the search for knowledge for the sake of knowledge.

The driving force behind Mode 2 is that the knowledge shall be of use to someone – industry, the state, or society in general. The knowledge is developed in an environment which has the character of negotiations between parties. Efficiency in the process of producing knowledge and usefulness of the knowledge produced are the central criteria in Mode 2. The authors point out the complementary relationship between the two modes. Mode 1 is a necessary prerequisite for the problem solving in Mode 2. But Mode 1 is not always adequate and therefore the intradisciplinary criteria for quality control are supplemented by aspects of efficiency and usefulness in Mode 2.

During recent years considerable changes have taken place in the Swedish system for funding research. New sources of funds in the form of private research foundations and the research funds of the European Union (EU) Commission have entered the Swedish research arena. These new sources have the special aim of supporting research which is considered useful and which can improve the competitiveness of trade and industry, that is, research according to Mode 2.

Problem formulation

The problem which shall be analysed is how the universities, as autonomous organisations, manage to balance research work initiated by themselves according to Mode 1, and the external requirements on research work undertaken according to Mode 2. Three questions will be addressed:

1. In what way will research grants from external funders affect the management of institutions, especially the allocation of resources within the institution?

2. Will the funders of Mode 2 want to create new units within the universities, which are separate from the basic units, e.g. the subject-based departments?

    To be able to answer this crucial question of how universities regard the development of units which are separate from the basic units, the concept 'unit' needs to be defined. Here, everything is conceivable on a scale from loosely linked temporary networks to units which have premises and employees of their own outside the traditional institutional structure, for example, physically separate organisations. In the following I will refer to *network* as the loosest form of cooperation. The next stage on the scale is the special *centre*. These are somewhat more permanent than networks. A centre can be a separate unit from the accounting point of view (an account or profit centre) and in certain cases can have a part-time administrator or director. At the other end of the scale we have *institute*. These have permanent organisational resources in the form of staff and premises. In certain cases these institutes can have their own premises with the institute's name over the doorway.

3. Will the new external setting, with several different funding bodies, increase the autonomy of institutions? Or will there be an increased tension between the management of the institution and the academic leaders of the faculty board in defending different values in the system? (See the normative modes in Becher and Kogan 1992, p.10.) For instance, the management of the institution may pursue control and efficiency according to Mode 2, meanwhile the faculty board might defend values according to Mode 1.

Approach and methodology

The study is qualitative and is based on interviews with vice-chancellors and/or pro-vice-chancellors, and bursars, as well as with deans and other representatives of faculties. The interviews took place at the universities of Gothenburg, Linköping, Lund, Stockholm, Umeå, and Uppsala, and the Royal Caroline Institute, Chalmers University of Technology and the Royal Institute of Technology.[1]

The creation of a new funding arena

In addition to the funding of research by the government, research councils and sector organisations, new funders have entered the Swedish research arena since 1994. Amongst these are the foundations established by the non-Socialist Government with money from the so-called 'collective wage earners' investment funds'. In total, eleven foundations were established. Among them were the Foundation for Strategic Environmental Research, the Foundation of Knowledge and Competence Development, and the Foundation for Strategic Research. These foundations were established as private organisations. This meant that their operations lay outside the control of the government.

The foundations were created to support research according to Mode 2 in order to increase the competitiveness of Swedish industry and companies. The aim is to build research environments, organised on a more or less permanent basis, for universities and trade and industry. An explicit condition stipulated by the funders is that the knowledge shall have practical relevance and be useful. The Foundation for Strategic Research wants to contribute to the development of Swedish research and postgraduate studies with the objective of strengthening Sweden's competitiveness. The Foundation of Knowledge and Competence Development wants to support higher academic education, for example involving people with postgraduate degrees who have strong links with Swedish trade and industry. The Foundation for Strategic Environmental Research wants to promote the development of strong research environments

---

1   The study was conducted within the work of The National Agency for Higher Education in Sweden, at the request of a government commission on the financing of research, in the autumn of 1995. This article draws in part on that report published in Swedish in an Official Report of the Swedish Government (SOU). See SOU 1996:29. 'Forskning och Pengar', bilaga 5, 'Externfinansieringens påverkan på fakultetsanslag och organisation inom universitet och högskolor', by Maivor Sjölund and Stefan Odeberg.

of the highest international class of importance for Sweden's future competitiveness. Research shall be of significance for the solution of major environmental problems and for environmentally-friendly social development.

After heated political discussions in the autumn of 1996, the Socialist Government managed to turn the private foundations into public foundations. The members of the boards will now be appointed by the government. But the aims of the foundations have not, so far, been changed. They will still contribute to research useful for trade and industry.

In addition to these foundations, so-called 'competence centres' were established by a central government agency, the National Board for Industrial and Technical Development (NUTEK). These are funded by the government with the aim of building up centres for trade and industry and research. One of NUTEK's criteria for building a competence centre is that the work done there shall be of importance for industry and the centre shall include researchers working with companies on an exchange basis.

Moreover, as a member state in the EU, it is now possible for Sweden to apply for research funds administered by the EU. According to EU's Fourth Frame Programme relevance and usefulness are required for funding of research.

This implies that all the newly established foundations in the Swedish arena promote research according to the values in Mode 2. Another important condition on the part of the funders is that they require corresponding financing from the university for the project.

Strategic approaches

In what way will research grants from external funders affect the allocation of resources at the faculty board?

The aim here is to analyse whether there is a correlation between the ability of a basic unit, e.g. a subject discipline, to obtain external resources, and the allocation of money from the faculty board to the basic unit.

This correlation can be either positive or negative. A positive correlation implies that the faculty board wants to create an incentive structure for the basic units to compete, on scientific grounds, for external money. It can be seen as a quality label if the subject discipline in a peer-reviewed process gets money for research.

A negative correlation implies that the faculty board, from a scientific perspective, will support basic units who fail to gain money from external funders. The 'basic unit' may comprise small unique subjects or new subjects with few external funders.

The analysis shows that the norms for distribution of money at the faculty board will be decided by the faculty board itself. There are different norms and formulae developed by different faculty boards. There are differences between faculty boards within the same institutions, and there are differences between institutions as well. For instance, the faculty board of medical science in Stockholm will not use the same norms as other faculty boards in medical science at other universities.

However, it is clear from the interviews that there is a correlation between the ability of a subject discipline to gain grants in scientific competition and the money allocated from the faculty board. A successful basic unit will get more money from the faculty board. The norms and the calculation of how much money they will get as a reward will differ between the faculty boards, but there is a clear link in the majority of the cases.

But this is true only for grants obtained from research councils. The reason is the use of peer reviews for ranking applications. Grants obtained from funders such as the new foundations, described above, will not be supplemented by the same rewards from the faculty board. That implies that it is only research grants according to Mode 1 which will be regarded by the faculty board as high quality research projects.

With a few exceptions the faculties are using a direct and positive link between the ability of a subject discipline to get external, peer-reviewed money, as a criterion for allocating resources. However, it is worth noting that it is just 10 per cent of the resources of the faculty board which will be distributed in this way. The remaining 90 per cent is tied up in permanent positions and other costs.

Even though it is just a small amount of money that a subject discipline can get in the competition at the faculty board, the incentive system seems to work. The impression is that most elements are positive to the system. It is interesting to note that the government has refrained from implementing a similar system at the national level.

Is there a tendency to create new units externally financed according to Mode 2, alongside the subject-based departments?

In interviews with university leaders it has emerged that external financing has a tendency to create units beside the basic units. For the universities this means that a dual strategy must be adopted. On the one hand the universities are interested in attracting new research resources to the universities; on the other hand the universities want to retain the initiative and decide for themselves on the use of these funds.

The analysis shows that no permanent units have been established beside the basic units through the initiatives or demands of external financiers. The permanent units which do exist have, as a rule, been established by governmental decision. It can also be difficult to determine whether a unit has been established solely through the initiative of an external party. It is often a case of interaction between an individual researcher, or group of researchers, who have an idea for research work and a common interest with an external party.

Neither have NUTEK's competence centres, which are co-financed by NUTEK, the universities, and trade and industry, been given their own organisations with premises and employees. NUTEK's purpose has been to create a 'long-term (five to ten year) concentration of resources with a sufficient critical content'. The intention has been to create an organisational location and identity in these centres, with their own name on the door, so that companies can easily find their way in the research environment. However, following negotiations with the universities, these competence centres have, rather, been given the form of special centres in the university. One requirement on the part of NUTEK has been that the centres shall have a director and shall be an independent accounting unit. There shall also be a board of directors for each centre with representatives of trade and industry. But the study shows that the active researchers are employed by the university departments.

The analysis indicates that there is some tension between the ambitions of the external funders and the strategy of the faculty or university to create the right environment for education and long-term research. The principle behind the university's policy is that there shall be a very close connection between education and research. According to university leaders this connection can be weakened if research is transferred to units outside the basic units which are responsible for basic education programmes at the universities. There is a danger that the direct link to teaching and learning will be lost. Let us take a few examples from the Faculty of Social Sciences at the University of Stockholm.

The Institute for International Economics, which came into existence in 1962 on the initiative of Professor Gunnar Myrdal and which, during recent years, has been led by Professor Assar Lindbeck, is an internationally recognised research institute. However, the Department of Economics at the University of Stockholm tends to be overshadowed by this successful institute. It can therefore be difficult for the Department to attract the best researchers for research and education. This problem has been solved by the Department entering into agreements with researchers at the Institute so that they fulfil a teaching obligation at the Department. In this way the link between research and teaching is maintained. Other departments have also engaged researchers from institutes in a similar way for teaching basic courses.

Another problem which can arise through the establishment of institutes for specific research purposes is that the parent discipline can be depleted of research problems. At the University of Stockholm there is, for example, a Centre for Immigration Research, established by a decision of the government, and a centre for research into the public sector (SCORE) (decided on by the government after negotiations with the faculty). This means that immigration research and analyses of the problems of the public sector have 'left' their basic units. The departments can therefore be said to have been depleted, as far as the content of research is concerned.

This must be weighed against the fact that research work can develop positively in its own environment. But there is also a danger in establishing research fields which are too narrowly defined. In the long term the research environment itself can be depleted since the environment can become far too uniform. The lack of regular contact with students at basic level, as well as with research students, can also mean that in the long term the research environment will become diluted.

The practical strategy, which clearly emerged during the interviews, is that all people who are active in a university should have their base, their work and their identity in a subject-based department. This applies to both teachers and doctoral students. The foundation of the universities, and therefore their stability, is the subject-based departments. From this foundation, networks and special centres can be extended or closed as questions and fields of research change. Traditional research (basic research) and the search for knowledge takes place in the departments according to Mode 1 without regard to the direct productive usefulness of the knowledge. In the centres, researchers, doctoral students and practitioners meet to solve jointly formulated problems. In this process, which is similar to Mode 2, new knowledge is generated by problem solving. This knowledge can then be brought back to the departments. This takes place partly via researchers who take up and discuss the new knowledge in their teaching, and partly by doctoral students who apply and develop the new knowledge in their doctoral theses and teaching.

There are also organisational (accounting) reasons for this strategy. Administrative difficulties would arise if a person was to draw salary and take vacation from different organisational units at the same university. It is also complicated to account for doctoral students on different accounts. And not least the present 'payment by results' system in which the university receives a payment for every successful doctoral thesis tends to favour a permanent attachment of the students to one basic unit. If doctoral students are organisationally attached to a multidisciplinary unit which has research programmes of its own, the delicate task arises of allocating the performance of the students between this unit and the examining department.

This strategy means that the universities work against solutions which would result in the establishment of permanent units (institutes) with their own personnel and employees alongside the departmental structure. These types of units lead to the adoption of certain solutions which can obstruct future development and flexibility. When the research problems which were the underlying reason for the establishment of a special institute eventually become obsolete, inertia will set in and obstacles to change will arise. The dismissal of staff and the closing of premises usually has a draining effect on the resources and energy of an organisation. If all the staff have their base in a department they can return to their posts there or go to a new special centre to deal with new problems. In this way the subject-based departments represent stability in research work while the special centres create the flexibility which is necessary both for new ways of seeking knowledge and for spreading the new knowledge to new users and to society in general.

Another factor is the long-term development of knowledge. This chiefly takes place in subject-discipline research without the intention that the new knowledge shall have direct practical relevance. It is perhaps only in a perspective of 10 to 20 years, or even longer, that this knowledge may prove to have a more direct practical application. In the interviews, it has emerged that university management and representatives of the faculties feel a certain apprehension about pursuing the long-term development of knowledge. If this is to be possible, a balance in the amounts of faculty funds and external funding is necessary. The universities express the fear that faculty funds will decrease in proportion to external financing. This would diminish the capability of the universities and the faculties to run activities themselves.

Will the new external funding arena mean more or less autonomy for Swedish institutions?

There is a positive attitude among both vice-chancellors and deans to the new opportunities which the research foundations and external financiers can provide. Today the development of knowledge is complicated and complex. Researchers from several subject areas must cooperate in order to gain new knowledge. The new type of research financing makes such cooperation possible. This is particularly conspicuous in the technical, science subjects and medical faculties. In the same way there is a positive attitude towards the research schools initiated by the Foundation for Strategic Research. These are seen as additional facilities which create better conditions for doctoral students.

A certain change in attitude towards the financing of research of Mode 2 type can be seen among university leaders. Developments have meant that university leaders are now in a position in which they can negotiate more directly with external funders. This is different from the research council funds which is a matter between the individual researcher and the council. NUTEK, for example, wants to sign contracts with university management. The same demands can be made in respect of EU's research funds. The universities originally had a somewhat sceptical attitude towards negotiating on funding and on the organisation of research. Now the universities have a more proactive attitude where this role is concerned. There is a positive attitude towards linking research to external contacts who can contribute resources and contribute to the formulation of problems. However, this is mixed with concern over future conditions in respect of basic education and the long-term development of knowledge. This concern can be described with Georg Henrik von Wright's words on the dominance of the technosystem over social development (von Wright 1993). By technosystem Wright means an alliance between science, technology, and trade and industry. The technosystem threatens the independent search for knowledge for the sake of knowledge. In the technosystem research and academic education tend to concentrate to an ever-increasing degree on the objectives of growth, competitiveness and technical innovations.

The study detected some tension between the vice-chancellors and the deans. This tension should not be exaggerated. But in some cases the vice-chancellors seemed more eager to develop the institution by gaining funds according to Mode 2 than the deans, as leaders of the faculty boards. The deans were more devoted to research funded according to Mode 1. The vice-chancellors interest in research work according to Mode 2 can be explained by the so-called third task of the Swedish universities. By law they have an obligation to spread knowledge about their work, new knowledge and experience and how this can be applied. If research projects are conducted in cooperation with parties (industry, companies) outside the institution, this task will be fulfilled.

From another perspective the new setting of research funding at the national level may suggest that university leadership has become a more strategic task. The vice-chancellors will take on the role of chief executives rather than the *primus inter pares* of the scholarly community (see Becher and Kogan 1992, p.64). The new situation implies that they have to use more tools and new tools in order to exert control over external as well as internal demands on the institution. They are no longer solely dependent on resources from the central authority. They have obtained more freedom to negotiate different solutions with external funders in order to attract more resources to their institutions. The work of the vice-chancellor will thereby increase in importance. But there will probably be greater demands for accountability. The crucial question is whether the institutions will manage to maintain their academic value system and autonomy under the new circumstances.

A central implication of the study is the imbalance which has occurred between internal university resources for research and the powerful new funds for Mode 2 research. This imbalance may, from one perspective, jeopardise the possibilities of the universities to appear as autonomous organisations. Their own driving force may be undermined since faculty budgets are constantly decreasing in size compared to external funds. The universities are in danger of becoming reactive organisations instead of autonomous organisations governed by norms which they establish themselves.

The critical question is the balance between internal resources, such as governmental grants and grants from research councils, and external financing from the private funds and EU. Technology and medicine are areas which are now balancing on the borderline, with just over 50 per cent of their research funds coming from external financing. This implies that the grants from the government will be tied up in basic equipment and the universities will be more dependent on external resources when choosing topics for their research. The autonomy of the institutions will then be at risk.

A future strategy on the part of the universities to protect their basic work tasks (i.e. basic education and research, which is their unique function in the society) may be to make demands which mean that external funders have to pay for basic education and the long-term development of knowledge. These should be seen as overhead costs in contracts with external funders. In this way it would be possible for the universities to protect the departments, the long-term perspective and stability in operations at the same time as they are flexible and can participate in different forms of cooperation. Another assessment made by university management is that in the future it will be necessary to make more strategic considerations in the running of operations. Otherwise there is a danger that the universities will become organisations which merely react to external signals. It is therefore important to develop and maintain the autonomy of universities in order to be able to choose the emphasis of operations in the future.

The central authority, particularly the government, seems to have less control over the research agenda due to lack of resources. The governmental fund for research has decreased, not in size, but in importance as a tool to design the research agenda due to the introduction of private funds in 1994. These funds have substantial resources at their disposal to invest in research projects within their fields of interest. The universities are still totally dependent on the grants from the government for their basic research activities. But these grants are more or less tied up in fixed costs such as salaries, equipment and so on. Therefore it has been harder for the government to promote special research areas without increasing the total costs of research. Instead, the government strategy seems to be to re-allocate resources from research areas supported by the new external financiers to other areas of less interest for the private funds, such as humanities and social science (see SOU 1996:29). It is from this perspective that the action taken by the government in the autumn 1996 should be seen. By transforming the private funds back to public funds the government will take a firmer control of the funds. The strategy seems to be a reallocation of resources from Mode 2 to Mode 1.

However, increased significance of leadership is not the same as increased autonomy for institutions. There are more actors taking part in the game on the Swedish research arena today than before. Obviously this gives more opportunities for institutions to find a funder. But the number of financiers involved in the game is of less importance in the discussion of institutional autonomy. If there are many funders with the same set of criteria, the action taken by institutions will be of limited value. It seems more important to have a group of funders who will use different sets of criteria. That will give more freedom to institutions to chose different partners and thereby maintain autonomy. A balance between Mode 1 and Mode 2 among funders seems to create the best environment for institutions striving for autonomy. We should remember that Mode 1 is a necessary prerequisite of Mode 2.

Strategic management between Mode 1 and Mode 2

The interviews with the management of the universities indicate that there are three strategic approaches. The universities seek to create an organisation which meets the requirements of stability, flexibility and autonomy. These three strategic requirements are of importance to the universities since they make it possible for the universities to perform their duty to society, namely:

- to run educational programmes which are based on a scientific foundation and on well-tried and tested experience

- to run research programmes

- to spread knowledge about their work, new knowledge and experience and how this can be applied.

Stability is needed for the long-term, unbiased development of knowledge. The subject-based departments are the foundation on which this work rests. It is within the departments that the development of knowledge relating to the particular subjects in question and the intradisciplinary quality control take place. As organisational units the subject-based departments are responsible for basic educational programmes, research and postgraduate studies. They create, thereby, the conditions necessary to provide educational programmes which have a scientific base.

Universities try to attain flexibility in their activities by creating loosely linked networks or by establishing special centres in universities, between universities, or between universities and trade and industry. As a rule these are multidisciplinary and work to solve problems that have been jointly formulated. The special centres consist of researchers and doctoral students and, in certain cases, include the participation of companies and trade and industry.

The autonomy of universities and colleges is founded on the intradisciplinary criteria and the unbiased search for knowledge that form the basis of decisions on the emphasis of educational programmes and research. The interviews show that university management seeks to protect the autonomy of the scientific environment. This is done in the first place by safeguarding the conditions under which the universities can perform research according to Mode 1, for example by increasing the budget of faculties which have received external funds from research councils since these have undergone an intradisciplinary examination. At the same time the universities are positive to the idea of creating and developing forms of work according to Mode 2.

References

Becher, T. and Kogan, M. (1992) *Process and Structure in Higher Education.* London: Routledge.

Gibbons, M., Limoges, C., Nowotny, H., Schwartzman, S., Scott, P. and Trow, M. (1994) *The New Production of Knowledge. The Dynamics of Science and Research in Contemporary Societies.* London: Sage.

Popper, K. (1989) *Conjectures and Refutations: The Growth of Scientific Knowledge*. London: Routledge.

SOU 1996:29. *Forskning och Pengar (Research and Money)*. Stockholm: Utbildningsdepartementet, bilaga 5.

von Wright, G.H. (1993) *Myten om framsteget: Tankar 1987–1992 med en intellektuell självbiografi. (The Myth of Progress: Thoughts 1987–1992 with an intellectual autobiography)*. Stockholm: Bonniers.

CHAPTER 12

Evaluation of Higher Education in Europe[1]

John Brennan

Introduction

In most European countries over the last few years, we have seen the introduction of national systems and procedures to evaluate, control, and improve the quality of higher education. The longest established system is in France – dating from 1984 – and Britain, the Netherlands and the Scandinavian countries have all had national quality systems in place for several years. The Mediterranean countries are in the process of establishing quality systems. Also, in the former communist countries of central and eastern Europe, national systems for the assessment and assurance of quality in higher education have been, or are in the process of being, established. Indeed, only Germany is standing apart from these developments but, even there, some of the individual *Länder* are taking initiatives on quality in higher education.

So evaluation can fairly be judged to be a Europe-wide phenomenon. It is one which is obligatory: all publicly-funded higher education institutions and most academic staff must participate. It is controversial and it is changing academic and institutional life.

This chapter will describe briefly what is happening in Europe, consider why it is controversial, and discuss the impact of evaluation upon European higher education.

---

1   This chapter is based on a paper given at an international seminar on the Evaluation of Higher Education, held in Uberlândia, Brazil, 22/24 October 1997. It also draws on the Introduction to Brennan, deVries and Williams (1997).

A 'general model' of quality assessment[2]

Discussion of quality in European higher education has created its own specialised (and confusing) terminologies. I will refer to issues of language regarding quality later. For the moment I am using the term 'quality assessment' in a very general way to describe systems and processes designed both to assess quality and to assure its maintenance and, if possible, its improvement.

In 1993, the European Commission sponsored two Dutch researchers, Frans van Vught and Don Westerheijden, to undertake a review of national quality assurance systems for higher education in the countries of the European Union. This review summarised recent national developments as representing a 'general model' of national quality assurance (van Vught and Westerheijden 1993). The elements of the model were as follows:

- a national coordinating body

- institutional self evaluation

- external evaluation by academic peers

- published reports.

Usually such arrangements involve the creation of some kind of national agency to oversee and to coordinate the assessment process. The assessment process is generally in two stages: the first a process of self assessment carried out within the institution; the second a process of external peer assessment involving the visit to an institution by a group of academic peers drawn from other institutions. During the visit stage, the visiting academics engage in discussion with the home institution's academic staff, with students and perhaps with employers; they review documentation about academic programmes and management; and all of this results in some form of published report.

---

2   Quality assessment is used here and throughout this chapter as a generic
     term for processes of evaluation in higher education.

This so-called 'general model' of quality assessment obscures as much as it reveals about what is going on in these processes. Nevertheless, the essential and common elements of the model are not unimportant and they are worth emphasising. It is an approach which places its emphasis upon *educational process* rather than inputs and outputs. Certainly in Western Europe, it is an approach which is largely *qualitative* rather than quantitative. The use of performance indicators appears to be quite limited. It is an approach which involves a strong element of *academic self-regulation*: the self assessment stage within the institution, the external peer assessment outside the institution, but within the academic community as a whole.

Recent developments are virtually all in accord with the main elements of the model although there are also significant differences between countries in how their systems work.

Variations in context, method and purpose

The first source of important differences lies in the *context* of external quality assessment: how and why the current arrangements were set up, what they were replacing. Central to contextual issues are relations between higher education and the state, how these have been regulated traditionally, the kinds of changes which are taking place in these relationships. These are questions primarily of power, of how power is exercised and by whom. This can be considered in terms of levels: the relative power of the individual professor through to the powers of national government via the powers of departments, faculties, institutions, intermediary agencies, regional governments. But the question of how power is exercised can also be considered in terms of what, drawing on the work of Martin Trow, is the relationship between accountability, trust and the market in regulating higher education. Trow suggests that it is the absence of trust and markets which creates the emphasis upon accountability and the creation of forms of quality assessment which, whatever their formal purposes, appear to those on the receiving end of them as processes of control and interference. Thus, apparently quite similar methods of quality assessment can be experienced quite differently according to *contextual* features of how power is exercised and the relative importance attached to accountability, markets and trust (Trow 1994).

The second source of important differences between national quality assessment systems is also related to power. It is the question of *who* undertakes quality assessment. Where a national agency for quality exists, who owns it, who controls it, how is it funded, what are its powers? The two most common forms of ownership are the state and a country's higher education institutions collectively. But there are complex intermediate positions, the aim of which is frequently to create an appearance of independence in the work of the agency. Questions of ownership are frequently connected to questions of scope: teaching and/or research, institutional or subject level. Ownership of quality assessment is a strong determinant of the uses of quality assessment. These affect scope but they also affect methods.

Self assessment and external peer assessment are the common elements of method but important differences exist regarding each. Self assessments can vary considerably in scope and focus, but perhaps the more important distinction concerns whether the self assessment is seen as primarily a descriptive and administrative process or as an academic and evaluative process. A related point is whether the self assessment is written primarily for 'self', that is, the department or subject group undertaking the assessment, or whether it is written primarily for others, that is, a visiting committee from a national agency. The external peer assessment visits themselves vary considerably: in duration – anything from a single day to three/four days; in composition of the peer group – subject specialists or non-specialists, senior academics or 'all ranks'; in focus – subject, pedagogic or procedural issues; in methods – dialogue, inspection, observation. These variations in the practice of quality assessment combine with variations in context to produce significant differences in 'experience' for those involved in quality assessment.

A further source of difference between national quality assessment systems is in the intended outcomes of the process. Some form of public report is common to most systems but reports vary in length, content, in whether they refer to a single institution or to a subject area across a range of institutions, and in whether they offer a summative evaluation in numerical or other form. As well as written outcomes, the results of quality assessment in some countries link to funding, or to accreditation decisions, or to regulatory or other decision making by the state.

Underlying these differences in context, ownership, methods and outcomes of quality assessment are the various purposes which are claimed for quality assessment. Some combination of the following seven purposes has been identified from the national quality assessment systems of OECD member countries (Brennan and Shah 1997):

- to ensure accountability for the use of public funds

- to improve the quality of higher education provision

- to stimulate competition within and between institutions

- to undertake a quality check on new (sometimes private) institutions

- to assign institutional status

- to support the transfer of authority between the state and institutions

- to make international comparisons.

While accountability and improvement are referred to in virtually all cases, the balance of emphasis differs and other purposes are stated in combinations unique to individual countries and circumstances. Purposes reflect national contexts but they also reflect differences in the balance of accountability, markets and trust in the relationships between higher education and the rest of society. And even within a single system, different interest groups tend to emphasise different purposes.

If the form which quality assessment takes varies, the reasons for its establishment are more universal. They reflect changes in the external environment for higher education which in most countries is marked by expansion, diversity and resource problems, and which are provoking changes within individual higher education institutions. These are changes in both substance and management. The links with quality assessment are multifaceted but they include:

- the inadequacy of exclusiveness as the primary quality control mechanism in expanded higher education systems

- the loss of consensus about purposes and standards in diverse higher education systems, leading to the replacement of informal, implicit approaches to quality by approaches which are formal and explicit

- the difficulty of state management of diverse and rapidly changing systems leading to the replacement of controls through regulation by controls through evaluation.

The introduction of quality assessment into the higher education systems of European countries has been controversial. Although there are local reasons and circumstances applicable to individual countries, more generally I think that we can detect three different sources of controversy about quality. They are controversies concerning language, power, and change.

A controversy about language

Part of the problem lies with the term itself. 'Quality' has become all-pervasive in modern society, almost a totem of postmodernism and mass culture. As a prefix, it attaches itself to everything: from automobiles to baked beans, from plumbing to lager. The adjectival use of the term evokes the marketplace, the advertising hoarding, the 'ad' in Yellow Pages. It is part of the none-too-subtle 'hard sell'. It is noticeable that its use has not, on the whole, been adopted by the more élite professions and social institutions: there appear to be relatively few 'quality' solicitors, priests and doctors. Thus, its adoption by higher education might suggest to some the invasion of the marketplace, and a particularly 'down market' invasion at that, bringing with it alien concepts and practices which take no account of higher education's special characteristics.

Much of the language of quality reflects contemporary management theory as developed in manufacturing and service industries. It is a language which can turn students into customers, academic staff into producers/providers, universities into businesses and their departments into profit centres. Of course, many of these trends have less to do with quality initiatives and much to do with cuts in funding, competitiveness and the need to secure new sources of income. But for many academics, quality initiatives are implicated in these broader trends which they see as threatening to undermine higher education's 'special' characteristics and status.

The language of quality has, of course, acquired its own experts, experts who know the difference between quality assurance and quality control, between quality improvement and quality enhancement, between assessment and audit, between evaluation and appraisal. But this is a language which exists outside of the specialist discourses of academic staff, socialised into and owing a primary loyalty to, specialist disciplines. To them, the language of quality can appear imperialistic, a spurious quasi-discipline with suspicious links to management.

Of course, higher education has its traditional language of quality reflecting notions of standards, of academic coherence and progression, of attainment and understanding. But the meaning of such terms is frequently implicit, perhaps even fuzzy, and not readily communicable to people outside of the discourse of the specialist discipline. The outsider might feel: never mind the coherence, are the customers happy?

Much of the language of quality appears to have been imported into higher education from elsewhere and, as such, emphasises and strengthens what have been termed higher education's extrinsic functions over its intrinsic functions, for example, servicing the economy over the creation and transmission of new knowledge. Some of the language of quality requires us to change the way we think about higher education: the controversy about language is about more than words.

A controversy about power

Systems of higher education in different countries vary in the extent to which things are decided by the state, by individual institutions, by faculties and departments, by individual academic staff (with considerable additional variation in the power of seniority and professional status), by students and by various external stakeholders. These different sources of power reflect respectively the state, the academic profession and markets. Notwithstanding a near universal emphasis on 'autonomy', in practice higher education institutions are subject to all sorts of controls – political, economic and cultural – from many different sources. In some higher education systems, the complex balance of power is such as seemingly to reinforce the status quo forever. In particular, the power of interest groups to block rather than to initiate change is an important source of either stability or inertia, depending on your point of view.

Quite a lot of the controversy about quality assessment in higher education has been about who should 'own' it. Where ownership reflects the existing balance of power (e.g. a state-sponsored agency in a system where the ministry has traditionally decided most things) controversy over ownership may be limited. But where ownership suggests a significant change in the balance of power (e.g. the introduction of a state-sponsored agency in a system where there have been relatively few mechanisms of state control) controversy over ownership is likely to be high. In some cases, it may be resolved by the creation of a symbolically 'independent' agency, balance secured through the composition of its governing body.

The controversy about power is reflected not only in questions of ownership; it also embraces questions of method. Thus, a preference for self evaluation is expressed by representatives of institutions while representatives of government emphasise a need for externality in the assessment process. These preferences may have less to do with the proven efficacy of any particular assessment method and have everything to do with the exercise of power.

The controversy about power can sometimes appear to be between only two interest groups: higher education institutions and the state. But a rather different kind of controversy exists at the institutional level: the controversy of so-called managerialism. From the perspective of the individual staff member, local controls and constraints can appear to be far more powerful than anything that exists at the system level. Thus, approaches to quality assessment which emphasise institution-level responsibility tend to be accompanied by the introduction of institution-wide procedures and policies which have the effect of shifting power away from the basic unit or department towards the institutional centre.

Power at the institutional level also impacts on attitudes to method. On the whole, an assessment method which focuses on the institutional level is likely to reinforce the power of institutional management. It does so by concentrating on matters which are largely management preserves: resources, policies, procedures. Conversely, an assessment method which focuses on the subject level will tend to reinforce the importance of subject values and academic work, thereby enhancing the power of the subject group.

Thus, much of the debate about quality assessment at both system and institutional levels is a debate about power. All parties to the debate are in favour of quality but each feels that it, better than the others, knows best how to achieve it (and what it is); and, at least in some systems and institutions, each mistrusts the motives and agendas of the others.

A controversy about change

Much of the mistrust reflects the scale of the changes occurring in higher education, changes which themselves have relatively little to do with quality assessment directly. The changes have involved expansion – new institutions, the growth of existing ones, larger class sizes; they have involved diversification – different kinds of students, different kinds of courses and new ways of teaching and assessing them; they have placed greater emphasis on higher education's extrinsic functions – to do with training people for jobs, greater relevance in research; and they have been accompanied by declining resource levels and greater accountability for the use of them. All of these changes are interconnected and, in the eyes of many academic staff, are linked to the most painful change of all: a decline in the status, remuneration and conditions of work associated with academic life.

Quality assessment is associated with these changes in a variety of ways. First, its introduction is a reflection of the greater costs, visibility and assumed social and economic importance of higher education. Governments want to know what they are getting for the resources invested in higher education. Relatedly, in some countries at least, governments have relaxed other forms of control which they have traditionally exercised over higher education. In large part, they have done so to encourage the process of change, freeing institutions to respond more rapidly and effectively to new demands. This movement towards greater autonomy of higher education institutions has brought with it requirements of greater accountability. The introduction of quality assessment has been an important part of this. (There are some notable exceptions to this trend: the introduction of quality assessment in the UK was part of a much larger process of greater centralisation and state control.)

Second, quality assessment has been associated with institutional issues raised as a result of expansion and diversity. Are institutions, and the staff within them, sufficiently equipped to deal with new kinds of students with new kinds of wants and needs? Developments such as credit systems, modularity, greater interdisciplinarity, and calls for teacher training for academics, are all responses to a perceived need to change in order to meet new kinds of demand. The process of quality assessment can contribute by questioning the appropriateness of existing practice to changing circumstances; it can provide a forum for the exchange of practice and experience across institutions; it can provide a reference point for change in a single institution by disseminating system-wide information and recommended good practice; in short, quality assessment can contribute towards the maintenance and improvement of quality in changing circumstances.

Third, quality assessment can contribute to institutional problem solving. Although a lot of the debate about quality has focused on the work of national agencies, this neglects the volume of internal assessment activity generated within higher education institutions quite independently of the requirements of external agencies. Institutions are having to review their activities and practices for all of the reasons cited above. They are faced with hard decisions and with a need for better information to inform them, and perhaps also to legitimise them. Thus, many institutions have undertaken evaluations or internal reviews of specific aspects of their work (sometimes concerning individual departments, sometimes concerning cross-institutional functions, and sometimes concerning organisation and management) in order to inform decision making and institutional change. Sometimes these reviews are instituted on a regular basis, more often they are ad hoc. They are perhaps rarely regarded as being about the assessment of quality as such, but the processes involved are hardly distinguishable from many of the processes of quality assessment.

Quality assessment is both a response to change and a mechanism for managing it at both institutional and system levels. Controversy can therefore arise from the substance of change (many current changes are unwelcome ones to large numbers of the academic profession) and from the question of steerage: whose hands are on the steering wheel?

Conflict of interests?

Quality, therefore, is controversial and recognising the controversy is perhaps a first step towards resolving it. The assessment of quality is called upon to perform different functions by different interest groups. Not all interests may be reconcilable. Choices may need to be made.

It is worth recording some of the main interest groups involved in these debates. First, there is government, within which politicians and civil servants may have different perspectives. Second, there are intermediary bodies, including quality agencies, which have their own professional staff, their own constituencies or sponsors, and their own coopted 'members' from other institutions; each will have its own interests and perspectives. Third, there are the higher education institutions within which senior managers, academics and administrators can be distinguished as representing distinctive interests and concerns. Fourth, there are interest groups within institutions which also have influential system-wide representation: staff developers are important in some countries in this respect.

There is every reason to expect these various groupings, representing different interests, values and experiences, to find things to disagree about. It is these disagreements which provide the basis for the debates about quality.

The impact of institutional evaluation

Quality and evaluation systems have been established for a sufficient length of time in several European countries for an assessment of their impact to be possible. My own centre has undertaken a project in England on the impact of quality assessment (Brennan, Frederiks and Shah 1997) and is currently completing a project for OECD on the impact of quality assessment and institutional evaluation in 15 OECD member countries (Brennan and Shah 1997). I shall draw upon these two studies in considering the impact which institutional evaluation may be having upon European higher education.

As part of the OECD project, nearly 40 higher education institutions have prepared case studies of the impact of evaluation on themselves. A common framework was provided for the case studies consisting of:

- the *contexts* for quality assessment e.g. national system features, government policies, external quality assessment requirements, institutional characteristics

- the *internal quality assessment methods* that are in place in institutions e.g. external examiners, student feedback, regular review and monitoring of courses

- how quality assessment (both internal and external) affects the *management and decision-making processes* e.g. relationship to planning and resources, curriculum development

- the *impacts* of external quality requirements upon the institution at structural, curriculum and governance levels

- the *interpretation* of outcomes from quality assessments and how the *future* of an institution's mission, policies, structure and culture are related to this.

Authors of the case studies were asked to address all of the above in the context of institutional and systems change. Where possible, institutions have undertaken *internal case studies* (within the overall institutional case study) *of recently evaluated departments or disciplines.*

An initial analysis of some of these case study reports suggests the following:

- quality assessment has raised the profile of teaching and learning in higher education institutions

- impact takes a very different form in each individual institution and the nature of this impact is related to the distribution of authority in the higher education system, i.e. what is typically decided at what level

- overall impact of quality assessment is greater where it achieves legitimacy at the basic unit (department/ faculty) level, i.e. individual staff members accept the conclusions and the processes on which they are based

- impact at the institutional level results in more centralisation of procedures and greater managerialism

- much quality assessment within individual institutions appears to be unrelated to external quality assessment requirements of national agencies

- quality assessment activities within institutions are being undertaken in order to meet institutionally-defined needs, generally to do with managing change and frequently in response to funding crises.

Within some institutions, quality assessment activities are becoming increasingly important management tools. In some countries, this may involve the strengthening of the powers of administrators and senior managers in relation to the powers of academic staff. But in other countries, the management tier within higher education institutions is too weakly developed to be able to wield any such tools effectively. This is where the direct impact of external quality assessment systems can become important.

We are now trying to analyse the case studies using a model which distinguishes three types of impact (namely rewards, structures and cultures), and four levels of impact (namely individual, programme/subject, institutional and national).

Rewards might be financial or reputational and be found at individual, programme or institutional levels. Of the countries we have looked at, quality assessment in Mexico is most closely linked to financial reward systems, particularly at the individual level. Reputational impact seems to depend quite largely on the nature of the public outcome of assessment with numerical scales, as favoured in the UK, having the most effect. For individuals and programmes, a further 'reward' from a good quality assessment might be greater influence and respect within their institution.

Structural impact might be on organisational or curriculum structure and on the roles and responsibilities associated with them. In this respect, and not surprisingly, the method of assessment matters a lot. Internal assessments probably have greater structural impact than external assessments, in that they are more likely to be about change than compliance. It is worth noting, however, that in some countries, for example Denmark, assessments can have a potential structural impact at national level by feeding into decision making concerning the scale and distribution of subject provision across the entire higher education system. Assessment systems linked to accreditation, as is becoming popular in central and eastern Europe, are associated with structural impact at national levels.

Cultural impact can occur at individual, programme and institutional levels. The conditions under which it is most likely to occur vary according to both context and method. But, perhaps rather obviously, it is likely to be greater when quality assessment embodies norms and values that are different from prevailing ones within the institution or department. We see this clearly in the English case of quality assessment where a method of subject assessment which emphasises teaching skills confronts prevailing cultures which emphasise research (notably in 'old' universities) or which emphasise curriculum content in disciplinary terms. Other forms of subject-based assessment, for example the Dutch system, seem to contain fewer tensions between the assessment values and subject values and so have less capacity to change culture and are more likely to find acceptance with academics.

We shall, in the remaining stages of our project for OECD, attempt to relate empirically different types and levels of impact to differences in assessment method and context.

Conclusions

I will conclude by returning to the controversies which have surrounded evaluation and quality assessment in higher education. Part of the reasons for them can be found in the *values* of evaluation and whether these are in line with or seek to threaten existing academic values.

We have distinguished four basic types of quality systems in terms of the values of assessment: of course, actual systems are unlikely to accord completely with only one type. But we believe that the emphasis of a quality assessment system is likely to reflect one of the types.

The four types are as follows:

1. *Academic*

- subject focus
- professorial control
- disciplinary values, vary across institution
- institution as 'holding company'.

2. *Managerial*

- institutional focus, procedural
- quality produced by 'good management'
- quality characteristics invariant across institution.

3. *Pedagogic*

- focus on teaching skills, classroom practice
- strong link to training and staff development
- quality characteristics invariant across institution.

4. *Employment/professional*

- focus on graduate output characteristics
- takes account of 'customer' requirements
- both 'core' and 'subject specific' characteristics.

In the case of England, traditional type one values of academics were challenged by external systems which placed a dominant emphasis on types two and three. (Changes currently proposed to the system of quality assessment in England appear to reflect type four values.)

In other systems, for example the Dutch, quality assessment appears to have largely shared the type one values of the academics, has been more closely controlled by the academic community and does not appear to have had quite the same traumatic consequences for those on the receiving end.

In European higher education, national systems of evaluation and quality assessment are tied up with pressures upon institutions and academic staff to change. In the steady-state institution or higher education system, evaluation will be neither required nor effectual. But in most European countries, change is being required of higher education: to meet the needs of more and different kinds of students, to contribute to economic prosperity, and to do so with often substantially reduced funding levels. We find examples of evaluation being used by the academic community as a defence mechanism to prevent unwanted change. We also find examples of it being used by governments and institutions to drive forward change. Evaluation and quality assessment are as much about power as they are about quality. Thus, who owns and who controls the evaluation process matters quite a lot for the future of higher education.

References

Brennan, J., Frederiks, M. and Shah, T. (1997) *Improving the quality of Education: The Impact of Quality Assessment on Institutions.* Bristol: Higher Education Funding Council for England/Quality Support Centre.

Brennan, J. and Shah, T. (1997) 'Quality Assessment, Decision-Making and Institutional Change.' *EAIR Journal, Tertiary Education and Management* (TEAM), 3, 2.

Trow, M. (1994) *Academic Reviews and the Culture of Excellence.* Stockholm: Universitetskanslern.

van Vught, F. and Westerheijden, D. (1993) *Quality Management and Quality Assurance in European Higher Education.* Enschede: CHEPS.

CHAPTER 13

Academic Responses to Quality Reforms in Higher Education
England and Sweden Compared[1]

Marianne Bauer and Mary Henkel

In his depiction of the rise of quality assurance in higher education, Brennan draws our attention to one particular mark of its importance: 'it provides a link between higher education's "inner world" and the wider social, economic and political forces that shape its institutional forms and structures.' (Brennan 1997) This chapter seeks to bring into focus changes and continuities in that inner world in the face of quality assurance policies in two countries, England and Sweden. It explores how academics have responded to these policies and their implications for professional roles and professional values. It thus brings the examination of state-higher education relationships into the centre of academic working lives. To do so, it draws on data from a collaborative international research programme on higher education reforms, conducted from 1994 to 1997 by an English, a Swedish and a Norwegian research team.[2]

Policies to strengthen accountability and quality assurance have played a key role in the process of transforming higher education in both England and Sweden, although there are significant differences

1   An earlier version of this chapter was published in *Tertiary Education and Management 3* (1997), 3, 211–228.
2   The Swedish and English components of the research programme were sponsored by the Swedish Council for Studies in Higher Education and by the Swedish Government's Committee on Follow-up of the 1993 Higher Education Reform (RUT-93). Supplementary support was derived from the Spenser Foundation, USA and from the Leverhulme Trust, UK. The research teams were based in Brunel University, England; the University of Gothenburg, Sweden; and the University of Bergen, Norway.

between them. The most conspicuous of these was the drive by the Conservative government in Sweden to devolve power to the higher education institutions, while English universities were subjected to more centralised control.

These policies constitute the frame within which the central question of the chapter is addressed: how far academic values and conceptions of the academic profession have been changing in the face of higher education reforms in the two countries and how far they are resisting, and thereby affecting the outcome of those reforms.

More specifically, we compare and contrast the two countries on three subsidiary questions:

- Have the reforms generated new responsibilities and new patterns of authority for academics in their institutions?

- What are the implications in each case for some traditional academic values and assumptions about what it means to be a member of the academic profession?

- How far are academic conceptions of quality changing in response to the reforms and in which respects are they resistant to change?

The analysis will be developed within a conceptual framework that embodies these traditional values and assumptions, and what appear to be key challenges to them, in changing approaches to the governance and administration of academic institutions, and in new thinking about quality and its systemic implications.

Conceptual framework
The discipline, the institution and the academic profession

Our starting points are the models of higher education regulation and governance that have dominated the literature and the academic values, and self perceptions derived from them. They depict academics as living in worlds of their own making, where the dominant influence on their organisation and on the formation of their values and assumptions is the nature of knowledge or the cognitive practices developed for the production of knowledge. Such analyses typically either ignore the political and economic conditions which make possible the power and independence depicted, or assume a stable exchange relationship in which society cedes power to the academics in the belief that in this way it will receive, in return, the forms of knowledge and advanced education which will be of most value to itself. Individual independence, collective self regulation, and collegial forms of governance are perceived to be the essential and mutually reinforcing conditions for the central tasks of academic organisations: the production, testing and transmission of knowledge.

Clark's classic formulation of academic systems as essentially matrix structures, the prime components of which are disciplines and the enterprise (or academic institution), is based on these assumptions, as is his further contention that within these structures the disciplines are the dominant force (Clark 1983).

But as other contributors to this book have argued, it cannot be assumed that the relationship between the disciplines and the institution will remain stable. The central role of the single discipline in individual academic practices, in the organisation and development of knowledge (Gibbons *et al.* 1994; Scott 1997) in the delivery of the curriculum (Boys *et al.* 1988; de Weert 1990; Jones and Little Chapter 7) and in the governance of institutions is under challenge (Scott 1995). Equally, changing relations with the state, a changing resource environment, the promotion of market principles, growth in student numbers and growing mission complexity put pressure on the existing equilibrium. They make institutional cohesion both more salient and more difficult to achieve.

The continued strength of the discipline-institution matrix and the principles of governance underpinning it are, therefore, on the agenda and, with them, questions about the consequences for academic values, professional roles and responsibilities.

Conceptions of quality

The word quality has traditionally had little place in the language used by academics. However, the demands on higher education institutions for accountability and quality assurance and the changing contexts in which these are occurring, have generated a substantial discourse on concepts of quality and the systemic implications that follow.

Our analysis of processes or systems for quality assurance will draw on the threefold categorisation used by Rolf, Ekstedt and Barnett (1993):

- *market systems* in which results are dependent on transactions where supply and demands meet

- *administrative systems*, which are given the resources and authority to steer others by rules or goals

- *professional systems*, in which the same category of actors (in this case academics) combine the functions of producing work and supervising the quality of one another's work.

These three types of system may be seen as complementary in the differences of emphasis placed by each on input, process and outcome factors. They also vary as to whether their major focus is on individuals, systems and knowledge respectively.

In both countries, market systems and, even more, administrative systems for quality assurance have been strengthened by the policies introduced during the past decade. Changes in the professional system for quality assurance and development are more difficult to detect, partly because this system has been implicit in the academic culture (Frackmann 1992), but also because the academic profession is fragmented between at least two different roles: the disciplinary expert and the teacher. The degree of professionality in the two roles, and in particular the extent to which control of quality criteria has been achieved, may differ both within and between institutions and subjects.

Data, processes and methods

The data on which this paper draws are derived from documents and from semi-structured interviews. They include government reform documents, material from central agencies responsible for quality audit and quality assessment, and accounts from the higher education institutions in the study of their systems for quality assurance and development.

Semi-structured interviews were conducted during 1995 in six English, and four Swedish, universities, together with two other higher education institutions in Sweden. The 105 English, and the 85

Swedish, interviews cover institutional leaders, deans and heads of departments, administrators and academics from six disciplines (biochemistry, economics, history, modern languages or English, physics and sociology).[3] The study thus concentrates on the more theoretical fields of knowledge and excludes, for example, faculties of Law, Medicine and Technology.

In England inquiry focused on three main developments, the funding councils' research assessment exercises (RAE), the Higher Education Quality Council's (HEQC) academic audit, and the Higher Education Funding Council for England's (HEFCE) teaching quality assessments (TQA). In Sweden, the interviews focused on academic values, concepts of quality and measures for quality of undergraduate education and the request for public quality assurance in the higher education reform of 1993. The empirical research was completed before the replacement in 1997 of HEQC and HEFCE quality assessment division by the new Quality Assurance Agency in England.

The national contexts of reform: an overview

The English and Swedish systems for higher education originated from different basic models and have developed within different traditions. The broad patterns of legitimate power at government, institution, and faculty levels within higher education systems in Britain and Continental Europe in the mid-twentieth century have been characterised by Clark and Youn (1976). In the Continental system there are two almost equally strong centres of power, namely the government and the faculties, but little university-level control or authority. In the British system, power has been concentrated in the basic units, while central control, both by government and by university leadership, has been weak, although the polytechnics had more centralised structures. During the second half of the century there have been tendencies in both kinds of models towards increasing the authority of the institutional level (Kells 1992).

---

3   A seventh, chemistry, was included in the English study in order to take one
science that had been subject to the HEFCE assessment of the quality of
education.

The most conspicuous difference between the present reform movements in the two countries, devolution of power to the universities in Sweden and increased central control in England, must be looked at from the perspective of these earlier power structures. Although the movements seem to be in opposite directions, the goals may be identical: increased institutional independence and effectiveness; more openness to society and interaction with external interest groups; and raising quantity and quality.

The difference in the size of the respective systems is also important. The Swedish system comprising six universities, three university institutes and 36 university colleges, of which some are very small, may appear easy to survey compared to the 70 English universities, especially from the point of view of the national agencies that have to supervise their quality or quality measures.

There are differences in the status of quality in the reforms in the two countries. Quality was installed as the central theme of the 1993 'Freedom for Quality' reform in Sweden, even though it had been subject for concern earlier, contributing to incremental changes towards increased self regulation. In England, quality was one of a number of reforms, the dominant one of which was probably massification. On the other hand, the quality assessment and audit policies have been in place substantially longer, and the tangible consequences of the assessments have been much more significant in England than in Sweden. It is important to take this into account when comparing the responses and reactions to them by English and Swedish academics respectively.

There was an essential difference in the governments' approaches to quality control in the two countries, which has been described by Bauer and Kogan (1997) and incisively analysed by Trow (1993a,b). In Britain, the government has taken a firm grip on assessment and control of quality in both research and education. Quality assurance has been centred on external assessments and their power to affect internal systems. In Sweden, the government strategy has been to emphasise the responsibility of the higher education institutions themselves for quality assurance and development, and to challenge them by requesting them to construct their own systems and demonstrate their functionality at the triennial audits of the Higher Education Agency (although at this point there was some convergence with the work of the British HEQC).

Thus, while the British government established central systems for carrying through quality control, the Swedish government stimulated a pluralistic approach, in that each institution was to build up from within the model and procedures for quality care that suited them best. This difference was observed in an early comparison between Britain and Sweden with the following hypothesis: 'there is perhaps a difference in the purpose of evaluation here between the contrary tendencies applying respectively in Sweden and Britain: decentralization for better learning, centralization for better control?' (Bauer 1988).

The most salient features of the reforms in the two countries are set out in more detail in the following section.

Quality reforms in higher education in England and Sweden

England

Until well into the 1970s, institutions on the two sides of the binary line had markedly different forms of governance and relationships with the state. The universities' autonomy was largely unchallenged. By contrast, the polytechnics and colleges of higher education, established to meet the growing demands for higher levels of technical and vocational education, depended on regulation by the Council of National Academic Awards (CNAA) and on local authority governance. However, CNAA was becoming increasingly liberal by the 1980s (Kogan 1996) and the Conservative government was in sympathy with the desire of polytechnics and colleges to be free of local government control.

But a main concern of government was to harness higher education to national needs. By 1987, their determination to forge higher education institutions into a massively enlarged national system, whose primary function was to be an instrument of the national economy, was becoming plain (Department of Education and Science (DES) 1987). In 1992, the binary structure was abandoned in favour of a unitary system that would, however, accommodate a diversity of students and institutional missions.

The tradition of university self regulation of standards in research and educational provision was transformed during the 1980s and 1990s, first through the institution by the UGC in 1985 of the first research assessment exercise. Quadrennial research assessment is now the basis of an increasingly selective policy of research resource allocation by the funding councils. Second came the development of performance indicators. Third, in 1990 a collective system of quality audit was established by the Committee of Vice-Chancellors and Principals (CVCP). More radically, in 1992 the new national funding councils were mandated systematically to assess the quality of education being provided by the institutions.

The Academic Audit Unit set up by the CVCP had been an unsuccessful attempt to pre-empt the imposition by government of an external system of quality control. The key task of the unit was to conduct audits of universities' own arrangements for quality assurance. At the ending of the binary line in 1992, it was incorporated into the HEQC, again under the aegis of the CVCP, and its remit extended to the new, as well as the old, universities. Audit methods combined documentary analysis and institutional visits. Auditors were drawn from the institutions themselves, by nomination.

Meanwhile, in response to government concern to introduce external assessment of the quality of higher education, the funding councils embarked in 1993 on subject focused assessments of teaching in all the universities. Assessment was based on self assessment, documentary analysis and institutional visits. It was carried out predominantly by subject peers. Following a revision of its methods by HEFCE in 1995, subject providers were scored against a six-dimensional profile.

Of the three policies that form the subject of this paper only the RAE carried significant resource implications, although teaching quality assessments (TQAs) were also intended to do so in the longer term. All were regarded in the universities as external assessments, despite the formal ownership of HEQC by the institutions. RAE quality criteria were predominantly those of discipline-based excellence, while TQA and quality audit defined quality in terms of 'fitness for purpose'.

A major function of the assessment systems, particularly the RAE, was to sustain stratification and selective state resource allocation between universities (Kogan 1996). But they were also important for government's aims to reduce the universities' dependence on state funding and to instill market mechanisms into higher education. Universities were under increasing pressure to generate wealth, to compete with one another for alternative sources of funding and so, in some senses, to become more autonomous.

Institutions' performance in the various forms of quality assessment was now crucial to them in this new world of markets. Competition was stimulated by media publication of institutional performance, particularly in RAEs and TQAs, in the form of league tables. Assessments in some ways conformed to an information deficiency model of quality regulation (Dill 1995, 1996), although the purpose of informing the public was explicitly built into only teaching quality assessments (HEFCE 1993). Customers, for research as well as for education, could make more informed choices as a result of these exercises.

Both academic audit and teaching quality assessments emphasised the importance of systems, codification, and internal and external scrutiny and so strengthened the administrative approach to quality. At the same time, academic audit drew attention to the balance to be sustained between central control and devolution of responsibility and between generic and specialist criteria and systems (HEQC 1994). For its part, the revised teaching quality assessment framework tilted towards holistic criteria of quality as distinct from those of individualistic professionalism.

Sweden

The development of today's Swedish higher education system can be characterised by three phases: the build-up phase (1950–77), the phase of consolidation (1977–92) and the phase of transformation and renewal (1992–?) (Bauer and Franke-Wikberg 1993).

The dynamic build-up phase involved the funding of new universities and colleges and strong expansion of university research. Student numbers in higher education multiplied ten times within a period of 20 years. The rapid growth of interest in higher education was prompting a reorganisation. In order to manage the quickly multiplying teaching task, a new position of university lecturer was introduced with a total teaching duty and no opportunity for research. And in the so called UKAS-reform at the end of the 1960s, a number of study lines within the philosophical faculty were designed in order to secure a more effective throughput of students with degrees relevant for the job market. The reforms during this period implied major attempts to provide uniform solutions by central means to the current problems caused by the expansion.

The U-68 Committee's work – in the spirit of rational planning and central management – leading up to the higher education reform of 1977, resulted in the design of an integrated and uniform system of higher education. The urge to reduce differences in status within postsecondary education was fundamental to the policy of a single comprehensive system of the six universities and the approximately 30 institutes and colleges. The system was internally differentiated, however, and still is, in that only the universities and the university institutes of medicine and technology have an established research organisation and postgraduate programmes. Furthermore, there are separate funding systems for undergraduate education and for research and research training.

Thus research and teaching in higher education became separated at both institutional and individual levels. This caused constant problems and a continuing discussion about their solution.

The key national goals of the 1977 reform were 'distributive fairness' and 'equivalent quality'. The means to reach these goals were a unitary institutional organisation, central access rules and admission system, further development of national study lines, and a detailed resource allocation system. In this rule-regulated system no further measures for quality assurance were considered necessary. This reform, however, was followed up through an evaluation programme, the results of which anticipated and portended changes contained in the reform to follow.

The strong confidence in higher education during the build-up phase was, however, gradually shaken in the 1980s. The whole public sector was subject to increasing critique, on the grounds of ineffectiveness and deficient quality. The failure of the existing centralised steering system seemed indisputable in a society characterised by a steadily growing complexity.

Decentralisation and the limiting of the central regulation were identified as the solutions to the problems. Decentralisation, however, had also been part of the previous reform. But Askling and Almén (1993) observed how the concept of decentralisation was changing. In the 1977 reform, the vertical transmission of authority was brought about through the introduction of intermediate bodies, that is, influence was distributed downwards to boards and committees but not directly to the professionals within the academy. Decentralisation thus included influence for, and devolved policy formulation authority to, new groups both inside and outside the system and was intended to play an essential part in its democratisation. Many academic teachers, on the contrary, perceived it largely as an increase in bureaucracy (Lane 1987).

In the 'phase of transformation and renewal' under the 1993 reform of the higher education system a more profound decentralisation was on its way. It implied radical reduction of central regulation, devolution of considerable responsibility and authority to the higher education institutions on matters of institutional organisation, allocation and disposal of resources, the offer and organisation of undergraduate courses and programmes, and appointment and employment of professors. Thereby differences in resources, competence and profile between higher education institutions were intended to increase and the system to become more diversified (Bauer 1996b).

This shift from a system of rule steering to a system of steering by goals and results also meant strong demands on institutional accountability.

A new performance-based resource allocation system for undergraduate education, introduced in connection with the reform, emphasises the institutions' responsibility for results. In this new system 40 per cent of the resources are based on the number of FTE students and 60 per cent on students' performance.

At first the resource allocation system was intended also to include a mechanism for quality assurance in that 5 per cent was to be dependent on national quality indicators. That idea had to be given up, however, as unrealistic and ineffective. Instead, each higher education institution was to develop and demonstrate its own system and procedures for quality assurance, and a national higher education agency was given responsibility for auditing local quality assurance systems. It was also to carry out national evaluations, without intruding upon the area of institutional responsibility.

The funding of research and postgraduate education for the universities and the university institutes was not changed in principle. It was allocated to the institutions for each faculty area. Further state funding for research was distributed through the research councils after application from individual researchers or research groups. Quality control by the research councils was effected through both *ex ante* peer judgements of proposals and *ex post* evaluations of various kinds, often implying judgment of research areas by international peer groups. The previous government also set up a number of strategic research foundations. This meant that the total amount of state funding for research was considerably raised, while at the same time the proportion of funding made directly to the universities, and the proportion of funding primarily aimed at basic research, were diminished. Universities must rely more and more on external funding of their research. Since this was linked to the actions of individual researchers or research groups it strengthened the departments as against the institutions (Askling, Almén and Karlsson 1995).

The shift towards strengthened institutional autonomy, however, has been partly reduced by the present social democratic government. It has diminished the scope for local admission rules and reinforced the national agency for higher education, although its responsibility for auditing the quality assurance systems of the institutions and for evaluation is the same as before the change of government.

Study findings in the two countries

Our comparative analysis of our findings examines the implications of policy changes for academic professional roles and for conceptions of quality in higher education.

Shifts in professional roles and responsibilities

Academics have traditionally carried a combination of teaching, research and administrative roles in their own institutions, at the same time as having a stronger basic identification with their individual specialised form of knowledge and its knowledge community. However, the professional role of disciplinary expert has come under increasing challenge from internal and external demands and forces.

Despite the apparent differences in the macro policies for higher education in the two countries, the role of the institution became more important in each of them. The responsibilities of the institution expanded and the managerial tasks became more complex. Universities were perceived to need both stronger central management and also devolution of responsibilities to faculties and departments, although the emphasis as between these differed between the two countries. There was in consequence more involvement of academics in management at all levels in the institution: the centre, the faculty and the department. These developments created more awareness of the interdependence between individuals, departments and institutions. Quality policies were strongly implicated in these developments.

Responsibility for quality was a key component of the strengthening of the institution in Sweden. Universities were requested to set up their own systems for quality assurance and enhancement. All four universities in our sample established central committees for quality matters, led by respected senior academics within the university. They, to a greater or lesser extent, transferred this responsibility to the faculties and departments, thus enabling them to form quality assurance procedures that suit their varying size, character and contacts with society. (For examples, see reports from the universities of Uppsala (Engwall 1995) and Göteborg (The Delegation of Quality Assurance, Göteborg University 1995).)

In England, the perceived need to develop more corporate strategies and structures for academic development in universities meant a strengthening of the centre, in the form of senior management teams, strategy groups for the development of research and teaching, and a proliferation of cross-institutional and non-disciplinary academic support units.

The mediation of quality policies was described by one institutional leader as one of the academic development functions of the centre. External audit prompted those institutions without internal audit structures to develop them. In three of our universities, the centre took an active role in the management of teaching quality assessments. Centrally based units had strong connections with, and roles in, quality policies (quality assurance, teaching and learning, staff development, research strategy). But research assessment, teaching quality assessment and external audit of quality assurance systems also required a new level of collective action and its management at departmental level.

In both countries, therefore, new responsibilities were required of academics in the basic units. Explicit administrative tasks in connection with the roles of heads of departments and directors of studies increased. Less visible, but equally significant, was a growing administrative burden within the primary tasks of teaching and research. For example, the requirements for more systematic performance measures and quality assurance procedures entailed more administrative work for the teachers.

However, that was not the only source of pressure for reappraisal of professional roles. While the status and importance of research had been continuously increasing in society and in the universities over a long period, the strong growth of student numbers brought concern about the risk of comparative neglect of educational missions. The reforms in both countries gave great attention to student learning and development and therefore to the teacher role and training.

Within the role of the researcher it was mainly that demands for productivity and relevance for society were intensifying, while the teacher role was being questioned on grounds concerning its professionality. This renewed attention to the processes of teaching, learning and examination in turn involved a necessary engagement in pedagogics and quality criteria other than those emanating from disciplinary expertise.

These trends of growing demands on the roles and performances of the academic staff were similar in the two countries. Our key questions concern what impact increased collective responsibility for the institution, changes in demands of administrative work, and the challenge of teaching professionality have had on the apprehension of the professional role of academics in the departments.

Shifts in professional roles – comparative findings

In England, the ideal professional role for most academics remained that of the discipline-centred teacher/researcher in an essentially collegially-governed institution. However, as the policy and institutional contexts changed, academics were finding it increasingly difficult to sustain the combination of research, teaching and administrative roles. The demands in all three areas were intensifying.

Clark's observation (1991) that generic forces were everywhere fragmenting the relationship between teaching and research against the deeply held beliefs of academics had strong resonances in this study. In England, as elsewhere, pressures were mounting towards greater differentiation in conceptions of the professional role (Elton 1996; McInnis 1996), even if the resistance to them was strong.

In Sweden, the responses to these generic forces ensued from a different situation, due to the separation of the teaching and research roles in the 1960s through the introduction of the university-lecturer position with a total teaching duty. Since then there has been a struggle to regain opportunities for the lecturers to combine teaching and research. And it has not abated in spite of increasing pressure through a growing student population and competition for research funding.

Rather than a tendency towards greater differentiation in professional roles, the Swedish university teachers gave evidence of still trying to meet the many new claims on their professionality during recent years. 'It means that your work is split up and that you are expected to be professional as researcher, teacher and administrator. It is a bit too much to be professional in three occupations', as one of our respondents expressed it.

The already high status of research relative to teaching has risen as research has been designated the crucial factor for development of society. In Sweden, there has been a strong pressure on the universities to meet the growing requests for research cooperation with industry. At the same time they are supposed to extend the opportunity to do research to all university teachers and see to it that all attain their doctorate.

In England, the resource and status implications of the RAE, together with its reinforcement of discipline-based evaluative criteria, tended to support existing academic reward systems which give priority to research productivity and to underline the defining force of the discipline in conceptions of professional roles. Academics were even more strongly persuaded that career advancement depended on their research profile, if necessary at the cost of their commitment to teaching. Institutional strategies to improve research performance included more differential contracts and salaries, rewarding the research productive. Teaching and administrative responsibilities might be reduced or even eliminated for them. Meanwhile, young academics might be bought in on fixed-term, teaching-only contracts to fill the gaps created by a combination of research development strategies and increasing student numbers.

The Swedish reform put new emphasis on the quality of undergraduate education which brings to the fore the dual role of the academic as teacher and researcher, and challenged the adequacy of many academics' strong identification solely as disciplinary experts (Bauer 1996a). Very few of our respondents, for instance, spontaneously included pedagogics and the training of teachers as an important condition for high quality teaching and learning, while a majority mentioned deepening of disciplinary knowledge as the best way to assure high quality teaching. However, the reform demands have contributed to a rising interest in pedagogical development and student learning and brought about different types of quality criteria than those used in peer review of research.

In England, partly due to the introduction of TQA, but also to rising student numbers and changes in the labour market for students, teaching and learning had also been given a higher profile in two of the four old universities and there were even signs that teaching was being accorded an explicit place in promotion criteria. Debates about pedagogy were opened up that had previously not been thought by most academics to be needed or to be of sufficient intellectual interest to them (see Gibbs 1995).

But belief in the importance of active involvement in research for good teaching constituted one of the most dominant themes in the interviews with academics in five of the sample universities. For many people in the humanities and the social sciences the reverse was also true: teaching was an important source of stimulus for research. Changes in student populations and in the pressures upon students were also recognised. Academics were concerned about their students' employability but most felt that their best contribution to this was to make stringent demands on them within their own discipline.

Differences between staff in new and old universities were not clear cut. Certainly, there were more staff in new universities whose professional identity was centred on their teaching role and whose thinking about teaching was less dominated by ideas about its interdependence with research. Yet the discipline remained important to most of them. And, indeed, in this setting, it might be the younger staff who held more traditional views. It was they who had been recruited to enhance the research profile of institutions and for whom the values and practices of élite institutions were more alive.

But the strains on traditional concepts of role were evident. It seemed to demand either further differentiation of staff (some English academics were, for instance, attracted by the possibility of research-only contracts) or some kind of qualitative integration between roles. An example of the latter is a most interesting development of the quality concept in higher education that has been initiated in one of the Swedish sample universities (Marton 1995). This sees the formation of knowledge within a discipline, collectively produced by research and individually attained through student learning, as having common epistemic roots, something which carries a deeper pedagogical or didactical meaning, making teaching an intellectually more challenging task. Such development would imply that the role of the disciplinary expert would constitute a more integrated profession of teaching/learning and research.

The main conflicts, however, were perceived to be those between administration and academic work. It was becoming more difficult to persuade staff to take on departmental or institutional administrative responsibilities, at the same time as these were expanding. But the most concern was with the growing weight of administration within both research and teaching, some of which was laid at the door of quality policies.

In England research selectivity and RAE criteria put a premium on competition for external research funding, particularly in science and social science. As financial support for research became harder to obtain, academics were spending more time on identifying funding sources, on making research grant applications, on accountability for research monies, on developing research partnerships and on maintaining research infrastructures.

Meanwhile, the most common complaint about teaching quality assessments and the internal quality assurance systems that were increasingly geared to them was the time needed for documentation, coordination, evaluation and presentation, which most continued to regard as burdens superimposed on their 'real work'.

In Sweden there was a similar worry concerning the growing proportion of time for research that had to be devoted to the kind of administrative duties mentioned, not least to the *per se* positive development of increasing international cooperative projects.

The Swedish national quality audit by the Higher Education Agency was still, at the time of our interviews, at a very early stage and had therefore not had such an obvious impact as the English audits and assessments. The demands on the institutions to develop more systematic internal quality assurance were met with a mixture of positive reactions to a system of self control and of scepticism, mainly due to the risk of a heavy administrative burden. Since Sweden has not had a system of external examiners and has relied on *ex ante* regulation of undergraduate education, the new system implied a significant change and, in consequence, some uncertainty. There were other reasons for increased administrative work within the teaching role, quality measures were also mentioned, mainly connected to the growing student numbers, and also the strongly developing international student exchange.

The academics in our study thus testifed to considerable pressure on their traditional roles from raised collective responsibility for the institution, new demands of administrative work, and a challenge to their teaching professionality. There were signs that academics' thinking about their role was changing. The competing demands on time meant new consciousness of the need to make effective use of time. And as the roles of dean and head of department became more demanding, holders of these posts had to define again for themselves their attitudes towards them. The external pressures also highlighted the need either to acquire new managerial skills of financial management and academic planning or to recruit specialists for these functions.

The two countries provide examples of 'solutions' both in the direction of a more integrated professional role and in increased diversification of staff for different professional tasks. For reasons indicated above there appeared to be a stronger trend towards diversification in English than in Swedish universities, and the opposite case concerning attempts at integration, although integration was also highly valued by many English academics.

Shifts in concepts of quality

Pressures, both external and internal, for changes in the basic, traditional academic tasks and conceptions of the professional role also challenge academics' concepts of quality. One way of addressing these issues is to ask whether there was movement from professional to administrative and/or market concepts of quality. But we suggest that it is also important to see whether challenge from, or interaction with, these two concepts has stimulated a development of ideas about professional quality.

Frackmann (1992) argues that demands to make criteria of quality explicit imply a move from a professional to an administrative model of quality criteria. But such demands also derive from moves towards market models: customers must be better informed about quality criteria and standards if there is to be effective competition (see also Dill 1995). Can we go further and say that these demands strengthen rather than weaken professional models of quality by requiring professionals to demonstrate the existence and effectiveness of quality processes and criteria to those outside the clan?

Our data tend to support the idea that market models of quality are perhaps more alien to professionals than administrative models but they also show that they constitute a challenge to them that cannot be wholly ignored. For example, debates about conceiving of students as customers raise salient questions about the balance of responsibilities for teaching and learning between students and staff and about what roles, if any, students should have in defining and assessing quality.

The increasing emphasis on the educational role of academics has challenged professional approaches to quality. Traditionally, academics have considered internal peer judgements and external peer reviews of research to be integral features of the academic profession and necessary procedures to guard scientific quality. But they often look upon the demands for similar processes of the evaluation of teaching and learning as bureaucratic devices of little importance. In other words, collective responsibility for, and control of, professional quality criteria are not equally acknowledged in the teacher role. It may be, too, that if they were acknowledged attention would have to shift from criteria connected with disciplinary skills and concepts to those of the teaching and learning process.

The changes analysed in the previous sections also raise the question whether concepts of quality used in higher education have moved to incorporate more holistic or more collective understandings of educational needs.

Shifts in concepts of quality – comparative findings

In Sweden, the setting up of their own quality assurance systems in the universities meant that the administrative model of quality was strengthened compared to earlier voluntary ad hoc procedures. Even though all four universities in our study provided scope for faculties and departments to create their own procedures, it was within a common framework of varying stringency. The triennial audit procedure by the central agency would compel further attention to the quality assurance system and to the collective responsibility for it. On the other hand, a strong emphasis on self evaluation reasserted the importance of the professional aspects of quality assurance.

The intention of the Swedish reform was to raise quality in higher education also by providing more scope for market-like mechanisms.

The reform expanded the possibilities for students to put together their own study programmes and resource allocation became dependent on students' choices and their performance. The few respondents who mentioned the occurrence of market models of quality all strongly repudiated them, especially the idea of students as 'customers'. On the other hand practically all teachers were aware that the impact of the new, performance-based resource allocation was a kind of market system, some stating that it had led to increasing effort and care for the students and for their study conditions, while others feared that it would lead to the acceptance of lower quality levels.

Similarly, in England external teaching quality assessments and the general adoption of internal audit systems entailed a substantial shift to administrative values in old universities. But the emphasis placed in both these developments on systematic course evaluation by students also signalled some movement towards market values in all institutions.

Administrative values were given some credence by academics, although most tended to think they were needed because of other developments, particularly the rise in student numbers.

Academics, at least those outside managerial circles, largely rejected market values. They were critical of conceptions of students as consumers or customers, considering that this would lower standards. They realised that students were contributing more financially to their education and that many saw the quality of their degree as critical for their future success in the labour market. These factors made students more prepared to complain. Academics applauded this, provided it did not imply they were encroaching on academic preserves.

Our interviews with Swedish teachers reflect a wide variety of awareness of the present demands for quality assurance, from some who knew nothing about them, to others who were strongly critical and considered it a bureaucratic device that would take away time and resources and thus lead to lower quality. But there were also those who felt that the new debate on quality issues was useful and stimulating and that a somewhat more systematic and collective approach to quality assurance would be good for the university.

Most teachers declared that quality was something that had always been cared for in the university and was best taken care of by the individual teacher or group of colleagues. A closer analysis of the meaning of such professional quality control was, however, difficult to obtain. An intrinsic, discipline- and research-centred view of quality in teaching was dominant among the Swedish respondents, and extrinsic aspects of quality were only rarely mentioned.

Teachers in England also held to an intrinsic model of higher education, in which the academics defined the goals and the requisite inputs, processes and outputs. A coherent and intellectually valid conception of the subject was essential to providing quality of education in it. Their thinking was strongly informed by élite systems of higher education and they stressed the importance of time for interaction with students individually or in small groups.

No informant, either English or Swedish, referred to the now considerable literature on the reliability of student evaluation, the high level of agreement between student and staff criteria found in studies of it (Harvey, Burrows and Green 1990; Centre for Higher Education Studies 1993) and its tendency to endorse educational research on what best promotes student learning (see, for example, Marton, Hounsell and Entwistle 1984; Ramsden 1991). A few English informants, mainly in new universities, had educational goals which did include the empowerment of previously disadvantaged students. Those who took this view tended to think that the higher educational agenda should start from an understanding of the needs of a much enlarged student population that would be defined primarily by the changing economic and social environment.

Have quality policies with their mainly administrative and market approaches had any positive effect on professional quality assurance systems?

In England the research assessment exercises have largely reinforced existing assumptions about peer review and quality criteria for research. As for the quality of education, opposition to the introduction of external quality assessments meant that assessors found they were often not accepted as peers and those being assessed tended to treat the experience as one of image management rather than participation in a legitimate academic evaluation (Henkel 1997).

However, the self assessment requirements of quality assessment had stimulated many academics to articulate their thinking about their curriculum aims, organisation and methods, and the quality or value of their work with students. The perceived need to give an account of themselves that included the experience of the students, and even the development of transferable skills, meant that aspects of their work that had remained implicit were now made explicit. Teaching quality assessments at minimum provided a mechanism for the reappraisal of approaches to education that the rise in student numbers and restricted resources were rapidly making imperative. Departments and institutions were setting up structures for the development and evaluation of teaching and learning and so providing a framework in which dialogue and experiment could take place.

In all the Swedish universities the central committees for quality assurance and development that were established arranged meetings and seminars for discussion of quality issues and recommended faculties and departments to do likewise. They also supported development projects in quality assurance and enhancement and published and distributed reports within the university on relevant and important issues. In interviews carried out for the RUT-93 Reform Follow-up Commission (RUT-93 1996) it was emphasised that there had probably never before been such a high level of consciousness in the university of the importance of upholding demands for quality. These new fora for professional exchange and discussion on quality matters, and for the development of collective responsibility within the university, can be seen as a most important effect of the quality policies.

There are important differences between the national quality systems in the two countries. While the earlier totally autonomous English universities have become the object of severe central quality control by funding councils, the Swedish universities, from a tradition of strong central regulation, have been challenged as self-regulating institutions to take responsibility for developing their own quality assurance policies and procedures. These two approaches might affect academic attitudes differently, but both imply demands for more systematic quality assurance and obligations of accountability, and both contain a challenge to largely implicit professional quality concepts and the often individual and non-public procedures of quality control.

Conclusions

While the starting point for this paper was provided by higher education policies in two countries, which seemed to be moving in opposite directions, the dominant theme has been convergence rather than divergence. In both England and Sweden, the expectations of higher education were intensifying, in the belief that it held the key to national survival and prosperity in the globalised economy. These factors led governments in both countries to conclude that substantial departures were needed from established relationships between higher education and the state, together with a higher profile for market forces in this field. Universities were required to become more accountable to a range of stakeholders.

There were clear policy differences arising, in part, from differences in political cultures and in the points of departure for the reforms. They centred on the British government's decision to rein in a previously highly autonomous system and the Swedish government's move to devolve more power to the institutional level.

In England, the impact of the quality reforms was powerful and felt by all university staff. While, at least until 1997, institutional audits remained in the hands of the institutions' own body, the HEQC, quality assessments of research and teaching were put into in the hands of the funding councils with the intention, already realised in the case of research, of linking quality with resource allocation. Thus these evaluations were summative, converted into national rankings and of intense significance to higher education institutions in the increasingly competitive drive for resources. The more recent introduction of quality reforms in Sweden has been more collaborative and designed to encourage pluralism and institutional control. The reforms centred on institutional audits and, although they were subject to evaluation by the national higher education agency, the evaluations were formative and not linked to the allocation of resources. At the time of our interviews academic awareness of the change was at a much lower level than in England.

But in both countries a variety of new structures, mechanisms and strategies were needed to develop an implementation system for new policies. And in both, much of the responsibility for such changes has been laid upon higher education institutions themselves.

In both countries, universities could be seen to be adopting some of the approaches of new public management, although this trend has been more pronounced in England, where moves to install stronger management into universities began in the early 1980s. Certainly the simultaneous pursuit of centralisation and decentralisation was a feature of institutions in both systems. In consequence, academics in both countries engaged with types of decision making that were new to them and challenged the definitions and knowledge base of their profession. Their own institutions were making demands on them, not all of which they were ready to meet. There has been a shift from the discipline to the enterprise in terms of the focus of academic attention and, in some cases, the locus of initiatives affecting academic work.

But higher education institutions are far from being simply implementation mechanisms of government policies. They also constitute policy arenas in themselves, in which 'academic tribes' (Becher 1989) have traditionally worked out their own goals within a broadly shared set of generic values and the belief that they themselves can assess, and adapt to, changing social, as well as intellectual, demands. Our data show how academics in both countries were seeking as far as possible to accommodate the new pressures on them, such as alternative definitions of quality, new educational needs and heavier administrative burdens, within their existing conceptual and value frameworks and traditional *modus operandi*.

In these circumstances, institutions have been, to some extent, mediators of the new policies, appraising them and measuring their responses to them in such a way as to protect the interests and values on which the institutions depend but also to see that these interests and values do not inhibit necessary change. In this chapter we have identified two broad approaches to the challenges: a structural approach, entailing more diversified institutions in which there is more professional specialisation, developed within different forms of contract; and an academic approach, involving attempts to hold on to a more integrated professional identity, through, for instance, the reconceptualisation of the relationship between teaching, learning and research within the discipline. The first is more strongly reflected in the English data and the second in the Swedish data, but it may be that elements of both will need to be adopted in each country, if new challenges are to be met. The overwhelming message of the research is that while institutional structures and strategies have become more critical for the health of higher education, academic values and academic disciplines remain a formidable cosmopolitan force.

References

Askling, B. (1994) 'Institutional Responses in Sweden' in D. Westerheijden, J. Brennan and P. Maassen (eds) *Changing Contexts of Quality Assessment: Recent Trends in West European Higher Education.* Utrecht: Lemma.

Askling, B. and Almén, E. (1993) 'From participation to competition: about changes in the notion of decentralization in the Swedish higher education policy.' *Tertiary Education and Management 3*, 3, 199–210.

Askling, B., Almén, E. and Karlsson, C.(1995) 'From a hierarchical line to an interactive triangle. A new model for institutional governance at Linköping University.' Paper presented at 17th Annual EAIR forum in Zurich, August.

Bauer, M. (1988) 'Evaluation in Swedish Higher Education: recent trends and the outline of a model', *European Journal of Education*, 23, Nos 1/2.

Bauer, M. (1996a) 'Quality as expressed in a Swedish reform of higher education and as viewed by University Teachers and Leadership', *Tertiary Education and Management 2*, 1, 1996, 76–85.

Bauer, M. (1996b) 'From equality through equivalence to quality through diversification: changes in the Swedish Higher Education Policy in the 1990s.' In V.L. Meek, L. Goedegebuure, O. Kivinen and R. Rinne (eds) *The Mockers and the Mocked: Comparative Perspectives on Differentiation, Convergence and Diversity in Higher Education.* Guildford: Pergamon.

Bauer, M. and Franke-Wikberg, S. (1993) 'Quality assurance in Swedish higher education: shared responsibility'. Paper presented at the First Biennial Conference of the International Network of Quality Assurance Agencies in Higher Education (INQAAHE), Montreal, 24–28 May.

Bauer, M. and Kogan, M. (1997) 'Evaluation Systems in the UK and Sweden: Successes and Difficulties.' *European Journal of Education 32.*

Becher, T. (1989) *Academic Tribes and Territories: Intellectual Enquiry and the Cultures of Disciplines.* Milton Keynes: SRHE and Open University Press.

Boys, C., Brennan, J., Henkel, M., Kirkland, J., Kogan, M. and Youll, P. (1988) *Higher Education and the Preparation for Work.* London: Jessica Kingsley Publishers.

Brennan, J. (1997) 'Authority, Legitimacy and Change: The Rise of Quality Assessment in Higher Education.' *Higher Education Management 9*, 1.

Centre for Higher Education Studies (1993) *Identifying and Developing a Quality Ethos for Teaching in Higher Education*, Newsletter 3, April, Institute of Education, University of London.

Clark, B. (1983) *The Higher Education System.* Berkeley and Los Angeles: University of California Press.

Clark, B. (1991) 'The fragmentation of research, teaching and study.' In M. Trow and T. Nybom (ed) *University and Society: Essays on the Social Role of Research and Higher Education.* London: Jessica Kingsley Publishers.

Clark, B. and Youn, I.T.K. (1976) *Academic Power in the United States: Comparative Historical and Structural Perspectives.* ERIC/Higher Education Research Report No 3, Washington, ERIC/AAHE.

The Delegation of Quality Assurance at Göteborg University (1995) 'A system for quality assurance for Göteborg University.' *Skriftserie*, 4.

DES (1987) White Paper: *Higher Education: Meeting the Challenge*, Cm. 114. London: HMSO.

de Weert, E. (1990) *Higher Education and Employment: the Case of the Humanities and the Social Sciences in the Netherlands.* Center for Higher Education Policy Studies, University of Twente.

Dill, D. (1995) 'Through Deming's Eyes: a cross national analysis of quality assurance policies in higher education.' *Quality in Higher Education 1*, 2, 95–110.

Dill, D. (1996) 'The positive and negative impacts of external assessment: a preliminary analysis of the regulation of academic quality in the UK'. Paper presented at the annual CHER conference, Turku, June 27–30.

Elton, L. (1996) 'Task differentiation in universities: towards a new collegiality.' In *Tertiary Education and Management 2*, 2, 138–145.

Engwall, L. (1995) 'Institutional responses to quality assessment – a Swedish approach to quality in education; the case of Uppsala University'. Paper presented at OECD/IMHE Conference, Paris, 4–6 December.

Frackmann, E. (1992) 'The German experience' in A. Craft (ed) *Quality Assurance in Higher Education: Proceedings of an International Conference, Hong Kong 1991.* London: Falmer.

Gibbs, G. (1995) 'The relationship between quality in research and teaching.' *Quality in Higher Education 1*, 2, 147–157.

Gibbons, M., Limoges, C., Nowotny, H., Schwartzman, S., Scott, P. and Trow, M. (1994) *The New Production of Knowledge: the Dynamics of Science and Research in Contemporary Societies.* London: Sage.

Harvey, L., Burrows, A. and Green, D. (1992) *Criteria of Quality*, Quality in Higher Education Project. Birmingham: University of Central England in Birmingham.

Henkel, M. (1997) 'Teaching quality assessments: public accountability and academic autonomy in higher education.' *Evaluation 3*, 1, 9–23.

Higher Education Funding Council for England (1993) *Assessment of the Quality of Higher Education, Circular* 3/93, HEFCE, February.

Higher Education Quality Council (1994) *Learning from Audit.* Birmingham: HEQC.

Kells, H. (1992) *Self-Regulation in Higher Education; A Multinational Perspective on Collaborative Systems of Quality Assurance and Control.* London: Jessica Kingsley Publishers.

Kogan, M. (1996) 'Government and the reform of higher education in the UK: a preliminary historical analysis.' Working paper no.B23, International Study of Higher Education Reforms, Brunel University.

Lane, J.-E. (1987) 'Against administration' in *Studies in Higher Education, 12,* 3.

McInnis, C. (1996) 'Change and diversity in the work patterns of Australian academics.' in *Higher Education and Management 8,* 2.

Marton, F., Hounsell, D. and Entwistle, N. (1984) *The Experience of Learning.* Edinburgh: Scottish Academic Press.

Marton, F. and Rovio-Johansson, A. (1995) 'What is a university for?' Translation of chapter in M. Bauer (ed) 'Universitetet: Ett framtidstema med variationer – Röster från Göteborgs Universitet'. Informationsavdelningen Göteborgs Universitet.

Ramsden, P. (1991) 'A performance indicator of teaching quality in higher education: the course experience questionnaire.' *Studies in Higher Education 16,* 2, 129–150.

Regeringens prop. 1992/93:1 *Universitet och högskolor-Frihet för kvalitet.*

Rolf, B., Ekstedt, E. and Barnett, R. (1993) Kvalitet och kunskapsprocess i högre utbildning, Nora: Nya Doxa,.

RUT-93 (1995) 'Universitet och högskolor i förändring: Ledningen, makten och vetenskapen.' *Arbetsrapport 1.*

Scott, P. (1995) *The Meanings of Mass Higher Education.* Buckingham: SRHE and Open University Press.

Scott, P. (1997) 'The changing role of the university in the production of new knowledge.' *Tertiary Education and Management 3,* 1, 5–14.

The National Quality Audit of Higher Education in Sweden (1996) *National Agency for Higher Education:* 10 R, Stockholm.

Trow, M. (1993a) *Reflections on Higher Education Reform in the 1990s: the Case of Sweden.* Studies of Higher Education and Research 1993:4, a Newsletter from the Council for Studies in Higher Education, Stockholm.

Trow, M. (1993b) *Managerialism and the Academic Profession; the Case of England.* Studies of Higher Education and Research 1993:4, a Newsletter from the Council for Studies in Higher Education, Stockholm.

CHAPTER 14

Academic and Administrative Interface[1]

Maurice Kogan

Introduction

This chapter analyses the changes in the infrastructure of higher education institutions in the light of changes in higher education's policy environment and reduced resources. Its focus is on the changes in the internal working of higher education institutions as revealed by the particular issue of relationships between academics and non-academic administrators. It must be noted that the material relates only to western Europe, the USA and Australia, and could be augmented and qualified by the current experience and intended changes in Eastern and Central European universities.

There is not much in our collective literature that throws light on these issues. What little there is tends to concern either the value positions taken up by academics and administrators, or the quantitative growth in administration and bureaucratisation. There is not much close analysis of the tasks performed by each side, and the connections between them.

Bureaucracy and collegium

Institutions respond to external changes and their responses become structured in terms of organisational and power structures. Many of the more important changes have been described as bureaucrat-

---

1   This chapter is based on papers given at the Consortium of Higher Education
   Researchers Conference, Turku, June 1996 and at the IMHE Seminar on
   Staffing and Institutional Interfaces at the Technical University of Budapest,
   August 1996.

isation. Some caution is needed in using this word. It is currently being used to mean two quite separate things. The first is the move from individual and academic power within the often mythic collegium to the system or institution, and a resulting new structuration of decision making. The second is the growth of power of non-academic administrators. In my view the first is the major phenomenon and the second a possible but not invariant consequence of it; indeed the opposite may happen.

Before looking at the changes in the interfaces between academics and non-academic administrators, we need to revisit old territory: the nature of the university as an institution. I confess that I am not too happy with some of the established literature which seems to me to represent academic organisation in a bureaucracy-free and romantic light. 'The community of scholars remains as a myth of considerable strength and value in the academic world' (Harman 1990). Middlehurst comments that, although weakened by the requirement to compete, collegial behaviour can be seen in the sharing of information, ideas and tasks, and in the professional critique of each other's work before it enters the public domain (Middlehurst 1993). These ascriptions are, however, mainly modal and stylistic, and, moreover, can also be used to describe behaviour in enlightened hierarchies. The nub point is where authority is exercised. Here we need a more parsimonious description than that provided by Middlehurst of the collegium. I define it as a group of academics of equal decision-making power acting together to determine standards of entry and accreditation, to share collective resources, and to determine divisions of labour and reward systems.[2] This is minimalist, but to say much more includes categories of power which could be equally found in other forms of organisation.

The earliest descriptions of university organisation assumed the dominance of academic ways of working, and the arguments in favour of them were convincing. Academics constitute the main production units, and their ability to produce requires considerable freedom. Stated in maximum terms (Templeman 1982) the academy's desired state was one in which 'academic autonomy, whether defined and

2   Collegia in some systems include non-academic staff, students and outside representatives. In this paper the traditional restriction to academics is observed.

guaranteed by law, by financial independence, or by customary tolerance, is thus the necessary safeguard for the free and unfettered discharge of every university's primary duty, which is to permit intellectual nonconformity as the means of advancing knowledge.' Nonconformity implies lack of hierarchy, although that assumption about academic life allows for a highly selective account of what actually goes on in professor-led systems where the subordination of already competent academics has frequently been the norm.

Hence the depiction of academic organisation as a structure of 'organised anarchy', which is a necessary condition for the existence of 'the garbage can model'. This romantic view of academic government did not, however, show how essential collective decisions were reached. Later work showed how decisions made within diffuse sectors of the university became regularised as procedures and eventually structures (Baldridge *et al.* 1978); thus political and organisational models of decision making were bridged.

The dominant descriptions depict university organisation as dual: the collegium (an ascription which often occluded the great power of the *ordinarius*) and the hierarchy/ bureaucracy constituted the Janus face of university organisation (Moodie and Eustace 1974; Becher and Kogan 1992). This theme is elaborated in Mintzberg's *Differentiation between the Collegium and the Bureaucracy* (1983) and is now an oversimplification. If these early, and formative, ascriptions were accurate, and they need to be tested, the recently changing tasks of higher education have led to changes in internal power relationships.

The influence of centralisation and decentralisation

The changes which I discuss later must be viewed within the context of the changing relationships between the state and universities. Observation of systems both western and further east suggests that wherever systems either centralise or decentralise, authority at the head of the institutions is strengthened. It seems as if systems need a minimum of authority at one level or another if they are to hold together disparate concerns and priorities. Whatever space central government or the collegium yields is occupied by the rectorates. In all but the Anglophone countries, that need for cohesion was previously met by the regulations laid down, and decisions made, by national authorities. A recent analysis by Christine Musselin shows how in France, ever the deviant case and in this matter the extreme example, the national authorities operated directly with faculties and thus virtually 'denied' the existence of universities (see Chapter 3). The opposite was true in the Anglophone countries where the university was the cohesive level, inasmuch as there was one at all. In the collegium, as most purely exercised in the Oxbridge college, it could be the college itself, but as soon as the colleges became part of a university they accepted collective arrangements for the admissions to membership of the university and for the award of degrees.

The interesting point is that it is not only in decentralising systems, but also in newly centralising systems, that authority shifts increasingly to the institutional level. That is because the target of reforms is not so much the central state or the institution as the professoriat. In the old centralised systems, the state controlled the universities rigorously. Even now in one country, perhaps more, universities must seek permission before buying a typewriter or allowing a room to be used for a conference. But the state did not press hard on the professoriat. Centralisation in those countries means or meant something quite different from current forms of centralisation in the UK or those following the UK's new models. In the UK it does not mean pettifogging and legalistic regulation but rationalistic planning through resource and quality assurance frameworks. But both centralisation and decentralisation bring a changed status for academics.

So the tasks falling on the rectorates of the centralising and the decentralising systems will come close together. Both must ensure that their institutions conform to wide span policies that have to be accepted by them and their academic staffs. The common coinage in these apparently opposite trends is the insistence on quality assurance, though insistence on the market is equally ambiguous and usable by both ministers wanting to decentralise and by those wishing to shed the welfare state concepts of deficiency funding.

The main changes

Some of the changes in higher education's governmental frames, and in the relative reduction in resources, have led to changes in internal management. The external forces have been so often depicted that I need hardly recite them here, but in continental Europe decentralisation has reduced formalistic central power (sometimes wrongly described as rationalistic planning) in favour of market behaviour and normative control through evaluation. In the UK, the change has been from decentralisation to more decisive planning and quality assurance. The changes have led to the following changes in management structures:

- growth in total managerial and administrative work at institutional and infra-institutional level

- changes in the tasks and relative power of academics and administrators within universities

- increased range of tasks for non-academic administrators as well as increase in their numbers

- development of academic administration: the bureaucratisation of the collegium.

These changes cannot be typified as simple transfers of functions and power. Thus the remark of one UK administrator in 1981 after big cuts 'there is now no academic veto' is an example of what has been typified as being a statement that is both true and untrue. What evidence do we have?

Growth in total managerial and administrative work at institutional and infra-institutional level

First, in some systems at least, there has been growth in the numbers of those rated as administrators as a result of the growth in administrative work. In Finland, for example, between 1987 and 1992, the numbers of teaching staff increased by 5.5 per cent whereas the totals of non-teaching staff rose by 20 per cent and administrative staff by 39 per cent (Visakorpi 1996). But while forms of control and administration may have grown within universities, these functions are being taken up by academics as well as by non-academic administrators. I will return to this point later.

Changes in the tasks and relative power of academics and administrators within universities

In order to analyse what is at present emerging we can think of the distinctions between the work of academics and administrators as definable in terms of differentiations in tasks, values, knowledge, and power or authority. Some of the dichotomies that one can note are:

- regulatory/ developmental functions

- production/ control and other secondary functions

- technical/ generic or systemic functions.

These differentiated functions tie in with what we can say about the nature of the university as an organisation. Traditional organisational theory (see, for example, Brown 1961) would start with the analysis of diffuse values and missions in universities and divide them between frontline production and secondary control of supporting functions. Crudely put, the academics are the producers (of knowledge and education) but either they, or non-academic administrators, then have to ensure that production takes place within a common frame of law and resources. If we go to industrial examples, we would also say that there are non-producers who occupy the essential roles of marketing and selling products, as well as making sure that the raw material and environment of production are there.

From these primary, operational, secondary or non-operational distinctions, we get a more secure sense of how academics and administrators interconnect. So far I have not preempted the issue of whether the secondary tasks should be undertaken by either. The answer is that some should certainly be undertaken under the eye of academics. Personally, I am wary of anybody else offering to market my products.

Work on professional organisations other than universities (e.g. the British National Health Service) has led some of us (Joss and Kogan 1995) to conclude that institutions depending on the use and generation of knowledge engage in three kinds of quality assurance. They are quoted here, with some adaptation to academic life, because they denote the different value positions that can be found in both parallel and in contingent relations with each other:

- 'technical quality', concerned with the specialist quality of care applied by individual providers in their work

- 'generic quality', concerned with the common aspects of quality in the way that work is organised and managed, its results and relationships as applied by whole services or management units (includes behaving with a respect for agreed procedures, punctuality, relationships with colleagues and customers and respect for the delivery of the service)

- 'systemic quality', concerned with the quality of a comprehensive and integrated set of services, as applied by whole services or management units.

In academic institutions, the technical values have seemed to dominate. The creation and certification of knowledge and its transmission according to academics' epistemic assumptions are the ultimate end of administration. As we move, however, into the market and state corners of Clark's triangle (Clark 1983) so institutions move towards more corporate concerns. They become more concerned that clients will receive services and enjoy relationships with the institution and its parts that will guarantee continuing market shares. Other forms of generic behaviour derive from the requirement to conform to external legislation and expectations of institutional behaviour in appointments and the like. They are required by outside forces and the pressures of resource constraints to think and behave systemically in terms of planning, portfolio building and resource use.

Increasingly, academics cannot hide from the generic and systemic aspects of their institutional being. Nor can institutions do other than strengthen their non-academic expertise and working in order to meet these demands. A further set of distinctions exists between the regulatory and developmental tasks of administrators to which I return in more detail later on.

This depiction of complex organisation leads us to deeper issues. Academic work is underpinned by certain value positions. The classic depictions are the disinterested search for the truth and the certification of knowledge on the criteria of logic, evidence and demonstrability. The secondary functions also have value bases. Administration has to have a concern for public accountability and for predictability which is not at the top of a research scientist's head. There are also value positions which may be shared territory, such as a concern for equal treatment of clients, or advancing the university beyond the good of individual academics or their departments. Certainly that has been a powerful tradition in British public administration (Kogan 1973).

All of this invites us to divest ourselves of some of the earlier simple diarchical assumptions. Academics move into systems management and administrators increasingly help create the policy and procedural frames for academic work. The structural consequences are:

- In virtually all higher education institutions there are mixtures of collegial, academic-based decision making, and bureaucratic/hierarchical working. Those operating the bureaucratic lines can be, however, either academics or professional administrators

- Collegial working is not simply a coming together of peers, but is itself structured into hierarchical and bureaucratic formats

- For institutions to work effectively there are, and have to be, hinge or interfacial mechanisms which enable collegial decision making to be authorised, legitimated and resourced by the institution. These are put into effect at least in part through the activities of the administrators or bureaucracies

- As institutions become more complex so they elaborate staff or regulatory or developmental roles cutting through traditional academic organisations.

Functions of the collegium in its bureaucratic and hierarchical forms

To make the discussion more concrete, we should note how academics, working in the collegium, produce the following functions which can be described as 'bureaucratic':

- the collegium generates and then authorises the curriculum; this curriculum begins usually with small groups of teachers in course boards, or departmental committees, and then goes through successive stages of authorisation through faculties, senates or academic boards

- the collegium determines the content and, to some extent, the structure of assessment procedures, again going through hierarchies of committees

- the collegium determines the criteria and standards by which new appointments to faculty are made, which the total institution absorbs into its own criteria

- the collegium decides the resources that it needs, and presents them to the institution for determination – but in some of the best USA universities there is said to be effective collegial and non-hierarchical mechanisms for carrying this out (Dill 1996).

The functions described above, and many more could be stated, require academics not to act as free spirits but to undertake quite technical tasks in order to reach decisions that then, in effect, have the force of regulation. Their decisions are taken on delegation from the total university. For them to be effective, there has to be legitimating action taken by the university.

Academic decision making produces a large number of decisions some of which add up to substantial policies. These are collated and monitored by members of the parallel administration. Curricula, assessment procedures and the like are:

- determined by committees and put together by secretaries to committees who will also ensure that they are reported effectively to the next level in the academic hierarchy

- monitored by administrators to ensure that they fall within existing policies and are consistent with practices being developed in the rest of the university. For example, a challenge might be set up to achieve a particular balance between unseen examinations and continuous assessment. This could eventually lead to a report to senate through the administrative secretariats so that it can be resolved and common policies made.

This decision making takes place within rules and policies of the total institution which are mediated to the collegial decision making systems by administrators. These can be academic administrators (e.g. those drawn from academic staff such as deans and heads of departments) or non-academic administrators who monitor their observance on behalf of the university. My point is that the collegium does not stand free of its institution but many of its vital collective functions are part of institutional decision making, and by virtue of this become part of a due process and inevitably bureaucratised.

Thus it is not realistic to assume that there are two clear cut organisational lines of collegium and a bureaucracy. Several collegia within an institution are held together by bureaucratic and hierarchical forms. A central bureaucracy assists and monitors academic decision making whilst undertaking other tasks which are not within the remit of the academic bureaucracy, such as the maintenance of the physical aspects of the university.

There are differences in the internal governance of teaching and research. Teaching is a largely individual activity undertaken, however, within consensus arrangements, although curriculum development may be a more explicitly collective activity. Teaching and associated activities are governed by institutional rules, not on content but time frames, assessment procedures and the like. Research is almost always individually generated, the funding sought for it is individual with researchers going on the resource awarding market on their own account, and then governed by academic procedures or, in the case of applied research, by the requirements of external sponsors. Voluntary association with compatible colleagues is, however, encouraged by research councils, and it is being reinforced by the scale and expense of scientific equipment and because of the challenges of interdisciplinary problems.

Structural position of the administrator

Administrative structures vary according to country. In the English speaking countries, the vice-chancellor, president or principal is seen as both the chief academic and the chief executive (but see also Chapter 15, Smith *et al.*). The chief administrative officer is accountable to him or her in his chief executive role. Vice-chancellors have been appointed until retirement ages, although all contracts are term contracts in Australia and some are so now in the UK. They have always been a feature of university presidential appointments in the USA. In some countries, a director, appointed by the Ministry of Education, has been parallel to the rector who is elected by the collegium, but, in most countries, the director is now subordinate to the rector, although some are still appointed by the Ministry. The rector is elected for a period from two to five years, and therefore politically vulnerable, whilst the director is a permanent appointment; this may still affect the power relationships between the two lines. Powerful directors have been known: the late Director of the University of Bergen was acknowledged to have set that institution onto its path of excellence and viability. In the 1960s, the role was established in Sweden, to the discomfort of some academics, because 'the government wanted to handle the growing university sector' and 'a strong university director was needed to establish enough confidence in the capacity ... of the universities to handle their new tasks in a professional way' (Karlsson 1996).

With Swedish decentralisation in 1993, the appointment of directors became a local decision; four of the six universities have retained the position. But while forms of control and administration may have grown within universities, these functions may be taken by academics as well as by non-academic administrators. The acceptance of the need for strong institutional administration and management is leading to the creation of stronger positions among some senior academics. Thus, a case study of the University of Joensuu (Höltta and Pulliainen 1991) shows how policy propositions which had been made by academic committees and individuals were prepared by officials who shared legal responsibility for them. This gave them considerable power as compared with that of the academics. But changes in structure led to an increase in the power of academic leaders. Decentralisation to the universities in Scandinavia brought 'an academic recovery of power; this change has primarily affected a few academic leaders, not the whole academic staff' (Karlsson 1996). Whilst this may ensure that new forms of strategic policy making are well informed by academic values and knowledge, a potential downside can be noted:

> The contemporary environmental pressures for strategic policy making can lead to an alteration in the structure of authority within academic institutions. In its most dysfunctional form, this change in structure can result in an administrative centralisation or autocracy. But in the case of faculty participation reviewed (in six esteemed USA institutions) the response to strategic change appears in the most effective instance to have led to a reassertion of academic meritocracy over pluralism and democratic participation. (Dill and Helm 1988)

In the UK and Australasia most universities now have pro-vice-chancellors taking functional responsibility for such areas as academic development or research. Similar functional arrangements have long been part of the USA scene in the roles of provosts or academic vice-presidents. It must be assumed that they thus place a boundary round the powers and functions of the Director or Registrar who remains as an expert administrator not drawn from the ranks of the academics. This does not preempt the issue of whether both roles have grown. There is plenty of new decision making to go round, but administrators may feel themselves squeezed by newly empowered academic administrators (Lockwood 1996).

Functions of the administrator

When contrasting the role of the academic bureaucrat working within the collegial committee and bureaucratic system and that of non-academic administrators (directors in Scandinavian universities, or registrars or secretaries general in other systems) we must assume great variations between systems and institutions. But before treating the matter a bit more theoretically we can shade in some of their characteristic tasks.

These exemplify the extent to which administrators are concerned with both regulatory and developmental issues. Examples (largely adapted from Middlehurst 1993, p.110) of work at the most senior levels are as follows:

- advice and guidance to the vice-chancellor/rector (VC) on the development of institutional policy, strategy and tactics
- policy execution
- interpretation and delivery of internal and external intelligence to the VC and the senior management group
- income generation
- preparation of papers and reports to committees
- development, monitoring and coordination of systems and procedures
- responsibility for the management of non-academic staff throughout the university and for the physical and service resources of the university.
- responsibility for the university's estate.

A recent comparative study by de Boer and Goedegebuure (1995) confirms that whilst academic expertise remains dominant on the primary processes of teaching and research, 'the role of the central institutional administration is an important component in higher education governance and management, especially for the non-primary process issues such as financial management'.

Some of the tasks listed above are regulatory whilst some are developmental. On the regulatory side, if the collegium, through Senate and its infrastructural echoes at faculty and departmental levels, creates whole institutional rules on matters that are inherently academic these rules have to be administered to ensure conformity and legality throughout the whole institution. The administrators, then, whilst not concerned with the intrinsic academic judgements that might be made within the rules, monitor and ensure conformance to policies on modes of academic appointment, admission of students, assessment of students, and recent policies such as non-discriminatory practices.

They provide the expertise on the plethora of employment, safety and anti-discriminatory law. They enforce institutional and national legal rules on the spending of money. They may have a fiduciary role in ensuring that resources are spent with propriety. There is a Company Secretary role which provides 'a legal and ethical check upon the activities of the rest of the senior management of the institution' (Lockwood 1996). Chief administrators may be protected in the statutes (as in the UK) as the secretary of council and senate when they have a fiduciary role. For example, it would be their duty to warn a vice-chancellor if he or she were infringing regulations or council or senate policies. There have been cases when chief administrators have felt it necessary to act as 'whistle blowers' when their senior colleague acts outside powers.

Increasingly, the interest of the state in matters of academic substance brings administrators to the boundary of the academic domain. Requirements placed on institutions to defer to quality evaluation increasingly bring departmental performance under institutional review. This can cause administrators to come quite close to monitoring academic performance.

On the developmental side, they may have the task of ensuring an adequate flow of resources to the university or of maintaining and developing the 'personality' of the institution by promulgating it effectively in the external environment. Increasingly they are concerned with activities which may change the boundaries of the institution, such as developing entrepreneurial activities, 'going into Europe', and sharpening and marketing the institution's capacity to get research contracts and grants.

Normative basis of administration

This brings us to look at the normative aspects of the administrator's role. Normative statements inevitably state the ideal, but give us a reasonable clue as to what motivates the best examples of those who operate in systems. A recent thoughtful rendition (Lockwood 1996) has resonances of what I tried to analyse for the value base of the British Civil Service whilst it was still enjoying its golden age in the 1970s (Kogan 1973). Lockwood starts with the observation that it takes place within an institution which 'places responsibility mainly on individuals of high academic quality functioning within a comparatively non-hierarchical and pluralistic structure of both work and management'. In this environment, and one of massive external changes, 'the expertise of the in-house professional administrator functioning in structures which provide for continuity has been an important factor in facilitating transition or adaptation at the institutional level.' It is possible to score continuity as a function that translates into such values as predictability and reliability, taking a longer view and, ultimately, contributing to organic and social solidarity. If it goes bad it spells stagnation.

Lockwood maintains that permanency gives the administrator the capacity to act as a change agent. He or she can '(adjust) the institution to new economic conditions, (cope) with internal conflicts, (steward) the estates against short-term internal demands, or (press) for changes in working practices uncomfortable for current employees'. And 'the low external allegiance of administrators makes for high commitment to the employing institution'. These ingredients of the internal administrative model, however, are in Lockwood's view being eroded.

Interfacial working

In this chapter an attempt has been made to delineate the two kinds of decision making and the two forms of bureaucracy, administrative and collegial, that work together in universities. It is too easy, however, to assume that what is analytically separable is also separable in actuality. It has been rightly emphasised (Hardy *et al.* 1984) that 'many important decisions, however, can be made neither by individual professors nor by central administrators, but require rather the participation of various actors with different interests and expertise. Decisions in these cases emerge from complex collective and interactive processes. In this, Hardy *et al.* assumed that university structures are decentralised and loose coupled and that many different people become involved in the process of decision making, ranging from the professor who sets a precedent to the administrator who reinforces the existing pattern.

The mechanisms for working together between academics and administrators exist partly because the formalised work of the collegium as described in this paper is serviced by the non-academic administrators, and partly because of the increased use of senior academics as administrators, at least in Australian, Scandinavian (Karlsson 1996; Hölttä and Pulliainen 1991) and UK universities.

The point being made in this paper is that the dichotomous categories too easily assumed in the past are more complicated, and to some extent less dichotomous, than has hitherto been the case. This does not mean that conflict has passed away, or that individual academics will not continue to be uneasy about those who promote institutional and policy generalisations which might override the specialist characteristics of the subject areas. Nor will administrators, whether lay or academic, cease to be restless at academics pursuing individual and specialist ends at the expense of what they see to be the more collective good. But reality about the extent to which both 'sides' are involved in policy making which inevitably becomes bureaucratised seems overdue. The remaining issue is, however, how far the majority of those at the specialist base of research, scholarship and teaching can or should be involved in those total systems. This point is being pursued by other authors (see, for example, Dill and Helm 1988).

Concluding points

Some issues arise from the foregoing analysis as follows:

1. Universities increasingly depend upon central administrative bureaucracies because resources are scarce and allocations have to be made, and the challenges from the external environment in the form of quality assessments and the like are more severe. Could this mean that bureaucratic values of predictability, conformity to set rules, due process and collective productivity overtake the individualistic and creative values assumed for academic work?

2. A general drift to bureaucratisation can be discerned (Gornitzka, Kyvik and Larsen 1996). This leads to an increase in administrative staffing and increased work for the academic bureaucracies. The full-time academic bureaucrat throughout institutional levels is becoming more common. This might lead to increased disassociation between them and their academic peers. Might not the fact that they are academics change the value orientation of academics more generally as they see status and rewards going to those who manage rather than perform? Does this matter and can anything be done about it?

3. Does the rise of the academic bureaucrat make redefinition of the non academic bureaucrat necessary? Does their distinctiveness rest in specialist knowledge or in the objectivity claimed for them by Lockwood? Or both?

4. The development of major tasks for bureaucrats such as institutional planning may also lead to some dislocation of power from the production base towards the central bureaucracy where other values than those of the individual decision making and power hold. Some universities are structuring dual mechanisms in an effort to forestall this danger. Could and/or should more be done?

5. The increased range of tasks for non-academic administrators raises questions about their recruitment and training. Of what should these consist? Those canvassed include technical knowledge of finance and personnel, information technology, and planning as well as political and negotiating skills (Davies 1979; Porter and Padley 1982). A balance between generic training and individualised staff development, perhaps related to organisational development, needs to be struck.

References

Baldridge, J.V., Curtis, D.V., Ecker, G. and Riley, G.L. (1978) *Policy Making and Effective Leadership.* San Francisco: Jossey-Bass.

Becher, T. and Kogan, M. (1992) *Process and Structure in Higher Education.* London: Routledge.

Brown, W. (1961) *Exploration of Management.* Harmondsworth: Penguin Books.

Clark, B.R. (1983) *The Higher Education System. Academic Organisation – A Cross National Perspective.* Berkeley: University of California Press.

Davies, J.L. (1979) 'Administrator training and development in European higher education: problems and possibilities.' *International Journal of Institutional Management in Higher Education 3,* 1, 95–108.

de Boer, H. and Goedegebuure, L. (1995) 'Decision making in higher education: a comparative perspective.' *The Australian Universities' Review 38,* 1 I.

Dill, D.D., Personal communication, 12 July 1996.

Dill, D.D. and Helm, K.P. (1988) 'Faculty participation in strategic policy making.' In J.C. Smart (ed) *Higher Education: Handbook of Theory and Research* Vol. IV.

Gornitzka, Å., Kyvik, S. and Larsen, I.M. 'The bureaucratisation of universities.' Paper given at CHER conference, Turku 1996.

Hardy, C., Langley, A., Mintzberg, H. and Rose, J. (1984) 'Strategy formation in the university setting.' In J.L. Bess (ed) *College and University Organisation: Insights from the Behavioural Sciences.* New York: New York University Press.

Harman, K.M. (1990) 'Culture and conflict in academic organisation.' *Journal of Educational Administration 27,* 3.

Henkel, M. and Kogan, M. (1996) 'The impact of policy changes on the academic profession.' Paper given at Society for Research in Higher Education Annual Conference, Cardiff.

Hölttä, S. and Pulliainen, K. (1991) 'Management change in Finnish universities.' *Higher Education Management 3,* 3.

Joss, R. and Kogan, M. (1995) *Advancing Quality, Total Quality Management in the National Health Service.* Buckingham: Open University Press.

Karlsson, C. (1996) 'The academics and administrative interface in Scandinavian universities.' *Higher Education Management 8,* 2, 29–36.

Kogan, M. (1974) 'Social policy and public organisational values.' *Journal of Social Policy 3,* 2, 97–111..

Lockwood, G. (1996) 'Continuity and transition in university management: the role of the professional administrative service.' *Higher Education Management 8,* 2, 41–52.

Middlehurst, R. (1993) *Leading Academics.* Buckingham: Open University Press and SRHE.

Mintzberg, H. (1983) *Structure in Fives: Designing Effective Organisations.* New Jersey: Prentice Hall.

Moodie, G.C. and Eustace, R. (1974) *Power and Authority in British Universities.* London: Allen and Unwin.

Porter, D. and Padley, J.S. (ed) (1982) *Training University Administrators in Europe.* Aldershot: Gower Press.

Templeman, G. (1982) 'Britain: A Model at Risk.' *Cré-Information* 2nd Quarter.

Visakorpi, J.K. (1996) 'Academic and Administrative Interface Application to National Circumstances.' *Higher Education Management 8,* 2, 37–40.

CHAPTER 15

Vice-Chancellors and Executive Leadership in UK Universities
New Roles and Relationships?

*David Smith, Peter Scott, Jean Bocock
and Catherine Bargh*

Introduction

This chapter examines the changing roles of university vice-chancellors in the UK. It draws on some of the initial results of a research project funded by the Leverhulme Trust designed to test two broad hypotheses.[1] The first is that new forms of executive leadership in UK higher education have emerged based on managerial expertise rather than collegial or charismatic authority. The second is that there has been a power shift in universities with vice-chancellors becoming the dominant figures in defining their cultures and determining institutional missions and performance. These hypotheses were informed by a previous study of university governors which highlighted the often informal and ambiguous relationship between governance and management and the key role, particularly in taking policy initiatives, played by the executive (or senior management team) and the vice-chancellor (Bargh, Scott and Smith 1996).

Our research posed a number of questions about the appropriateness of the title 'chief executive' in the context of universities. Are vice-chancellors essentially senior managers with certain leadership roles attached? Or are they primarily leaders, not quite in the heroic mould of a Rupert Murdoch or Richard Branson, but still

---

1   The authors are grateful to the Leverhulme Trust for funding the study on which this article is based.

'individuals' occupying great strategic command posts of influence and prestige rather than members of a network or system? In the quasi-collegial and professional setting of the university, the notion of leadership, typically organised around concepts of 'superiors' and 'subordinates' or 'leaders' and 'followers', may seem inappropriate, no matter the resurgence of interest in leadership as a tool of organisational performance. On the other hand, precisely because of the culture and values of universities, vice-chancellors may be (still) accorded a degree of symbolic authority that is in part academic prestige (derived from the notion of *primus inter pares*) and in part functional. Such authority, symbolic or otherwise, is closely associated with power and authority. Since vice-chancellors occupy the occupational space at the apex of the university hierarchy, they have access to varying degrees of social influence both within and beyond their organisation.

We present some preliminary results of our research into these issues. It is arranged in four sections. The first outlines the evolution of the vice-chancellorship within the context of the broader policy environment and developing ideas about organisational leadership. The second asks who are the vice-chancellors, discusses our approach to profiling the educational and career characteristics of vice-chancellors as an occupational group, and reports briefly some of our preliminary findings. In the third section we consider the nature of vice-chancellors' work and identify some of the key issues and relationships which define their roles. The final section reviews the changing nature of the vice-chancellorship and discusses the contested and contingent nature of executive leadership in the university setting.

The evolution of the vice-chancellorship

Policy context

The research is located within a broader set of policy issues. The first relates to the legacy of new-right thinking which has exerted a decisive influence on, once taken for granted, understandings about the wider relationship between universities and the state. Mounting government deficits and attempts at reconfiguring welfare and public sector funding arrangements have impacted heavily on universities and other local public spending bodies. Internationally, governments are using deregulation as a means of promoting new forms of self regulation which are strongly responsive to government priorities (Baird 1997; Tapper and Salter 1995). As a result, governors and managers of universities are expected to restructure and change their educational processes in line with available resources (Schmidtlein and Taylor 1997).

The roles of university leaders need to be viewed in the context of this wider restructuring which has changed many of the familiar post-war practices, processes and structures of the state. With marketisation of public sector services now deemed a core building block of the restructured state, there has been a resultant shift towards the adoption of new practices and methods borrowed from the private sector – sometimes referred to under the generic title of 'corporate managerialism'. Managing for results describes the essence of corporate managerialism. It is about delivering more efficient and effective services: its watchwords are value-for-money, efficiency, outcomes and results (Taylor *et al.* 1997, p.78).

While the implementation of the new public management approach has brought about a narrowing of policy goals, set at the top, responsibility for their achievement has been devolved to front line institutions. Within the higher education sector this has been reflected in the focus on corporate planning procedures, strategic mission statements and objectives, performance indicators and so on. Vice-chancellors occupy the nexus between these two, often opposing, sites: the centrally determined policy framework on the one hand; and the self-governed/self-managed university on the other. Because of their pivotal position, vice-chancellors can exert a decisive influence over the direction of the university and the shape of its policy.

The second policy issue arises out of the growth of mass higher education systems and of the redefinition of the university itself. In the UK, the number of universities has increased from 31 to 93 since the Robbins Report and the total number of students in higher education from around 400,000 to over 1.5 million (HESA 1996/97; Robbins 1963). A national system has replaced a collection of autonomous institutions and universities have become much more complex institutions. At the same time, the word 'university' has ceased to be a straightforward descriptor. This is seen in the emergence of a sub-set of 'modern' universities – the former polytechnics, lacking, often by design, the customary attributes of their older peer institutions. Their presence represents a challenge to older conceptions of the university. It is also seen in the imperative of 'management' in universities. As new funding systems are devised and ever more ambitious economies of scale demanded, as expenditure totals rise and as the external environment, including university-state relations, becomes more complex, so the pressure to 'manage' effectively and efficiently increases.

There are other expectations. Universities have taken on new roles that extend beyond teaching and research as once conceived. Intervention in social and technical innovation is increasingly expected. New student constituencies, informed by enhanced consumer sovereignty, have to be appealed to and recruited; their needs accommodated alongside (or in place of?) engagement with traditional élite scientific and scholarly cultures. Broader engagement with the community or 'stakeholders' locates universities as critical agents for regional regeneration and/or as national champions in global economic competition. Finally, the university is no longer a monopoly provider of higher learning, but increasingly one of a widening range of providers obliged to position and reposition themselves in a marketplace full of semi-regulated 'differentiated' institutions.

Nor are the boundaries of the institutions themselves always clear. Emerging institutional linkages, embracing both old-style mergers and franchising arrangements and technology-based global connections, provide novel means of competing in diverse learning markets. Higher education systems increasingly comprise a web of rival institutions stretched across a new landscape of post-compulsory education and learning. Responsibility for steering or leading institutions through this changing and challenging landscape is vested in large part in their executive leaders (though in conjunction with governing bodies), the task described by one vice-chancellor as 'moving the herd generally west'.

Organisational leadership

The literature of leadership demonstrates a particular concern with the identification of traits, styles and situational contingencies. There has also been a heavy emphasis on the structured observation method designed to allow measurement of activities and comparison of managerial 'events' (see the work of Bussom *et al.* 1981; Martinko and

Gardner 1990; Mintzberg 1973). Other work, however, has shifted the focus of attention from the analysis of quantitative categories such as traits or contingencies towards how leadership is socially constituted: 'the process of leadership as a social and organisational phenomenon' (Knights and Willmott 1992, p.762; see also Bennis and Manus 1985; Bryman *et al.* 1988; Hosking 1988; Hunt *et al.* 1984; Hunt 1991; Strong 1984). Studies in this genre draw attention to how leadership qualities are socially defined rather than unproblematically given, how they depend on relations of power and tend to stress the importance of the management of meaning in the social practice of leadership. Leadership can be seen as a process for guiding values and beliefs. In order to be properly understood, therefore, attention needs to be given to the cultural assumptions and understood ideas which underpin leadership processes.

Viewed as a process for guiding values and beliefs, leadership is a contested area since it addresses issues surrounding the production of consensus, dealing with resistance and the general structuring of relationships. This paper develops this theme and argues that changes in the relationship between state, society and its universities have reconfigured the nature of managerial leadership in contemporary higher education systems. Earlier charismatic or collegial models of university leadership have been replaced by a new model which emphasises managerial skills that are both bureaucratic and entrepreneurial. This shift has been less dramatic in the USA where the university president has always possessed powerful executive responsibilities; and most dramatic in continental Europe where the rector has traditionally been regarded as *primus inter pares* with predominantly ceremonial functions.

The UK case, arguably, stands somewhere between these models. Unlike the rector, the vice-chancellor is not selected (or elected) from among the professors of the university and is (usually) a permanent appointment. But, unlike American university presidents who have devolved many of their academic and domestic functions to provosts, UK vice-chancellors are still expected to combine the roles of institutional manager and academic leader. However, the nature of the emerging model of executive leadership in UK universities remains underresearched (see Middlehurst 1993 for an exception).

The evolution of the vice-chancellorship has been a complex phenomenon. Leadership roles need to be viewed alongside other, potentially rival, foci of institutional authority: lay members of council and professional administrators in the case of the 'old' (pre 1992) universities; and local authorities, both members and officials, and since 1989 the independent members of the governing bodies in the case of the 'new' (post 1992) universities. Before 1960, the direction of the old universities was influenced by a small number of powerful vice-chancellors. This pattern was continued in some of the new universities founded in the era of Robbins where founding vice-chancellors played decisive roles in shaping their ethos. In the 1970s, the influence of many vice-chancellors was compromised by more democratic styles of academic government, while oversight of the management and direction of the expanding university system often slipped into the hands of registrars and other professional administrators. After the 1981 cuts in university budgets, and especially after the 1985 Jarratt report on university efficiency, a different model of institutional leadership emerged with the vice-chancellor as chief executive at the head of a senior management team.

Thirty years ago, therefore, the role of the vice-chancellor remained largely unquestioned and could still be styled 'chief academic and administrative officer' – something akin to the Victorian position when the post was more like that of a headmaster. (Moodie and Eustace 1974, pp.126–127). Since then the vice-chancellor's post has been progressively transformed. Analysis of a sample of recently advertised posts of vice-chancellors gives more than a hint of the nature of the changes, for they now routinely state that candidates must be able to demonstrate all or most of the following qualities: academic leadership; research standing; a sound knowledge of higher education; senior management accomplishments; and evidence of interaction with a wide range of private and public bodies. Traditional concerns with academic leadership remain strongly in evidence, but to them have been added formal expectations about managerial experience. These requirements are evident across the spectrum of universities and are illustrated by two examples from recent, publicly advertised posts in old universities:

> Candidates must be able to demonstrate successful experience of leadership and management of organisational change. In this re-gard it is vital that the next Vice-Chancellor and Warden possesses the capacity to innovate and to think imaginatively in strategic terms whilst at the same time demonstrating a clear commitment to the ethos of the University.

> In seeking its next Vice-Chancellor the University is seeking to appoint an individual of exceptional calibre to provide academic and executive leadership ... The University is a complex organisation ... It therefore requires a first class Chief Executive with skills in financial management and in income generation, able to guide the organisation in an uncertain environment.

This shifting orientation of job requirements has been reflected in pay and pensions packages. One survey reported that, by 1993, six-figure packages were becoming commonplace among UK vice-chancellors, with 28 universities declaring remuneration of more than £100,000 and a further 15 more than £90,000. Although these figures were lower than comparable private sector rewards various commentators noted that the trend was upwards (*Times Higher Education Supplement* 9.2.96).

Our research was designed to test our broad hypotheses about the changing nature of executive leadership in universities by examining vice-chancellors from a range of perspectives. These included the historical evolution of the role of British vice-chancellors, the literature on institutional management, the development of theories of organisation, and notions of 'leadership' generated in other commercial and professional settings. The intention was to explore the evolution of new patterns of leadership in British higher education in the context of, first, the changing goals and organisation (and demands on) universities; and, second, parallel developments in university leadership in the rest of Europe and the USA.

Who are the vice-chancellors?

Previous sociological studies of élites have identified vice-chancellors as members of an occupational élite (Giddens 1974; Perkin 1978/9; Rubinstein 1987). Although we did not investigate changes in the social origins of vice-chancellors, we thought it legitimate to try to establish the main influences on their career development and to chart the main pathways to the top in terms of education and career experiences. Our approach was to construct databases of biographical information of all British vice-chancellors appointed since 1960. Construction of these databases commenced at the start of the project. This has proved a demanding and time-consuming task but is now substantially complete. These data comprise 341 separate cases in two independent, but linked, databases.

The first database contains up to 77 numeric variables per case detailing the characteristics of the vice-chancellors appointed since 1960. These variables are grouped into three main descriptive categories. First, the demographic characteristics of vice-chancellors such as age and gender together with the honours and titles they hold; second, the principal features of their previous educational, career and recruitment paths; and, third, their participation in the life of the university sector and wider public and private sector organisations. The second database comprises nine tables of qualitative data which provides greater insights into the latter category of numeric variables.

These databases have been constructed mainly from data drawn from successive editions of *Who's Who*. Although these data may be incomplete in some cases, overall they provide the only accessible and comprehensive social profile of this élite occupational group. At the time of writing, our database has only 32 'missing' cases of vice-chancellors known to have occupied office since 1960. Exploratory analysis of the 341 complete cases has already begun and we are satisfied that the databases will enable us to chart changes over the past 37 years in the composition of successive cohorts of vice-chancellors and to link changes in career patterns to the expansion in the number and diversity of UK universities in the post-1960 period. Wherever possible we have tried to ensure that the categories of analysis in the biographical databases are compatible with those of the only other previous study of UK vice-chancellors which presented data for 1935 and 1967 (Collison and Millen 1969). This will enable us to comment on longer-term temporal variations in the social profile of vice-chancellors.

The purpose of this phase of the research was to enable us to investigate changes in career experiences which could be related to the development of the office of vice-chancellor. For example, we wanted to test whether the shift from academic and administrative towards executive and managerial interpretations of the post were reflected in educational and career experiences. Beyond this, it would be useful to examine the extent to which the university's articulation with new social groups and occupations was reflected in the officeholders of vice-chancellorial posts.

Initial results

The data demonstrate some broad similarities in the characteristics of
vice-chancellors and the typical ways into the top job:

1. The vast majority, over 90 per cent, are appointed to their
    posts after careers in academia. Prior to taking up their posts
    they had been university professors, pro-vice-chancellors in
    old universities or deputy directors in new universities. Only
    a small proportion were recruited from industry or the civil
    service.

2. Only 12 per cent made horizontal career moves from being a
    vice-chancellor at another institution.

3. Historically, the Oxbridge institutions have exerted an
    important influence on the recruitment patterns of
    vice-chancellors. Once 'the principal source of
    vice-chancellors,' Oxbridge influence has declined slightly
    but remains prominent. Nearly a third of vice-chancellors
    appointed since 1981 were Oxbridge undergraduates. When
    postgraduate and academic/teaching experience is taken into
    account Oxbridge influence increases still further.

4. Most vice-chancellors are appointed from a different higher
    education institution, but a third did achieve promotion
    within the same institution. There was almost no movement
    from new to old universities. Amongst vice-chancellors of
    new universities, one in five had come from the old sector.

5. The average age of vice-chancellors at appointment is 52
    years. Vice-chancellors of the old universities tend to be
    slightly older at appointment than their new university
    counterparts (53 and 50 respectively). There is little
    evidence to suggest any marked change in age at
    appointment over time.

6. The average period of office for the entire population of
    vice-chancellors appointed since 1960 is just under eight
    years. Over time the periods of appointment are getting
    shorter in both old and new universities. In old universities
    the period in office has declined from 11–15 years before
    1960 to under five years in the 1990s. Duration in office has

been generally lower in new universities and has shown a similar long-term decline.

In identifying the previous educational and career experiences of vice-chancellors, particularly the continued durability of the London–Oxford–Cambridge axis, our data suggest that they display at least a potential for a similarity of outlook or 'life space' (F. and J. Wakeford 1974). Historically it has been shown also that at national level, vice-chancellors chair Royal Commissions, specialist committees, research councils and so forth, they sit on boards of directors in other sectors. Locally, they occupy key posts on governing bodies of a range public services and charities. They appear at élite gatherings and mix with other prominent members of local and national élites. It is legitimate to ask how this potentially close alignment of élite groups and shared set of curriculum values might influence the direction of university business and the shaping of its policy.

This is linked to Clark Kerr's notion of the 'multiversity' and the assumption that it is possible to accommodate many varied and conflicting demands within the system and its institutions (Kerr 1963). Whilst we might expect élite universities to be led by members of the élite and continue as producers of leadership cadres, mass systems might be expected to be less focused in this respect. As Trow has argued, there is a struggle between the autonomous and popular functions of contemporary universities. While the autonomous functions involve a commitment to a broad liberal education, the transmission of élite values and preparation of candidates for membership of élite groups, the popular functions involve a commitment to provide higher education for as many students who want it, not as a privilege but as of right (Trow 1973). The extent to which the executive leaders of 'old' and 'new' universities might diverge in terms of their educational and career backgrounds could be interpreted as one test of a reconfigured system no longer focused so single-mindedly on the autonomous functions of the university and specific élite social groups and occupations.

Even if, as the figures suggest, Oxbridge is no longer 'the principal source of vice-chancellors' it has still provided nearly 30 per cent of vice-chancellors in the period since 1981. It has been argued that higher education is not an appropriate indicator of the social background status of élite position-holders (Rubinstein 1987). An

Oxbridge education does not necessarily indicate evidence of 'family wealth and high status' because entry to the colleges had been successfully infiltrated since the late 1800s by the new middle classes, and to a large extent a meritocratic system had replaced one of privilege. Since we have not analysed school background, which incidentally is subject to the same argument, and higher education is an insufficient indicator of privileged social status, we cannot necessarily infer that many of the vice-chancellors have indeed come from an élite social class. However, even if we accept that attendance at Oxbridge cannot in itself be used as indication of privileged family background, we can surely argue that accompanying an Oxbridge degree are certain social and employment advantages derived from the prestige associated with the institutions. Vice-chancellors are hardly immune from these processes. While it may be the case that the majority of Oxbridge graduates have to be content with 'more modest professional positions' (Anderson 1992), 'élite studies' have underlined the dominance of Oxbridge graduates amongst the top strata of professionals (for example, see Boyd 1973 and F. and J. Wakeford 1974).

The fact that there is virtually no cross-sectoral movement from the new to old sector (if we limit our investigation to respondents' immediate preceding post) is one of the important findings of this element of our research. Although a lack of movement from new to old may not be very surprising, it is nevertheless rather stark in terms of its consistency across all the previous post categories. How can this finding be explained? We can speculate that while the binary divide between the sectors has been, or is being, eliminated through the process of convergence, in terms of leadership recruitment the gap between old universities and the former polytechnics remains wide (and significant?).

On the basis of our data it is reasonable to speculate further that the future development of the 'popular' and 'élite' functions of universities will be strongly influenced by the continued prevalence of traditional career and educational pathways into the vice-chancellorship. Once in post, of course, it is a moot point how far particular educational and career experiences influence the actual practices of managerial leadership. All we can say at this stage is that research into managerial leadership in other settings suggests that there are strong links between these early experiences and the formation of leader and manager identities which, in turn, are likely to influence behaviour in the job (Hall 1997).

The full results of our investigation into the educational and career influences on vice-chancellors are not yet available. However, once complete, the data will provide a comprehensive picture of changes in the profile of vice-chancellors since Collison and Millen's study of the 1930s and 1960s (Collison and Millen 1969). It should be possible also to compare with similar studies of career patterns of vice-chancellor equivalents in the USA, Canada and India (Desai 1983; Moore 1983; Muzzin and Tracz 1981).

Vice-chancellors' work

Although leadership is an important aspect of the vice-chancellor's job, it is only one of a broader set of managerial responsibilities. In order to understand leadership in the context of the university, therefore, we need first to comprehend the vice-chancellor's job as a whole and the place of leadership in it. Based on our fieldwork, the present section attempts to provide an overall impression of the vice-chancellor's job. It concentrates on the linkages between *interpretations* of the responsibilities of vice-chancellors and the sorts of actions which demonstrate how they engage with these responsibilities.

Fieldwork comprised two elements: first, semi-structured interviews with a sample of serving vice-chancellors together with senior managers and chairs of councils/governors in ten representative institutions; second, extended periods (two working weeks) of non-participation observation of three vice-chancellors. The purpose of the fieldwork was to enable intensive study of the nature and practice of managerial leadership, the interviews focusing on the perspectives of vice-chancellors and their colleagues about roles and relationships, non-participant observation affording an insight into the social practice of leadership.

Through observation in particular we hoped to be able to 'get inside' organisations and understand their practices in much greater depth (Tomkins 1997). In one recent study of Australian vice-chancellors, non-participant observation was deliberately eschewed on the grounds that the researcher would not be given free access to a sufficiently wide range of matters, most notably those concerning personal and disciplinary matters (Sloper 1996). Whilst there were some periods of exclusion in each of our field study sites, overall our observational studies, in combination with supplementary interviews of other key figures and documentary analysis, produced a wealth of data detailing the work of vice-chancellors: their objectives, strategies and styles.

However, while our methodology afforded a unique insight into the behaviour and cultural norms of our case study leaders, at the same time it imposed certain limitations on how it can be reported. Privileged access into these worlds of work necessarily encompassed a wide range of circumstances, people and events, from the openly public, often mundane, to the highly confidential and private nuances of organisational life. In seeking to interpret and report these data we have consciously striven to ensure that the individuals, organisations and events observed remain as anonymous as possible. In the summary of vice-chancellors' work which follows, therefore, wherever possible we have referred to issues generically and changed the names of participating organisations and people.

The data suggest that despite the differences in the historical and organisational backgrounds of universities, the work patterns of vice-chancellors bear some major similarities. The layout of their work, in the operational sense, is embedded in a meetings 'culture'. Diaries are tightly scheduled, given shape by a combination of formal meetings arising out of the committee and managerial structures of the institution and informal meetings with key groups and individuals involved in its governance and management. In the operational sense, it is primarily through these forums that the exercise of academic and executive leadership can be observed. It is also in the pattern of meetings with external constituencies, that we can see how vice-chancellors attempt to engage with their ambassadorial and representational roles.

These meetings and the use of the spaces between them afford some insight into certain common characteristics in the patterns of behaviour of the vice-chancellors. All work long hours, spend most of their time with others, engage in a broad spectrum of topics, many of which do not necessarily connect directly with the core business of the organisation and will rarely be seen issuing orders or making big decisions. In the same way, the ideas, imagination, ability to think strategically or manage change successfully, all of which are routinely recited in job specifications as the major requirements of the vice-chancellor's role, are unlikely to find obvious expression in the confines of a majority of these meetings. Nor did we find evidence of vice-chancellors overtly issuing orders or making decisions. On the contrary, there appeared to be conscious avoidance of the use of formal authority and official power.

Although this summary provides a broad impression of what vice-chancellors tend to do and how they spend their time, it conveys very little sense of why they engage in these activities and how they approach them. The literature on the work of general managers/ executive leaders suggests that they tend to approach their jobs in broadly similar ways. Kotter provides a useful framework to understanding their work. He suggests there are essentially three key problem areas or dilemmas associated with the responsibilities of managerial leadership: setting goals, policies and strategies; balancing resource allocation; and coping with the diversity of activities. In his own study of general managers, Kotter found that they all concentrated on 'developing agendas for their businesses and on developing the networks of resources needed to accomplish those agendas' (Kotter 1982, p.60). Our own observations of vice-chancellors concur with this analysis. They have key roles to play, particularly in attempting to provide the vision which connects with day-to-day decisions inside their organisations. But this element of leadership is tempered by the demands and dilemmas of the job.

In the remainder of this section we attempt to illustrate how two of these key roles can be played out in practice. In the first the focus is on issues of vision and strategy and the vice-chancellor's role in providing both corporate or strategic leadership and positioning the organisation within the sector. In the second the focus is switched to the problem of scarce resources, a perennial problem for universities, and discusses how various vice-chancellors appear to tackle the problem. These examples attempt also to engage with some of the key concerns set out by Carlson in his seminal study of executive work, namely to connect with the factors which determine the leaders' actions, the goals they strive for, and the attitudes they have towards the goals and situation (Carlson 1951).

Vision and strategic direction

At one level of generality all the vice-chancellors participating in our research identified vision, the question of where the institution is going, as a key element of their leadership role. Their focus is on long-term decisions about the positioning of the university within the higher education market or, as one vice-chancellor expressed it, strategic thinking 'beyond the millennium'. An essential part of this task is to introduce longer-term vision into the culture of the senior management team. Our observations suggest that vice-chancellors now routinely engage with this issue at senior management 'away-day' seminars, more usually than not held in local hotels. Such occasions, in the words of one vice-chancellor, provide valuable opportunities for 'radical and deliberately provocative thinking, a chance to think the unthinkable'. What did he mean?

In part the answer is to do with positioning universities post-Dearing: conscious attempts to crystal ball gaze and anticipate the place of universities in general, and their own institution in particular, within the spectrum of needs expressed by constituency groups – the government, employers and students. Away-day seminars, therefore, are concerned with the university as a corporate entity (how the vice-chancellor and senior managers see their institution within both higher education and broader society) and provide an opportunity to try to develop, from often fragmentary beginnings, a corporate image which, ideally, will come to be shared internally, by colleagues, and externally, by the broader constituency of users.

Our interviews and observations presented plenty of evidence about how vice-chancellors identify this task and set about influencing the cultural norms and behaviour of their senior management colleagues. Introductory sessions of 'away-days' afford vice-chancellors a chance to take the lead and set the tone, often in the form of a personal view of the present and future state of higher education. Often this might involve elaborating on sometimes informed, occasionally speculative, hunches.

For example, at the time of our research, the Dearing Report was eagerly awaited and much anticipated. As one vice-chancellor confided to his senior managers, Dearing would not be a report about the mechanics of funding, but a chance to build on the radical thinking of 16–19 qualifications. It would give to higher education a focused vocational slant which would take into account the needs of employers for graduate skills. The university of the future would be accountable for the development of society's key skills. For the new universities, however, there were other dangers, two in particular: the

Harris report on research funding and the machinations of the Russell group of universities.[2]

Ensuring the compliance of other senior managers with the leader's vision is a key, but far from straightforward, task. Not all will share the vision, let alone 'live' it. The vice-chancellor may well be questioned. For example, on one of the away-day seminars one senior manager of a new university, a former polytechnic with a strong tradition of access, thought there was a strong incentive to leave these historical roots, become élite, share traditional values and opt out of the '21st century NVQ brigade'. The vice-chancellor's response was unequivocal: 'There's no time to grow the ivy.'

Vigorous debate about how to translate vision into strategies and task objectives might take place on the occasion of away-days. Indeed, one vice-chancellor deliberately tries to engender debate by kicking-off so-called wild-time sessions in which many sacred cows of organisational norms are butchered. Such 'wild-times' are designed to open the well of ideas from other senior managers. However, we observed also how the emergence of collective ownership and identification with the cultural norms underpinning the vision might leave some individual senior academics/managers in a quandary. Do they move with the collective will of the group, even when they have misgivings that new, sometimes radical, ideas have not been sufficiently thought through? Or do they resist their leader and risk isolation from the group and possible loss of favour and downgrading of future promotion prospects. For the individual concerned, a difficult and ultimately personal choice. For the vice-chancellor, too, a difficult situation to assess and control. From our observations of, and discussions with, vice-chancellors, it is not unknown for individual managers to be allowed to wander in isolation: 'to learn', as one vice-chancellor explained, 'they're on their own'.

Translating vision, which may have certain ethereal qualities, into more specific strategies designed to position the university in a

2 The Harris report recommended that the HEFCE should limit research funding in respect of postgraduate research students to departments (mainly those located in 'old', pre-1992 universities) with a grade 3 or above rating in the most recent Research Assessment Exercise [RAE] (HEFCE, CVCP and SCOP 1996). The Russell group is a self-styled 'club' of 'old' universities, so-called because their vice-chancellors meet informally for breakfast at the Russell Hotel, London. The group comprises 17 of the top research-led universities. There is no official secretariat.

changing higher education 'market' has become another key task objective of vice-chancellors, particularly in those institutions outside the élite. The search is for image and the sort of words necessary to describe adequately what each university will do for those engaged in its various activities. What sort of graduates should the university produce both now and in the future? In an increasingly marketised and massified system of differentiated institutions, such concerns are routinely discussed by many vice-chancellors and senior managers.

We observed discussions about the relative merits of words such as vocational, employability, knowledge and learning skills; debate about how to align the university with sophisticated knowledge based companies located in the local area; and, more generally, how to achieve the objectives set: in short, how to 'lift the vision'. As one vice-chancellor admitted, the university was expert at what it did, but the problem was how to communicate it. What he wanted to see from his senior colleagues was a commitment to develop an institution with the 'public self-confidence which will communicate with various markets'. The contrast and, paradoxically, the goal, was Oxbridge, where in his opinion things were done with an air of 'effortless superiority'. The search was for quality.

The extent to which 'away-days' really change strategic thinking is debatable and difficult to assess. Wild ideas (thinking the unthinkable) might have more to do with letting off steam than shaping the real agenda facing universities. It might also have more to do with developing senior management teams, influencing the culture, values and norms of the team and providing opportunities to assess the potential of available human resources. It is in such settings that individuals are likely to move up and down the pecking order, when reputations as 'blue-eyed boys' (and girls) are played out, sometimes confirmed, sometimes lost, in front of colleagues. Our own observations and the evidence of several respondents suggest that such occasions have more than a hint of self-fulfilling prophecy about them. Vice-chancellors almost inevitably bring to the forum of strategy seminars thoughts developed elsewhere. While research provides a valuable snapshot of the dynamics involved, it is unlikely to capture the medium to longer-term processes that contribute to the emergence of ideas and reputations.

In several universities, various members of the senior management team concurred that strategy steering groups and consultation exercises are instrumental in developing medium to long-term positioning and that, in some cases, the vice-chancellor stands outside this process. One pro-vice-chancellor interviewed felt that in his university many academics felt a sense of bewilderment and desire for directive leadership, a view which he expressed as: 'Why the bloody-hell doesn't someone write it and tell everybody what to do?' He was not alone in describing internal debate, between those who wanted the university to consolidate in the market for 'quality students' (defined mainly by higher A level points scores) and those more anxious to develop access missions and commitment to students with alternative qualifications.

All the vice-chancellors in our research acknowledged that a key responsibility of university leadership is to provide vision and guide the strategic direction of the institution. Grounding their vision in a subtle combination of reality and prescience is an important part of the task. Its translation into a set of meanings and firm strategic objectives creates a major dilemma for it requires others to 'share' and then ultimately 'lift' the vision. But senior colleagues may not share the vision, they have to be converted or, in extreme cases, replaced by those who do. How this 'conversion' process is tackled will reflect differences in individual leader styles and approaches. It will be influenced also by the organisational history and culture of the institution concerned.

Old universities with their more entrenched traditions of collegiality may present vice-chancellors with more ingrained resistance to new visions and cultures. There is evidence, too, that the practice of temporary tenure of pro-vice-chancellorships may provide a more enduring bastion of resistance to the ideas, radical or otherwise, of vice-chancellors, particularly where the leader lacks the full confidence of many, even if the backing of the university's council is not in doubt. Conversely, new universities, with their permanent senior management teams, may present the vice-chancellor with rather fewer impediments to change, even if, as one new university respondent lamented, 'change takes time'. The key difference, then, may not be the symbolic authority of the vice-chancellor's office, important though this may be, but the ways in which specific leadership practices interact with the context and dynamics of the vice-chancellor's actions.

Scarce resources: the problems of funding

Budgetary constraints emerged, not surprisingly, as a major responsibility and dilemma facing most of the vice-chancellors participating in the research. The key task objective is identifying the resource problems and possible solutions, even before difficult decisions about their allocation are considered in any detail. Nor could budgetary issues be easily compartmentalised since invariably there was a complex intermeshing of historical and organisational contexts which might constrain the scope for action.

In some cases the problem of constraint had clearly escalated into mounting budgetary crisis. The tensions created were aggravated by a shifting terrain of funding and other policy issues within preexisting structures and cultures of management and control. For example, in the setting of old universities, a strong tradition of committee and collegial decision making can set operating units and the 'corporate' centre on a collision course. Under these circumstances the credibility of the vice-chancellor's intervention in budgetary allocations may be undermined by a perception that historically the vice-chancellorship has been the site of administrative rather than executive prerogatives. It would be neither comfort nor surprise to several vice-chancellors to discover that several of their closest senior colleagues harboured sometimes grave doubts about their ability to provide the calibre of leadership required during hard financial times, no matter their capacity for long hours of work. Indeed, the mounting menace of financial stringency had caused several chairs of council/governors to reassess and readjust, usually in consultation, the amount of time spent by their vice-chancellor on external or ambassadorial business. As one respondent explained:

> I mean, if you're chief executive of anything normal you have got to spend so much time on the job. But you see, they still say well we can toddle off and give a lecture in Mexico City or somewhere. Well, I'm afraid that is not compatible with being a vice-chancellor. If you're going to be chief executive you've got to really run the business, which means spending time on the business and not on other things.

Other chairs of councils/boards of governors and most vice-chancellors concurred, some very strongly, about the importance in the prevailing financial climate of being on the job rather than being diverted by too many external commitments.

Vice-chancellors' interpretations of budgetary problems tended to be influenced by two sets of perspectives. The first was appreciation of the sector-wide reality, confirmed in the Dearing Report, that there has been a long-term decline in the unit of resource per student (a fall of 40 per cent over the last 20 years, Dearing 1997). The hope of many vice-chancellors was that Dearing, once perceived as resistant to the idea that this decline was too problematic, would acknowledge the limits to efficiency gains.

The second set of perspectives tended to be filtered through the particular lens of the institution. Although the enormous increase in financial pressures as a result of successive government reductions in funding was readily acknowledged, the impact on individual institutions had been far from straightforward. Even where they expressed a particular interest or expertise in financial planning and management, as a group few vice-chancellors tended to view the issues surrounding funding in isolation, rather as an admixture of academic and financial issues. As one vice-chancellor (of an old university) explained:

> The first thing I have to do is make sure we don't get into a mess financially. This may seem a mechanical sort of thing, but the point is if you get in a mess financially you cease to be master of your own fate academically. So it's an academic issue.

Some claimed to enjoy being immersed in the detail, others, like the vice-chancellor above, less so. But the important point is that none could afford to ignore the financial dimension of any activity. Involvement in the Research Assessment Exercise (RAE) was one potent example. Even if the institution was involved in the exercise more for Brownie points than hard cash, the demonstration effect and potential for developing consultancy and access to 'dirty money' was scarcely lost on vice-chancellors.

Nor could vice-chancellors ignore the issue of allocating scarce resources internally. At meetings of senior management, vice-chancellors presented hard facts and talked about new methodologies for allocation. Histories of unequal funding across schools/departments, generated in times of less constraint, were scrutinised rigorously. Hence, in one case, the imposition of a 10 per cent cut in overall funding, made up partly of government reductions and partly in the decision by the university to set aside several million pounds for strategic development, had to be accommodated. The vice-chancellor delegated to a deputy the presentation of the 'facts' to deans of school. Fears were expressed by several that cuts of the magnitude envisaged could not be managed. The vice-chancellor drove the meeting forward nonetheless, requiring all deans of school to produce plans of action to cope with the cuts. Indeed, early reports were demanded of the most hard-hit schools.

These financial constraints assumed added importance because it was the area most likely to bring the vice-chancellor and senior members of the university in contact with members of the council/governing body. It is an area also in which many chairs and sometimes individual members feel they have particular expertise or advice to offer. Chairs were unanimous that the financial affairs of universities were becoming increasingly central to the work of vice-chancellors. However, these are frequently some of the most sensitive areas of activity, taking senior managers and lay members alike into the darkest recesses of finance. We found evidence to suggest that vice-chancellors were necessarily re-examining accepted customs and practices of budgetary allocations.

Those under extreme financial pressures saw no ring fence as sacred. As a consequence, the potential for conflict between vice-chancellor and those constituencies within the university likely to be affected raised the stakes of the managerial game considerably. Not surprisingly vice-chancellors are sometimes involved in secret and delicate negotiations with financial and legal advisors about the likely effects of certain courses of action. Such negotiations often took place away from the gaze of the formal apparatus of institutional governance, though we have no reason to suppose that key members of management and governing body were not aware of the actions of their chief accounting officers. As the chair of one new university board explained:

> Vice-chancellors are becoming more and more preoccupied with the financial viability of institutions. That does tend to bring you down to the more managerial aspects of the job. Are you going to get rid of a hundred people? Are you going to continue to run with these same departments that seem to be losing money? More vice-chancellors are going to find themselves preoccupied with the nitty-gritty of keeping their heads above water.

Conclusions: interpreting executive leadership in universities

Our research has generated a number of detailed findings about the emerging roles of vice-chancellors:

1. In addition to discharging the traditional functions of academic and administrative leadership, he or she is now expected to be the active manager of a large and complex organisation with a budget measured in tens or hundreds of millions of pounds and in which academic and service functions can no longer be disentangled. Many vice-chancellors see themselves essentially as managing directors. Of our interviewees only one explicitly referred to himself as an academic. However, all stressed the need to focus, and thereby shape, the wider academic endeavour.

2. With the decline of donnish collegiality the role of the vice-chancellor has taken on the mantle of chief executive, a role which demands the shaping of the institution's strategic values and ensuring it recognises and adjusts to the rapidly changing environment.

3. This new role and the range of sophisticated intellectual and leadership skills it demands is distinct from the traditional notion of academic leadership grounded in distinguished service as a teacher, scholar and researcher. Nevertheless, as an occupational group almost all vice-chancellors continue to be recruited from the ranks of academics. The predominance of this career route makes an important statement about the changing demands of higher education leadership and the skills and expertise required of vice-chancellors.

4. Work patterns of vice-chancellors exhibit certain basic similarities. However, there are differences in the balance of activities displayed by individual vice-chancellors, particularly with respect to internal and external activities. These differences did not appear to follow a simple dichotomy between old and new universities, although more thorough analysis of the complete data may refine this view.

5. The vice-chancellor is now expected to interpret a bewildering variety of political and market messages, often contradictory, and play a leading role in the external representation of the institution – locally, nationally and internationally.

6. Issues of external accountability now have to be addressed and the vice-chancellor is a key agent of the governing body of the institution, the relationship with the chair and other leading members of the governors/council being a particularly sensitive issue.

7. Finally, the vice-chancellor must contribute to the collective government of the university system itself, through membership of representative bodies like the CVCP.

Empirical evidence has been presented which highlights two of the major responsibilities of the vice-chancellorship – vision and strategic direction and handling scarce resources – together with some of the dilemmas they create. The expectation that vice-chancellors will generate and articulate a vision for the future, set the destination of the university and map how it will get there is widely accepted by vice-chancellors and their senior colleagues as part of the job. Although the immediate executive challenges facing the vice-chancellor as leader were, by common consent, funding driven, particularly the need to adjust to a reduced unit of resource, their ability to tackle various issues was influenced by existing organisational cultures and decision-making structures. At the heart of this problem lies a familiar debate between the virtues of collegiate versus executive decision making. Our data demonstrate that despite the similarities in the nature of vice-chancellors' work, their behaviour was affected by certain situation-specific factors. Although some of the issues (budgetary constraints, corporate spans of control to name but two) were essentially the same, their leadership styles, their interactions and relationships with colleagues proved to be markedly different.

This conclusion points to the importance of developing a better understanding of the practical process of managerial leadership. Vice-chancellors are engaged in almost continuous (sometimes contested) negotiations with those to whom key tasks will be delegated and those with responsibility for implementing front-line change. These negotiations are complex and often subtle, involving the interplay of power and subjectivity: they are, in effect, intriguing struggles of minds in which differing interpretations of the social reality facing the university compete for ascendancy. These negotiations and the processes which underpin them are exceedingly difficult to capture and conceptualise (Knights and Willmott 1992). But it is important to attempt the task if we are to understand better the practice of executive leadership in the context of universities. While this is an important part of future work in this area, some interim conclusions about the nature of vice-chancellors' work can be drawn.

Because the nature and expectations of executive leadership have changed to reflect broad shifts in the relationship between universities and the state, the actual practice of executive leadership has become much more of a contested and contingent area. It is contested for two reasons. First, because the policy environment has changed significantly. It is turbulent and volatile and generally inhospitable to institutions with a history of stability based on closed and self-referential values. Second, because operating in this new semi-marketised and increasingly massified environment imposes often competing demands for entrepreneurship and strong management as well as attempts to preserve the existing ethos of the institution, including the vestiges of collegiality and professional autonomy. This view accords with an earlier study of leadership in higher education which noted that by introducing a species of managerialism institutions were able to survive (even prosper), but survival had been at the cost of collegiality and a resultant loss of ownership and shared professional responsibility (Middlehurst and Elton 1992, p.261).

The new (managerial) roles of vice-chancellors are contingent also in two senses. First, in redirecting responsibility for accountability and control down to agencies and ultimately institutions, the state has effectively inserted into the space between traditional 'academic' and 'administrative' leadership a new role for vice-chancellors who must now straddle both governance and management. The accomplishment of that precarious role depends upon the emergence of effective working relationships across the two domains of governance and management. It places particular emphasis on the relationship between the vice-chancellor and chair of governing body, key representatives of the executive and governors respectively.

Protecting institutions from inappropriate executive behaviour (and there have been some well-publicised cases of 'out-of-control' vice-chancellors) depends, therefore, on the effectiveness of governance arrangements which our previous research has already shown to be heavily dependent on good informal relationships rather than on constitutional processes.

The second source of contingency stems from the rump of collegiality. Despite the imperatives of 'control' and self regulation and the spectre of managerialism, all the participants in our study maintained the necessity of retaining the confidence of academics. In short, academic leadership remains an ambiguous yet vital component of executive leadership, a fact reflected in the comments of many vice-chancellors who stressed the importance attached to the academic board/senate. This has less to do with the role of the academic body in taking decisions than with the need to assure the academic community that its interests and concerns are understood and taken seriously. On serious or major issues it is clearly also something of a vote of confidence in a vice-chancellor and his or her judgment. Failure to win approval would send a strong signal that the temper of the academic community had been seriously misjudged.

Executive leadership, like arrangements for governance, comprises a set of social and political processes which are both contested and contingent. Since these processes may be obscure and difficult to monitor they pose particular challenges for researching and understanding leadership roles and practices. In our empirical investigations we have attempted to be sensitive to the more diffuse elements of power and subjectivity contained in the process of leadership. The evidence suggests, therefore, that executive leadership in UK universities can no longer be understood within a simple paradigm of collegiality in which the vice-chancellor provides academic and administrative leadership, first among equals.

References

Anderson, R.D. (1992) *Universities and Élites in Britain since 1800*. Studies in Economic and Social History. London: Macmillan Press.

Bargh, C., Scott, P. and Smith D. (1996) *Governing Universities: Changing the Culture*. Buckingham: SRHE/Open University Press.

Baird, J. (1997) 'Accountability of university governing bodies in Australia: issues for proponents of corporate models.' *Tertiary Education and Management 3*, 1, 72–82.

Bennis, W.G. and Manus, B. (1985) *Leaders: The Strategies for Taking Charge.* New York: Harper and Row.

Boyd, D. (1973) *Élites and their Education.* Windsor: NFER.

Bryman, A., Bresnen, M., Beardsworth, A. and Keil, T. (1988) 'Qualitative research and the study of leadership.' *Human Relations 41*, 1, 13–30.

Bussom, R.S., Larson, L.L., Vicars, W.M. and Ness, J.J. (1981) *The Nature of Police Executives' Work: Final Report.* Carbondale, Ill.: Southern Illinois University.

Carlson, S. (1951) *Executive Behaviour.* Uppsala (1991 reprint with contributions by Mintzberg, H. and Sewart, R.)

Collison, P. and Millen, J. (1969) 'University chancellors, vice-chancellors and college principals: a social profile.' *Sociology 3*, 77–109.

Dearing, R. (1997) *The National Committee of Inquiry into Higher Education: Report of the National Committee.* London: NCIHE.

Desai, U. (1983) 'University vice-chancellors: profile of the educational élites.' *Journal of Higher Education 8*, 3, 265–288.

Giddens, A. (1974) 'Élites in the British class structure.' In P. Stanworth and A. Giddens *Élites and Power in British Society.* Cambridge: Cambridge University Press.

Hall, V. (1997) 'Dusting off the phoenix: gender and educational leadership revisited.' *Educational Management & Administration 25*, 3, 309–324.

HEFCE, CVCP, SCOP (1996) *Review of Postgraduate Education.* HEFCE.

Higher Education Statistics Agency (1997) *Students in Higher Education Institutions: 1996/7.* Cheltenham: Higher Education Statistics Agency.

Hosking, D. (1988) 'Organising, leadership and skilful process.' *Journal of Management Studies 25*, 2.

Hunt, J.G., Hosking, D., Schriesheim, C.A. and Stewart, R. (eds) (1984) *Leaders and Managers: International Perspectives on Managerial Behaviour and Leadership.* New York: Pergamon Press.

Hunt, J.G. (1991) *Leadership: A New Synthesis.* London: Sage.

Kerr, C. (1963) *The Uses of the University.* Cambridge MA: Harvard University Press.

Knights, D. and Willmott, H. (1992) 'Conceptualising leadership processes: a study of senior managers in a financial services company.' *Journal of Management Studies 29*, 6, 761–782.

Kotter, J.P. (1982) *The General Managers.* New York: The Free Press.

Martinko, M.J. and Gardner, W.L. (1990) 'Structured observation of managerial work: a replication and synthesis.' *Journal of Management Studies 27*, 3, 329–357.

Middlehurst, R. (1993) *Leading Academics.* Buckingham: SRHE and Open University Press.

Middlehurst, R. and Elton, L. (1992) 'Leadership and management in higher education.' *Studies in Higher Education 17,* 3, 251–264.

Mintzberg, H. (1973) *The Nature of Managerial Work.* New York: Harper and Row.

Moodie, G.C. and Eustace, R. (1974) *Power and Authority in British Universities.* London: Allen & Unwin.

Moore, K.M. (1983) *Leaders in Transition: A National Study of Higher Education Administrators.* University Park, PA: Pennsylvania State University and ACE.

Muzzin, L.J. and Tracz, G.S. (1981) 'Characteristics and careers of Canadian university presidents.' *Higher Education 10,* 335–351.

Perkin, H. (1978–9) 'The recruitment of élites in British society since 1800.' *Journal of Social History XII,* 222–234.

Lord Robbins (1963) *Higher Education: Report of the Committee on Higher Education.* London: HMSO.

Rubinstein, W.D. (1987) *Élites and the Wealthy in Modern British History.* Sussex: The Harvester Press.

Schmidtlein, F. and Taylor, A. (1997) 'Processes employed in graduate/research universities in response to strategic issues.' *Tertiary Education and Management 3,* 1, 52–62.

Sloper, D.W. (1996) 'The work patterns of Australian vice-chancellors.' *Higher Education 31,* 205–231.

Strong, P.M. (1984) 'On qualitative methods and leadership research.' In J.G. Hunt *et al. Leaders and Managers: International Perspectives on Managerial Behaviour and Leadership.* New York: Pergamon Press.

Tapper, E.R. and Salter, B.G. (1995) 'The changing idea of university autonomy.' *Studies in Higher Education 20,* 1, 59–71.

Taylor, S., Fazal, R., Lingard, B. and Henry, M. (1997) *Educational Policy and the Politics of Change.* London: Routledge.

Tomkins, C. (1997) 'Corporate governance in a UK university: the case of the University of Bath,' unpublished paper, School of Management, University of Bath.

Trow, M. (1973) *Problems in the transition from élite to mass higher education.* Berkeley, CA: Carnegie Commission on Higher Education.

Wakeford, F. and J. (1974) 'Universities and the study of élites.' In P. Stanworth and A. Giddens *Élites and Power in British Society.* Cambridge: Cambridge University Press.

CHAPTER 16

An Institutional Perspective on Managing Change

Rob Cuthbert

Introduction

Most British studies of higher education policy and its effects have focused on educational experiences and policy processes, rather than institutional management and its significance (or not). One apparent exception, a literature on managerialism in higher education, has largely traded in ideological assertion and counter-assertion rather than drawn appropriately on an eclectic range of theoretical perspectives. In contrast, this paper presents a case study of change in one polytechnic/new university over 1988/97, interpreted in the context of changing government policies for higher education, using a range of theoretical perspectives. It argues that changes in the practice of higher education can be understood through the interplay of external and internal pressures, mediated by the institution's governors, managers, and the structures which they inhabit. The best-known theoretical account of change in this context is the academic drift thesis formulated by Pratt and Burgess (1974) and refined by Locke (1978). In this paper it is argued that the drift thesis is insufficient to account for more recent change, because it gives too little weight to the mediating influence of institutional management and strategic choice. While drift may have been the result of external and internal forces in the 1970s, in the 1990s diversification is the result, because of changes in the context, the scope for managerial discretion, and the nature of the higher education experience itself.

Rather like much recent British government policy for higher education, the paper does not flow from a rigorous research programme, designed in advance. It is a practitioner account which draws on a range of studies and analyses to interpret institutional experience and to derive a number of conclusions which are inevitably speculative. However, they do perhaps have the face validity needed to justify further research of a kind which has, to date, been underrepresented in the British literature on higher educational policy and management.

Fifteen years ago I was an academic running a Masters programme in Higher Education Management. After a grounding in policy studies and management theory, those Masters students were asked to write an assignment on the topic: 'What difference does government policy make to institutional practice?'. Their answers showed repeatedly how the question *could* be illuminated through a consideration of management and institutional processes.

Ten years ago I worked on the National Advisory Body's (NAB) Studies of Good Management Practice (GMP) (National Advisory Body 1987), which aimed to reconcile the wishes of the polytechnics and colleges for operational autonomy with the desires of local education authorities (LEAs) – their owners and creators – for a continuing stake in their governance. But the compromise embodied in the GMP report 'was pre-empted by the publication of the 1987 White Paper' (Pratt 1997, p.291) in which institutions were removed altogether from LEA control. This brutal exercise in the imposition of central political will left little doubt about the power of government to change the relationship between higher education and the state.

Turning to address the problems for higher education institutions in the process of becoming independent corporations (Cuthbert 1988a) I was invited to apply my academic concerns in practice, and joined Bristol Polytechnic, as it then was, in 1988. Since then, as a member of the institution's senior management group, I have helped to manage the processes of incorporation, change to university status, and many other aspects of institutional change.

Throughout this period the question: 'What difference does government policy make to institutional practice?' has had continuing relevance and resonance.

The longevity of universities might suggest that they are effective at managing or adapting to change. Universities do indeed show the entrepreneurial behaviour which typifies professional-dominated organisations, but at the same time they are in some respects intensely conservative organisations, which might account for the recent waves of government intervention and reform in higher education. Whatever its scope, this institutional capacity for adaptation and change management has been relatively neglected by academics as a focus of study, even though many academics have specialised in studying organisations and the management of change in other contexts.[1] In this chapter I offer a personal, practitioner's account which takes institutional capacities, processes, governors and managers as the focus for an exploration of change in the relationship between higher education and the state.

The voyage from Avon to the West of England

1997 was the 500th anniversary of Cabot's voyage of discovery from Bristol to North America in his ship *The Matthew*. My aim is to chart the voyage of Bristol Polytechnic from the 'old world' of LEA control under Avon County Council to the 'new found land' of university status as the University of the West of England, a voyage on the stormy seas of government policy and state intervention.

The events leading up to the Education Reform Act of 1988 were extensively analysed at the time (see, for example, Cuthbert 1988a, 1988b; NAB 1987; and Pratt 1997) has now provided a definitive history. The polytechnics' mission to provide socially responsive and accessible higher education (Crosland 1965; 1967; Robinson 1968; Pratt and Burgess 1974) had been nurtured in the relative plenty of the late 1960s and early 1970s. The Thatcherite reforms of the public sector in the 1970s had switched institutional attention to funding and control, without diluting their commitment to access. In their struggle for independence from what were in many places absurd local authority restrictions on their operational freedom (Locke *et al.* 1987) the polytechnics acquiesced in a shift in central government policy:

> Where once we were concerned with bottom-up control, growth and effectiveness, qualitative assessments of performance, education and the individual in society, we are now concerned with top-down control, contraction and efficiency, quantitative assessments of performance, training and the worker in the economy. There has been, in other words, a shift in emphasis from access and quality to funding and control. (Cuthbert 1988b, p.53)

---

1   This neglect is a phenomenon which deserves study in its own right, and is addressed in a separate paper (Thorne and Cuthbert 1997).

It was control which was the dominant feature of the 1988 Education Reform Act (ERA) in respect of higher education. The Act abolished all but a vestigial stake for local authorities in the continuing governance and ownership of the polytechnics. Bristol Polytechnic ceased to be a creature of Avon County Council and was recreated as the higher education corporation, Bristol Polytechnic.

The first phase of the post-ERA period was one in which the polytechnic began to come to terms with its new independence. I have argued elsewhere (Cuthbert 1992) that this meant a change of managerial culture for the polytechnic, a process summarised in Table 16.1.

Table 16.1 The cultural transition in Bristol Polytechnic 1988–1992

	Past		*Present*		*Future*
Structures:					
Resources	Centralised	→	Devolving	→	Decentralised
Programmes	Autonomous	→	Collaborating	→	Interdependent
Processes	Closed	→	Emerging	→	Open
Expected Performance	Ambiguous	→	Negotiating	→	Clear
Focus	Process	→	Reorienting	→	Outcomes
Culture	Dependence	→	Learning	→	Independence

Source: Cuthbert (1992, p.160)

Alongside the new sense of independence, reflecting the policy emphasis on control, went a new concern, at all levels of management in the institution, for cost. Government policy, realised through the ERA-created Polytechnics and Colleges Funding Council (PCFC), aimed to bring down unit costs while securing a rapid expansion in higher education student numbers. Within the polytechnic the sense of liberation after incorporation made it possible to accommodate the new financial restrictions at a time of expansion. Corporate owner-ship of assets meant that the polytechnic could rationalise its previously dispersed distribution of small sites, and the proceeds of rationalisation were also for the first time available as of right for investment in the institution's development.

Although the polytechnic shared in the national mood of resentment in higher education at government financial policy, this did not inhibit rapid development in both academic and financial terms. The polytechnic reconstructed its internal management processes to exploit its new independence, unifying previously separate consideration of budgets, student number projections, and staffing levels. An internal document about the planning process argued that:

> This is not meant in any way to weaken the emphasis on the academic and educational dimension, nor is it meant to inhibit academic diversity. Rather it aims to put educational objectives in the context of financial possibilities – to balance quality and cost. This means that managers at all levels will be expected to take a rounded view of performance against targets, to balance achievements against costs, and to compare income with expenditure. They will have more responsibility and more freedom to manage, but they will be held to account for overall performance – balance between quality and cost ... (Bristol Polytechnic 1990)

With these new internal management processes went a mission 'to excite and satisfy demand' for higher education of an applied and regionally responsive kind, in partnership with other higher education and further education institutions in the region (Bristol Polytechnic 1989). The outcome was a rapid expansion in which student numbers, on an ever-widening range of full-time degree programmes, increased from 6900 in 1989–90 to 14,200 in 1994–95, and topped 16,000 in 1996–97. Part-time student numbers also increased from 4800 in 1989–90 to 7800 in 1996–97. During the same period the average unit of funding per student was almost halved in real terms. Expansion reflected an institutional responsiveness both to student demand and to Funding Council mechanisms which provided incentives to growth. However expansion *per se* was not the prime objective; rather, it was the by-product of the aim to expand opportunity. In this sense the polytechnic (unlike some) might be said to have experienced mission-driven expansion rather than pursued an expansion-driven mission.

This institutional trajectory might be seen as vindicating Locke's (1978) refinement of the 'academic drift' thesis, whereby institutional development is seen as a rational response to the interplay between institutional (i.e. staff) desires for prestige and financial support, and external pressures, controls and incentives. However, that thesis gives insufficient weight to the mediating effect of judgements by institutional managers and governors. During the period from 1988, all polytechnics faced similar external pressures, and had to a considerable extent common staff concerns in respect of funding and status. Yet institutions developed in very different ways. Bristol Polytechnic, like some others (such as Sheffield, Newcastle, and Trent), grew rapidly as part of a declared strategy to become the dominant regional provider and supporter of accessible applied higher education. As a counterexample Oxford Polytechnic, which in the late 1980s was of similar proportions to Bristol, and often bracketed with it in terms of standing and mix of programmes, grew much less, so that, by the mid 1990s, the Bristol institution was almost twice as large as its Oxford counterpart.

This difference reflects major differences of both institutional mission and managerial judgement in 'reading' the significance of Funding Council funding mechanisms and positioning the institution to face an uncertain future.[2] Oxford Brookes University, as the Polytechnic became, continued to recruit most of its students from a national rather than regional catchment, and its strategy deliberately maintained its average level of funding per student significantly above the rapidly-falling national average. The difference from Bristol's trajectory exemplifies the significance of management as a mediating influence in institutional change. It also suggests that an organisation's environment must to some extent be seen as enacted, as well as imposed. Thus it challenges the deterministic version of the drift hypothesis, which takes external pressures as a given.

After independence and expansion came a further government policy change in the 1992 Further and Higher Education Act. The

2   This conclusion is drawn from public and private debate about Funding
     Council funding methods, in which Clive Booth, Vice-Chancellor of Oxford
     Brookes University was prominent, arguing against 'rewarding' the
     irresponsible expansion of a handful of institutions by retrospective levelling of
     the 'unit of resource' through a common funding tariff.

Act enabled polytechnics to acquire university titles and to award their own degrees. Each change was a predictable and widely-predicted sequel to the earlier 1988 reforms. Polytechnics had already gained academic accreditation to become largely self-validating under the Council for National Academic Awards (CNAA); thereafter degree-awarding powers were but a small step. University title had also been widely heralded, so that many polytechnics were immediately ready to tackle the Privy Council formalities to change their titles. Bristol, like other polytechnics located in university cities, took rather longer to settle on a new name. The Polytechnic nevertheless was able to relaunch itself as the University of the West of England (UWE), Bristol in October 1992.

The new University's vice-chancellor took the opportunity to restate the mission and vision for the new University, in a speech at a degree ceremony in 1991:

> ... I shall urge that we use the wider powers which will come with a university title ... to create a new University which:

- is distinctively comprehensive and inclusive in character, in the manner of the Polytechnic

- is student centred, in the tradition of Bologna as reflected in the University of Glasgow, rather than of Paris as reflected in Oxbridge

- uses its validating and degree awarding powers to extend its quality control umbrella over a regional network of educational opportunity provided locally by further education colleges

- aims to become the heart of a credit accumulation and transfer consortium, through which, in partnership with colleges and library services throughout our region, we might offer students a consolidated prospectus of modular opportunity

- conceives itself to be a civic institution, sharing the concern ... to assist a partnership between the local authorities, the Chamber of Commerce, and the Training and Enterprise Councils

- looks first to the needs of the local and regional economy and its communities, in a manner more characteristic of Scotland or Germany than of post war England (Morris 1991).

This could be seen as the natural development of the mission first articulated in 1989. In its distinctive emphasis on 'regional strategy' it was later criticised by some staff for giving insufficient weight to national and international dimensions, which became matters of increasing concern as the importance of research to the institution became more marked.

For government, university title for the polytechnics was a reward for their delivery of more higher education at lower cost, as well as a recognition of their range of work and the standing which they had achieved – which in most other parts of the world would always have been acknowledged with a 'university' label. For institutions like Bristol Polytechnic, apart from the entertainment of the name change and its associated logo swapping, it seemed that the new title would be less significant than the earlier process of incorporation leading to independence. However, almost immediately the new university title prompted raised expectations from students. These heightened expectations were not so much in terms of teaching and learning, where the quality of student experience was already well-recognised among students, if not always by the general public. But there were immediately higher demands for extracurricular provision of all sorts, such as residential student accommodation and sports facilities. These demands were fuelled by the emergence of guides and league tables such as *The Times Good University Guide*, which purported to rank all universities, old and new, on a range of criteria such as volume of student accommodation, as well as quality of teaching and research. Students, encouraged by government and the media to behave more like consumers, changed their benchmarks and rewrote the ground rules of inter-institutional competition – with significant effects on the emerging structure of the 'unified' university sector. Within the new universities, too, there was a fresh concern with and debate about institutional mission. At UWE a two-year seminar series explored *The New Idea of a University* (UWE 1996).

This was a period of continuing academic innovation and growth. UWE introduced a university-wide undergraduate modular scheme, after long debate, in 1991. The scheme was not intended to offer a cafeteria-style 'pick-and-mix' programme for students, but was designed to increase flexibility and economy in course design and redesign, and to facilitate interfaculty developments. It also aimed to promote consistent treatment for all students across the University's undergraduate programmes, for example in terms of credit for the volume of work done, and in assessment procedures. UWE's 12 faculties revised their programmes to fit the university scheme at varying rates, but by 1996–97 the twelfth faculty had admitted its first cohort to a revised modular programme. Modularisation can be seen as a major move towards standardisation of course offerings, teaching and learning methods, and assessment procedures. It was a process developed and delivered by the academic professionals within a managed institutional framework designed to facilitate the change.

Modularity also facilitated the accreditation of prior experience and learning and a move towards more fully credit-based degree programmes. This was reinforced by a Credit Review during 1996–97 which led to adjustments to the modular scheme and a shift towards a full credit accumulation culture. 'Full-time' students were relying increasingly on part-time employment to finance their stay at University, and the traditional distinctions between part-time and full-time students were beginning to break down. Students were also getting older; although there continued to be a significant proportion of A-level qualified school-leavers aged 18 or 19 enrolling on UWE programmes, increasing numbers of students were over 21, even over 25, when they first enrolled. Modularity and a credit culture were needed to accommodate this changing population and their changing needs for variably-paced study. The growing national debate about graduate standards was perhaps a response to the 'more means worse' criticism which always follows expansion of higher education, but it could equally be seen as a necessary part of a system in which individually paced flexible learning with credit accumulation and transfer becomes a major part of the overall activity.

The student body also became steadily more local or regional during the late 1980s and early 1990s. The Polytechnic had always recruited significant numbers of local students, most obviously to its large part-time programmes enrolling up to 6000 students each year. The full-time student population had also always had a local flavour, especially in vocational areas such as teacher training, social work and engineering. As government policy shifted the burden of student support from grants to loans in the 1990s, so more students chose to stay in their home region, and the proportions of local full-time students rose steadily. By the mid 1990s more than a third of all full-time students at UWE came from the West of England region, broadly drawn. The proportion was further boosted when in 1996 the University incorporated two local colleges of health alongside its own small faculty covering health and social work, to create the largest academic unit in the University. In the new Faculty of Health and Social Care, recruitment to full-time and part-time courses was almost entirely local, serving the region's health and social services. In 1997, the University added a thirteenth 'associate' faculty by forming a close academic partnership with Hartpury College, a small mixed further education/higher education college of agriculture with an international reputation for equine studies.

The changing student population also had more focused, if not narrower, expectations. Students 'working their way through college' understandably wish to concentrate their academic efforts on what is assessed, and what takes them towards their goal of a tradeable credential in the employment market. Commenting on the experience of the USA, Zemsky (1993) argues that student consumerism has bred demands for credentials and practical knowledge in a flexible package – a far cry from the pursuit of knowledge for its own sake by the willing apprentice to the community of scholars. The latter may always have been as much myth as reality for the majority, but the myth dies hard among higher education staff (and students and their parents) who have long cherished it. However, in mass higher education more does mean different in this respect. Modularisation and credit systems push the higher education experience steadily further away from the intensive, full-time, residential three-year honours degree experienced by a cohort who enrol, progress and graduate together.

The changing student demands coincided with the government's decision to 'consolidate' higher education student numbers, after the policy objective of expansion to accommodate one-third of the rising 18/19 year old cohort was met years earlier than planned, to Treasury consternation. A standstill in total numbers combined with continuing 'efficiency gains' (cuts in the level of funding per student) reinforced the former polytechnics' natural tendencies to develop their research in ways which attracted more public funding, and more academic prestige. The 1992 Research Assessment Exercise (RAE) had for the first time delivered significant funds, albeit still small in overall proportion, to the new universities. It was also clear that a high RAE rating had a 'halo effect' which extended far beyond its quantitative or financial significance. Increasingly, new university staff formed the view that RAE ratings also strongly influenced assessments of teaching quality, whatever the protestations of Higher Education Funding Council for England assessors to the contrary.

Among the new universities there were again discernible differences in response to apparently similar external pressures and internal forces. The central management group at the University of the West of England (UWE), known as the Directorate, aimed to play down the significance of research funding through the newly unified Higher Education Funding Council for England (HEFCE). This was a conscious attempt to preserve a balanced concern for all aspects of university operation, rather than to license a chase for research ratings and prestige at the expense of teaching quality, and ultimately of income. While some other universities developed elaborate institution-wide strategies for research development over five and ten years, UWE's planning process enabled different faculties to pursue quite different research strategies. In consequence the enabling university research strategy was perceived by some as not valuing research enough. It prompted recurrent anguish among the research community, who felt moved to state and restate the 'case for research' at regular intervals. While this was seen by some as the expression of 'old university' values, its manifestation, in the call for a tighter university strategy and policy, was very much part of the 'new university' culture of managed change. In any event, UWE's improvement in both quality and quantity in the 1996 RAE was better than the norm for former polytechnics, and involved a doubling since 1992 in the numbers of 'research-active' staff entered in the exercise.

The apparently similar achievements in the 1996 RAE of institutions with widely different explicit strategies suggests that the growth of RAE-oriented research was, across a wide range of institutions, a phenomenon fuelled by individual academic aspirations and relatively unsusceptible to 'management'. Here we can see the 1990s version of 'academic drift', in an apparently inexorable tendency among new universities to boost the volume and quality of their academic research. Just as in the 1970s, staff desire for academic prestige and more intrinsically rewarding work coincided with external funding mechanisms which rewarded institutional drift towards work of a kind already done in the old universities. The difference in the 1990s was that research, rather than teaching, was the growth area.

However this drift, although prominent in public debate, was not the most significant change in the expanded university sector.

Influenced by government policy, responding to student demand, but driven by institutional commitment and choice, the new university sector diversified as it grew. To see how, let us turn to a brief consideration of policy developments during 1988–1997, examining what difference policy makes to institutional practice from another perspective.

Higher education policy 1988/97: from new right to new universities

Marie Thorne and I have recently reviewed higher education policy developments over the last decade as part of the broader change in the public services brought about by the Thatcherite and 'new right' reforms of the 1980s. We argued that government policies aimed 'to increase efficiency in service delivery and limit professional autonomy, by strengthening market forces and promoting managerial control'. (Thorne and Cuthbert 1996, p.173). This section draws on that analysis.

The drive for efficiency was accompanied by an emphasis on management which often spilled over into an ideology of managerialism. In similar vein Trow (1994, p.11) differentiates between 'soft' managerialism, denoting a concern for efficiency, and 'hard' managerialism, which 'elevates institutional and system management to a dominant position in higher education'. The bureaucratisation of control in higher education was accompanied by standardisation which promoted performance measurement and league tables, whether through the RAE or the national press. Inevitably such processes circumscribe academic autonomy.

At the same time there were new policy pressures for competition between institutions, which went beyond the familiar competition for academic prestige, research funding and the best students. The funding councils created in the 1988 Act, and restructured in 1992, were established as purchasers whose role was to fund, not to plan. Initiative was to transfer to the institutions, who would compete in proposing, while the funders would dispose. The UWE case study shows the effectiveness of this policy in creating a new sense of institutional responsibility, while maintaining the effectiveness of the government policy thrust to increase volume and reduce unit costs.

Institutional autonomy increased at the same time that academics felt that their individual professional autonomy was being curtailed.

Each was an explicit aim of government policy. Incorporation of the polytechnics, to give them independence, was intended to empower institutional governors and managers, and it did. Funding Councils ensured that policy aims were followed through by requiring the regular submission of strategic plans from every institution. The very notion of a university strategic plan appears to be a blow to traditional academic autonomy and its organisation theory counterpart, the collegium as organised anarchy (Cohen and March 1974). However it can be argued that such concepts can flourish and make sense only in what Dill (1996) calls 'munificent' environments which in effect confer 'strategic certainty'. When resources are scarce, strategic uncertainty demands explicit attention to strategic choice. We can see this process at work in the development by Bristol Polytechnic/UWE of its 'regional strategy', contrasted with the national niche strategy of Oxford Polytechnic/Oxford Brookes University.

The cumulative impact of policy changes has, then, brought both 'new liberty' and 'new discipline', in Winter's (1996) terms. Increasing the significance of institutional management and of interinstitutional competition, reducing resource levels to promote efficiency and strategic choice, standardising academic operations and performance measures amounted to a significant shift towards controlling the professional academic workforce. 'Where professionals are controlled rather than controlling, it is meaningful to speak of clearer organisational focus – ... *concentration* on particular kinds of activity, leading to *diversification* of the sector' (Thorne and Cuthbert 1996, p.182).

Thorne and Cuthbert (1996) used a stakeholder model to map the emerging diversification of the higher education sector. Adopting a model developed by Winstanley, Sorabji and Dawson (1995), we argued that universities and other higher education institutions differ in the extent to which their stakeholders enjoy *criteria power* and *operational power*. Criteria power is the ability of stakeholders to define the aims of the service, design the overall system, influence performance criteria and evaluate performance. Operational power is the ability to provide the service and decide how to provide it, or to change the way it is delivered. In some institutions, for example, government and Funding Council may dominate in terms of what work shall be done (high criteria power); managers may have both high criteria power and high operational power. Teachers will then be relatively disempowered, while students have some operational power through consumerist forces. We labelled such institutions 'market bureaucracies'. At the opposite extreme, in some loosely-coupled collegial universities the professor enjoys high power on both dimensions. Government, Funding Council, Research Councils, senior institutional staff may all have limited criteria power by comparison. Students are disempowered, junior teaching and research staff not much less so. These are the 'autonomous professional' institutions, occupying the golden triangle of Oxford, Cambridge and London, and perhaps a few other places. These opposite extremes are, it is argued, diverging in the 'unified' university sector.

At the same time there is convergence in the middle 'mass' market where market forces meet head on with academic autonomy, and force a draw. Old universities, labelled 'professional market' institutions, are becoming increasingly similar to new universities approaching from a 'managerial market' position. This convergence is apparent at UWE, for example, in undergraduate student recruitment. The average applicant for a university course makes between five and six applications on the Universities and Colleges Admissions Service form. The institutions most often coupled with UWE include a number of former polytechnics, as one would expect, but also in the top twenty are Bristol, Cardiff, Exeter, Reading and several other 'old' universities. Within this mass market there are a number of significant distinctions, as for example between the large regionally-oriented comprehensive institutions such as UWE, and the various niche players such as Oxford Brookes, but also the many specialist colleges of art, music, and so on.

Other analyses are of course possible and likely to be equally valid. This analysis shows that diversification, perhaps even fragmentation, is a real phenomenon which urgently needs study, if only to enable public debate to move beyond the 'old' and 'new' university labels which conceal more than they reveal of the rapidly changing higher education landscape. I have argued that diversification is the consequence of the interaction of internal and external forces, mediated by institutional management. I will in the final section summarise the argument and draw on theories of strategic management and change to reinterpret and restate the proposition.

Summary: recognising managing for a change

In the 'academic drift' hypothesis as originally formulated there was little room for institutional managers. The irresistible forces of policy and external funding mechanism met the immovable object of academic self-interest and the polytechnics drifted in consequence closer and closer towards the binary line. The circumstances encouraged it: English higher education was notoriously undersupplied in comparison with most of the developed world. The hypothesis was adequate to account for the phenomenon.

In the late 1980s and 1990s, a succession of government policy initiatives brought about major change in the higher education sector as a whole, and within the institutions themselves. Those changes cannot be understood simply as the resultant of staff and student wishes and extra-institutional forces. The observed diversification of the supposedly 'unified' university sector can only be explained by acknowledging the possibility of mediation of those internal and external forces by institutional managers and governors, exercising discretion in making or influencing strategic choices by institutions.

Their influence lies not only in the choices themselves, but also in the way in which the choice opportunities are recognised and presented. The case study has suggested that institutional environments must be seen as enacted or socially constructed (Smircich and Stubbart 1985) as well as, or instead of, as a given objective reality which is 'out there'. In enacting environments, or making sense of them for the benefit of the institution, managers may take different approaches. A well-known categorisation of strategic management style (Miles and Snow 1978) differentiates between *defenders, prospectors, analysers* and *reactors*. *Defenders* are managers who concentrate on a relatively well-defined market area, strengthening their position in it rather than seeking out new opportunities in new areas, which is the hallmark of the *prospector*, who often also creates uncertainty and change. *Analysers* work in both stable and unstable areas; in the former they adopt more bureaucratic or formalised routines but in unstable areas they use a more organic or intuitive approach. *Reactors* recognise change and uncertainty but are unable to respond by developing a consistent strategy, in a way which would help to shape or enact the environment. Instead they act only when environmental pressure forces them to do so.

These ideal types are readily recognisable in practice, usually occurring together in different mixes in different institutions. UWE's management over the last decade might be described at first in terms of defending the well-marked territory of the growing 'regional' market. Later, a growth in prospecting behaviour led both to expansion of research activity in many faculties, and also at corporate level to the new developments in health and social care, and agriculture. Deans of faculties had to be analysers to maintain large and relatively standardised teaching programmes while also encouraging research in more organic or intuitive ways.

This characterisation is offered merely to sketch the possibilities for this kind of analysis, and to show that there were real opportunities for strategic choice, in which the exercise of managerial discretion inevitably played a significant part. To understand the process of change in higher education, it is necessary to recognise that institutional management plays its part. Change cannot be interpreted simply as the consequence of policy pressures interacting with institutional values, as the theory of academic drift once suggested. Theory needs to change because higher education circumstances have changed. The major changes include: the creation of greater institutional independence through incorporation; the encouragement of inter-institutional competition; declining resource levels which force institutions to make more and weightier strategic choices; changes in the student population and its expectations; and changes in the nature of the higher education experience itself, which has become more diverse and fragmented as mass participation multiplies the forms which are recognised as legitimate higher education experiences.

The consequence of these changes in higher education is that there are more choices to be made, and more influence to be exercised, at the institutional level. In the process of making strategic choices and exercising influence on development institutional managers and governors are inevitably prominent. When we ask, in the late 1990s, 'How does government policy affect institutional practice?', we can only achieve a satisfactory answer by recognising managing for a change.

References

Bristol Polytechnic (1989) *Mission and Strategy*, June 1989, Mimeo.

Bristol Polytechnic (1990) *The Bottom Line*. Report by the Head of Corporate Planning October 1990, Mimeo.

Cohen, M.D. and March, J.G. (1974) *Leadership and Ambiguity: The American College President*. New York: McGraw-Hill.

Crosland, A. (1965) Speech by the Secretary of State for Education and Science at Woolwich Polytechnic, 27 April 1965.

Crosland, A. (1967) Speech by the Secretary of State for Education and Science at Lancaster University, 20 January 1967 in J. Pratt and T. Burgess (1974) *Polytechnics: a Report*. London: Pitman.

Cuthbert, R.E. (ed) (1988a) *Going Corporate*. Bristol: Further Education Staff College.

Cuthbert, R.E. (1988b) 'Reconstructing higher education policy.' In H. Eggins (ed) *Restructuring Higher Education*. Milton Keynes: Society for Research into Higher Education and Open University Press.

Cuthbert, R.E. (1992) 'Management: under new management?' In I. McNay (ed) (1992) *Visions of Post-compulsory Education*. Buckingham: Society for Research into Higher Education and Open University Press.

Dill, D.D. (1996) 'Academic planning and organisational design: lessons from leading American universities.' *Higher Education Quarterly 50*, 1, 35–53.

Locke, M. (1978) *Traditions and Controls in the Making of a Polytechnic: Woolwich Polytechnic 1890–1970*. London: Thames Polytechnic.

Locke, M., Pratt, J., Silverman, S. and Travers, T. (1987) *Polytechnic Government*. London: Committee of Directors of Polytechnics.

Miles, R.E. and Snow, C.C. (1978) *Organisational Strategy, Structure and Process*. New York: McGraw-Hill.

Morris, A. (1991) Speech at Honorary Degree Ceremony, Bristol Cathedral 1991.

National Advisory Body (1987) *Management for a Purpose*, Report of the Good Management Practice Working Group. London: NAB.

Pratt, J. (1997) *The Polytechnic Experiment 1965–1992*. Buckingham: Society for Research into Higher Education and Open University Press.

Pratt, J. and Burgess, T. (1974) *Polytechnics: a Report*. London: Pitman.

Robinson, E. (1968) *The New Polytechnics*. Harmondsworth: Penguin.

Smircich, L. and Stubbart, C. (1985) 'Strategic management in an enacted world.' *Academy of Management Review*, 724–736.

Thorne, M.L. and Cuthbert, R.E. (1996) 'Autonomy, bureaucracy and competition: the ABC of control in higher education.' In R.E. Cuthbert (ed) (1996) *Working in Higher Education*. Buckingham: Society for Research into Higher Education and Open University Press.

Thorne, M.L. and Cuthbert R.E. (1997) *Management and Higher Education: Different Discourses in a Common Context?* Paper for the British Academy of Management Annual Conference, London Business School 8–10 September 1997.

Trow, M. (1994) 'Managerialism and the academic profession: the case of England.' In *Higher Education Policy 7*, 2, 11–18.

University of the West of England (1996) *The New Idea of a University.* The Programmes Office Seminars 1993–1995 Bristol: UWE.

Winstanley, D., Sorabji, D. and Dawson, S. (1995) 'When the pieces don't fit: a stakeholder power matrix to analyse public sector restructuring.' In *Public Money and Management 15*, 2, 19–26.

Winter, R. (1996) 'New liberty, new discipline: academic work in the new higher education.' In R.E. Cuthbert (ed) (1996) *Working in Higher Education.* Buckingham: Society for Research into Higher Education and Open University Press.

Zemsky, R. (1993) 'Consumer markets and higher education.' In *Liberal Education 79*, 3, 14–17.

CHAPTER 17

Decoding Dearing on Diversity

David Watson

Introduction

My night job, to which I have clung jealously as my various day jobs have grown and grown, is to read, think and write about the history of ideas. As a consequence, I have a fairly well-developed amateur interest in the history of science, and especially popular controversy in science. There is one such running at the moment in the *New York Review of Books*, which Stephen Jay Gould has elected to use to attack a brand of what he calls 'fundamentalist evolutionism' (Gould 1997a; 1997b).

There are two ways in which this controversy put me in mind of the topic 'managing diverse systems of higher education'. First the concepts of diversity and selective survival are common to both. Second, the popular discourse around both topics has often degraded into a slippery use of allegory and metaphor. On the latter, Steve Jones has some harsh things to say: Evolution is to allegory as statues are to birdshit. It is a convenient platform upon which to deposit badly digested ideas (Jones 1997).

The call to 'diversity' in UK higher education is often appealed to on evolutionary grounds. The emergence of diversity is apparently a sign of our strength and vitality; its continuation (for some seemingly without limit) is claimed to be necessary for our future health. Thus, it has much in common with popular theorising around biodiversity.

Here it is perhaps salutary to note that many evolutionary biologists are beginning to have second thoughts. There has been a rash of recent studies claiming that increasing the diversity and range of species does not necessarily aid the development of the ecosystem as a whole. More important for systemic health are the biological traits of the dominant species. These studies include examination of recovery from forest fires in Sweden, nutrient cycling in California grassland,

and the development of an artificially constructed reserve in Minnesota. Reviewing these in *Science,* J. P. Grimes of the University of Sheffield isolates the central issue as the discovery of the key species: 'The most immediate problem is to identify irreplaceable species and functional types and to discover whether there are situations in which ecosystem viability depends on unusually high biodiversity' (Grimes 1997).

I do not want to go much further in contributing to the allegorical fallacy myself (see Appendix I for further comments on the ecological analogy): but I do want to suggest that the dialogue about institutional diversity in UK higher education has missed two tricks towards which this controversy leads us: through first an unwillingness to tackle seriously the question of key institutional types; and second a reluctance to question a convenient article of faith for policy makers and those seeking to influence them.

The discourse on diversity

To be brutal, much of the recent discourse about diversity in British higher education has been at best loosely and ineffectively formulated, and, at worst, self-serving and politically manipulative. This is demonstrated by the isolation of three (relatively) unchallenged propositions that have structured the debate:

- that all participants mean the same thing by diversity

- that diversity is unambiguously good for systemic health in higher education

- that current policies and practice have inhibited or constrained diversity.

I will try to test each of these propositions.

On the first, I suggest that it is revealing that every positive official statement made about diversity by an institutional head is followed either by no examples at all (and hence represents an appeal to self-evidence) or only by examples which relate to her own institution. The appeal to 'diversity' is almost invariably a partial, positioning statement, rather than a framework for system-wide understanding or analysis.

The second proposition follows from this. Since diversity is relatively unexamined, and since it is regularly cast as 'us' against an undifferentiated 'other', it is easier to assume that it is infinitely permissible (or at least that we have no collective responsibility for what it includes).

Finally, we are told that diversity is constrained, usually by the actions of others (notably our funders). As I have argued elsewhere, this is an argument which it is difficult to sustain, not least when we examine funding outcomes (Watson forthcoming). The lists of 'winners' and 'losers' in Figure 17.1 below both seem satisfactorily diverse. (The question of the overall adequacy of these funds is another matter.)

Average unit of differential funding per student

FULL-TIME/SANDWICH		PART-TIME	
Oxford Brookes	+468	**Oxford**	**+2,559**
Leeds Met	+424	**Cambridge**	**+731**
Sheffield Hallam	+378	**UMIST**	**+678**
Oxford	**+313**	North London	+493
Liverpool JM	+300	East London	+448
Brighton	+299	**Birkbeck**	**+376**
Kingston	+266	Oxford Brookes	+350
Northumbria	+263	**Newcastle**	**+268**
Imperial	**+258**	Manchester Met	+261
Aston	**+238**	Brighton	+222
SOAS	**-268**	Middlesex	-446
Anglia	-308	**Leicester**	**-463**
Warwick	**-311**	Luton	-465
Humberside	-313	**Liverpool**	**-499**
Brunel	**-313**	**Sheffield**	**-499**
City	**-417**	**Southampton**	**-546**
Surrey	**-429**	**Lancaster**	**-587**
Birkbeck	**-465**	**Bristol**	**-617**
Derby	-471	**Exeter**	**-712**
Luton	-484	**Bath**	**-932**

*Figure 17.1: 1994/95 'T' Funding per student
    (above or below average funding)* ★

Source: Knight 1996
★ Higher Education Funding Council for England 'Teaching' element of grant

The outcome of this kind of approach has been a discourse that if subjected to academic assessment on philosophical, sociological, economic, or even literary grounds would result in resounding failure.

Analysing diversity

Most of my fire so far has been concentrated on a group who could be characterised as participants. The professional literature is not much more helpful. I would like to offer some examples of analyses of diversity based upon:

- institutional typologies

- institutional missions

- the relationship of institutions to the state.

1. Oxford and Cambridge	7. Scottish (ancient, civic, technological, old new, new new)
2. University of London	
3. Victorian Civics	
4. Redbricks	8. Wales & Glamorgan
5. Durham and Keele	9. Queen's & Ulster
	10. Open
	11. Old new
6. Technological (ex-CAT)	12. New new
13. Multi-faculty aspirants	15. Mixed-economy
14. Liberal arts	16. Specialised
17. HE in FE	

Figure 17.2: Scott's 17 varieties of university
Source: Based on Scott (1995)

Figure 2 is based on Peter Scott's analysis in *The Meanings of Mass Higher Education* (Scott 1995, pp.44–50). As is apparent, this is an extraordinary hodge-podge of historical, territorial and functional criteria; it reaches its nadir in the 'category' containing Durham and Keele (both are *sui generis!*)

Nor are the institutions much help in terms of what they say about themselves. As is now regularly recognised, unlike the post-Robbins expansion with its clear experience of (officially sanctioned) 'academic drift', the later 1980s surge of expansion world has given us mission spread. A good indicator of this was the use by institutions of succinct 'charity tag-lines' during 1993–95, as they took advantage of a loop-hole (now closed) to avoid VAT on advertisement. Figure 17.3 gives an overview of what the participants chose. Given the context of preparation for the 1996 Research Assessment Exercise the reference with the top frequency is perhaps understandable.

Key Words	'Old' universities (39)	'New' universities (28)	Colleges of HE (8)	Total (75)
Research	30	12	4	46
Excellence	21	12	2	35
Teaching	20	6	3	29
Education	9	14	2	25
Learning	12	3	2	17
Quality	3	1	2	6
Vocational/ Careers	0	4	1	5
Access	1	3	0	4
Knowledge	4	0	0	4
Lifelong learning	1	2	0	3
Training	0	0	2	2
International	2	0	0	2

Figure 17.3: Analysis of 'charity tag-lines'
Source: Analysis of advertisements placed in the *THES* and *The Guardian*

Finally, we have the broader analysis of Gareth Williams in Figure 17.4 (Williams 1992).

1. Self-governing, autonomous university, community of scholars
2. Public service corporation, students as trainees
3. Enterprises in the knowledge industry, serving customers and clients

Figure 17.4: Williams' three relationships between higher education and society
Source: Williams (1992)

This has all the strengths and weaknesses of Weberian ideal-types. I cannot find a pure example of any one in the real world. The great universities of the USA are mixtures of 1 and 3. Those of Europe are mixtures of 1 and 2.

Diversity and the Dearing vision

This was the 'conversation' that the Dearing Committee joined. Did they (we) do any better?

Paragraph 10.102 of the Report of the National Committee of Inquiry into Higher Education (the Dearing Report) reads (in part) as follows:

> The diversity of programme provision and of students will continue to be a valued element in higher education ... However, we seek to encourage diversity within a framework where qualifications are widely understood, standards are high and respected, and the quality of teaching and student learning is amongst the best in the world. In the absence of the infrastructure and arrangements of the kind we propose, pressures for increased and direct intervention from outside the higher education system will intensify.

In the remainder of this paper I attempt a critical reading of this vision of diversity within a framework, as well as an assessment of the likely effect of the relevant Dearing recommendations on the pattern of higher education institutions within the UK and their practice.

Decoding Dearing

The Dearing Committee's analysis and recommendations can be summarised in six main areas:

- the 'convergence argument'
- the scope for differentiation
- the implications for quality and standards
- the call for 'discipline'
- the 'territorial' complication
- the 'compact' concept and its implications.

Briefly, Dearing half-bought the argument for institutional convergence in response to funding and reputational pressures, urged the case for transparent and well-understood institutional differentiation (by title as well as function), recognised the difficulties of mutual assurance of quality (and especially output standards) in such a differentiated system while insisting that it should be achieved (especially at the threshold level), complained about aspects of actual and potential institutional indiscipline (as on quality, especially in respect of academic governance and franchising, and on titles – of courses as well as of institutions), and supported more systematic local and regional complementarity of mission while giving way to territorial exceptionalism on several dimensions (franchising in Wales, course length in Scotland, institutional designation in Northern Ireland etc.). (See Appendix II for relevant references to the main report.)

From diversity to plurality

In estimating the potential effects of these Dearing recommendations on diversity, I would like to propose a couple of changes in the terms of discourse. First, for me the key emergent concept seems to be something like 'disciplined plurality' rather than just 'diversity'.

Second, and to return to the 'ecosystem,' I suggest that we need to concentrate more on the identification of key types of species than on the myriad of possibilities.

This approach embodies something of a personal change of heart. I used to think (ideal-types again) more in terms of a continuum of possibilities, as in the following description of 'universities ancient and modern'.

Ancient	*Modern*
Élite	Open
Competitive admission	Accessible enrolment
Full time	Full time, part time, mixed mode
Highly structured	Flexible, modular
Single honours	Many levels, intermediate awards, CATS
Postgraduate research	Postgraduate amd post-experience, CPD
Traditional teaching	Innovative learning styles
Subjects and disciplines	Interdisciplinary Professional and vocational applications
Pure/basic research	Applied research, consultancy, 'technology transfer'
Graduates to research and further study	High graduate employment
The 'ivory tower'	Many partnerships
National/international reputation	Local/regional role
High costs	High value for money

Figure 17.5: Universities: ancient and modern
Source: Watson (1998)

I now think that history (especially relatively recent history) exposes this as a cop-out. The political, economic, and even some of the moral, arguments underlying the Dearing concept of a compact, mean that some policy dimensions and priorities are for the system as a whole. Among these I would list, as the inescapable agenda for higher education institutions:

- access and widening participation (it is no longer acceptable for élite institutions and competitive courses to be so overwhelmingly dominated by the affluent privately-prepared)

- funding (where the Report proceeds on a broad assumption of equal funding for equal work)

- community links (why should the walls around the ivory tower be higher and its treasures more exclusively guarded?)

- collaboration and partnerships (including across the further/higher education boundary – as will be required by sector-wide acknowledgement of credit)

- the scholarly environment (which Dearing argues is essential for genuinely higher education)

- attention to quality and standards (where the whole theory of the about-to-be-reinvigorated external examiner system is that closed shops, rings and isolation of groups should not be allowed to emerge).

If we concede the uniform application of this agenda, it makes the process of identifying key species much easier. Figure 17.6 is my initial (and deliberately short) first attempt.

| 1. The international research university |
| 2. The modern professional formation university |
| 3. The 'curriculum innovation' university |
| 4. The (headquarters of the) distance/open-learning university |
| 5. The university college |
| 6. The specialised/single-subject college |

Figure 17.6: Universities: essential species
Source: Author

Each of these institutional types is potentially problematic (for example, several of the 'curriculum innovation' universities which emerged in response to Robbins have found it difficult to renew themselves). Equally, 'hybrids' may in some respects be both possible and desirable.

The *Times Higher Education Supplement* leader of Friday 17 October 1997 had the headline 'Diversity: big issue Dearing ducked'. It outlined two alternative views of diversity (the 'market model', and 'managed diversity' – as always on the Californian model) and then went on to offer a characteristically robust attack on the Committee's view that the sector should take responsibility itself for the limits of diversity. That was indeed the Committee's position, and I believe it to be an honourable and effective one, fully in tune with the sector's historical commitments until they were wobbled by a decade and a half of officially encouraged and brutal competition (Watson 1997; Watson and Bowden 1997). I could list a number of issues on which the Dearing Committee either ducked or deferred key problems, not least because of pressure of time. This was not one of them. If the sector as a whole cannot manage diversity, a vital argument in the battle for self-regulation and self-determination is lost.

References

Gould, S.J. (1997a) Darwinian fundamentalism. *New York Review of Books,* 12 June 1997, 34–37.

Gould, S.J. (1997b) Evolutionary psychology: an exchange. *New York Review of Books,* 9 October 1997, 56–58.

Grimes, J.P. (1997) in *Chronicle of Higher Education* 29 September 1997.

Jones, S. (1997) in *New York Review of Books* 17 July 1997.

Knight, P. (1996) 'New currency proves worth.' *Times Higher Education Supplement,* 16 February 1996, p.6.

The National Committee of Inquiry into Higher Education (1997) *Higher Education in the Learning Society.* London: NCIHE.

Scott, P. (1995) *The Meanings of Mass Higher Education.* Buckingham: SRHE and Open University Press.

Watson, D. (forthcoming) 'The limits to diversity.' In D. Jary and M. Parker (eds) *The New Higher Education: Issues and Directions for the Post-Dearing University.* Staffordshire University Press.

Watson, D. (1997) 'Quality, standards and institutional reciprocity.' In J. Brennan, P. deVries and R. Williams (eds) *Standards and Quality in Higher Education.* London: Jessica Kingsley Publishers.

Watson, D. and Bowden, R. (1997) *Ends Without Means: the Conservative Stewardship of UK Higher Education 1979–97.* Education Research Centre Occasional Paper, University of Brighton.

Williams, G. (1992) as described in Radford, J. *et al.* (1997) *Quantity and Quality in Higher Education.* London: Jessica Kingsley Publishers, p.46.

Appendix I

The following comments on the ecological analogy have been very kindly suggested by Professor John Krebs, Chief Executive of the National Environment Research Council.

'If you plan to develop the ecological analogy further, it might be useful to distinguish three questions about biodiversity.

1. Why does diversity exist?

   A common misunderstanding amongst non-specialists is that diversity is somehow developed by ecosystems and communities as a mechanism of optimising the allocation or utilisation of resources for the community as a whole. In fact, the real picture is that diversity arises as a result of the competition between individuals. The observed mixture of species in a community is a dynamic-equilibrium outcome of avoidance of competition. There are some classic experiments and theory in ecology from the 1920s and 1930s that summarise this. One is the so-called "Gause's Principle" which says "complete competitors cannot co-exist".

2. How is diversity described?

   In the ecological literature, the diversity that allows different species to co-exist has generally been described in terms of 'niche separation'. Imagine the properties of a species being represented along different axes. For example the size of food items consumed, the depth of the water in which the species lives or the range of temperatures that it can tolerate. These "niche axes" can be used to represent in an n-dimensional hyperspace the characteristic ecological niche of the species.

3. How does diversity relate to stability of the community as a whole?

   This has been a knotty problem for ecologists over many decades. Some think that greater diversity begets greater stability because there is richer connectivity in the system and therefore more buffers. Others see it just the other way round, that diversity promotes greater instability because, like with an elaborate house of cards, pulling out one element of the system can cause the rest to collapse. The empirical evidence tends to support the view that greater diversity is correlated with greater stability, but it is not clear whether the relationship is causal.' (Personal communication with the author, 8.12.1997)

Appendix II: NCIHE Main Report

References to diversity

Term of reference 2: 'students should be able to choose between a diverse range of courses, institutions, modes and locations of study'

1.6

3.90–92:	'convergence of institutional ambition'
5.54–6:	diversity and standards
7.22:	diversity and widening participation
7.30:	Scottish successes
9.89–90:	curriculum breadth
10.11–12, 49:	course titles
10.46:	HNC/D
10.64:	threshold standards
*10.102:	'diversity within a framework'
11.26:	research funding
12.7:	regional dimension
13.2:	Communications and Information Technology
15.34:	governance

*   Chapter 16, passim, including recommendation 61 (16.13): 'We recommend to the Government and the Funding Bodies that diversity of institutional mission, consistent with high quality delivery and the responsible exercise of institutional autonomy, should continue to be an important element of the United Kingdom's higher education system; and that this should be reflected in the funding arrangements for institutions'

16.9:   autonomy

16.10:   declining discipline

16.24:   institutional innovation – 'a period of relative
    stability'

16.38–41:   HE in FE

16.46:   collaboration

20.105:   devolved decision making

22.13:   intermediate funding decisions

22.14:   mission-oriented funding

CHAPTER 18

Concluding Remarks

Mary Henkel and Brenda Little

The fact that the relationships between higher education and the state are changing is not in dispute. Our concerns have been the nature of the changes, the reasons underlying them, and the mechanisms for effecting change. We have not offered clear or simple explanations. Rather, through analysis based on research and practitioner reflection, our contributors have sought to illuminate the multiple and often conflicting forces at work in the relationships between higher education and the state.

Although we have been largely concerned with Western European countries, the issues raised by changing relationships are undoubtedly replicated elsewhere in the world; and they are not wholly new. Thirty years ago, a group of academics took as their theme for a series of lectures at York University (Canada) 'Is a fundamental change taking place in the relationships of governments and universities'? (Cooper *et al.* 1966). They identified some of the tensions that run through this book between, for example, academic freedom, legitimated criticism, collaborative knowledge formation and public accountability. From an American perspective, one contributor alluded to the dangers of too close an interdependence developing between universities and national governments, and government and industry such that universities had 'almost certainly lost some of their prerogative to criticise, some of their freedom to speak out on controversial political and economic issues' (McConnell 1966, p.90). He also predicted that the tension between institutional independence and public accountability would grow in intensity.

The analyses offered here certainly confirm tension between independence and accountability as a pervasive phenomenon. Conditions for sustaining such tension abound: not only are the forces pulling against each other strong but they are also multiple. We now seek briefly to summarise how we have depicted the sources of tension and the conclusions that can be drawn about where they are leading.

The starting point is the rise in the scale and significance of higher education. This is a taken-for-granted phenomenon in the societies with which we are concerned. The forces driving it have been political and economic. There have been normative political arguments for equity, inclusiveness and the sustenance of democracy; but equally powerful have been pragmatic political actions, responses to social demand. And during the last two decades the political arguments have frequently been subordinated to the economic: higher education as an investment for states and for individuals, although, as Williams has reminded us, those economic arguments are far from straightforward and eminently contestable.

Moreover, even if the returns are ultimately high for some or all concerned, the issue of who makes those investments and in return for what is sharpened in the context of massification. Other stakeholders than governments must be required to contribute in different forms: private companies and a whole raft of knowledge users; students will have to pay more, however this is organised. If the range of potential investors increases, does that enhance or reduce academic autonomy? Is finance necessarily a mechanism of control or can it be a source of freedom? For many institutional leaders, under pressure to act strategically in the face of this multi-stakeholder environment, the key task is to sustain a critical distance from one stakeholder and to retain some immunity from short-term external pressures and fashions (see, for example, Barnes, Teichler, Sjölund in this volume). Freedom to choose from a range of funding sources is seen as one way of increasing institutional autonomy.

Massification has compelled governments to develop new forms of regulation, which, in turn, may imply different degrees of freedom and control for different institutions. Massification entails diversification. It implies a wider range of institutions, of students and of university staff: different inputs will tend to produce different outputs, different types of graduate and different forms of knowledge. There will be more variation between universities as to the functions they perform. So universal regulation and central planning must give way to new forms of control: contracts; institutional self regulation within a more discretionary framework; incentives and sanctions; new and more extensive forms of evaluation; competition in quasi-markets. And even if the alternative, a more wholesale shift to real markets, is taken, most of these will still follow.

The other major driving force of change in higher education–state relationships is change in beliefs about knowledge. While the rhetoric of 'the knowledge society' and the 'information society' grows ever more fluent and persuasive, its implications are less certain. In what forms does knowledge become an engine of economic prosperity and how far are they compatible with the modes of knowledge production traditionally (some would say essentially) associated with higher education, modes which assume academic autonomy and academic organisation?

Universities are under more pressure to accept usefulness as the prime goal for the production of knowledge and to concede that this demands collaborative work with a range of interested actors. As several authors have noted, what Gibbons *et al.* (1994) have termed 'Mode 2' production of knowledge (knowledge developed with a view to application or problem solving within domains whose boundaries are socially defined (see also Trist 1972)) is competing with 'Mode 1' or discipline-based knowledge formation.

Sjölund has shown how universities in Sweden are attempting to sustain a combination of Mode 2 and Mode 1 knowledge. This has created some tension within universities, between institutional leaders and senior academics, the former tending to favour a shift of balance towards mode two, the latter expressing more caution. Although the tension should not be exaggerated in the Swedish context, and neither party would wish to undermine the authority of disciplinary knowledge, both this chapter and others (Smith *et al.*; Bauer and Henkel) remind us that academic autonomy is not an indivisible concept. The emerging role for vice-chancellors epitomises how the challenge to academic authority is being worked out in practice. Greater freedom of decision for institutional leaders does not necessarily mean enhanced individual or departmental autonomy. Institutional leaders may be clear that they must retain the confidence of the academics, but the more they come to think of their universities as corporate enterprises (Smith *et al.*) the more challenging is their task of sustaining academic motivation and identification with the institution.

Some of the issues of autonomy and control are raised equally in the context of the educational functions of universities. The right of universities to constitute a bounded sector of society in which they determine the education they provide is also under challenge. Jones and Little demonstrate how developments within the undergraduate curriculum are being influenced by the world of work. This influence is exemplified in the questioning of the nature of high level knowledge and skills, the location of their acquisition and who should control their certification. But as the analyses of Teichler, Connor and Dolton and Vignoles demonstrate, the complexities and vicissitudes of the labour market and the uncertainties of employers defy any simple redefinition of the location of universities in society or of the kinds of graduates they are expected to produce. If 'creative distance from society' can too easily be converted into an 'ivory tower' (Teichler) collaboration will be equally resisted lest it become incorporation.

It is clear that the combined forces of massification, diversification and changes in assumptions about knowledge have led to substantial instabilities in the balance of power and exchange between universities and not only governments but other sectors of society. As Välimaa's paper indicates, new mechanisms of control in a new, more pluralist context might put a severe strain on the integrative forces in society: a fundamental concern of the state.

In the face of the instabilities described, it is perhaps not surprising that most governments are to be found speaking in different voices; vacillating between solutions; exerting contradictory pressures; using constructive ambiguity as a tool of policy making. Governments have never been likely for long to speak with one voice: they are multimodal in their policies and operations, and frequently tribal in their cultures and organisations (Kogan and Henkel 1983). As many seek to embrace and promote various forms of market into the arena of the state, these tendencies are surely bound to be more in evidence.

Some of the strains will be devolved onto institutions – they in turn will have to manage the need for integration in the context of a wider range of conflicting pressures. Hence, again, the growing importance of institutional management and its mediating influences.

Taken together, the trends described constitute a significant challenge to academic authority and there have been shifts of power: from universities to employers (Jones and Little) from the discipline to the enterprise or from individual academics to academic leaders and administrators (Bauer and Henkel; Kogan; McNay; Smith *et al.*); and the introduction of more varied forms of control has not necessarily meant less power for government (Barnes; Bauer and

Henkel). The higher education landscape has been re-shaped by an overall movement on the part of governments towards outputs, performance and product control.

However, academics have also shown a continuing capacity to sustain power. Academics continue to control evaluative systems, even in the UK where these have been most removed from their hands. Criteria of educational evaluation remain those of process rather than product (Brennan) while research criteria are still strongly in the power of the academic élite (McNay). Academics have incorporated the new language of quality and new educational agendas into their own disciplinary cultures, even if the dominance of the discipline in education and research is being seriously questioned.

More fundamentally, the above discussion is framed within assumptions about the continued key role of national boundaries: self-regulating institutions operating within national evaluative systems of control, based primarily on notions of public accountability for public funds raised by the state. We have seen institutional activities being mediated by various influences and resulting in various responses, such that institutional diversity becomes something of a 'watchword'. And we have seen attempts to codify such diversity in terms of a common agenda for higher education institutions within which key species, essential for the continuing health of the 'whole' might be identified (Watson). But what we have not tackled in any depth is possible future scenarios.

Currently the national evaluative systems in operation hold sway by dint of their 'hold' on sources of public funds – but we are now seeing (admittedly 'at the margins') the emergence of higher education institutions which are not dependent on public funding, and thus are not susceptible to the 'public' evaluative mechanisms. We are also seeing (albeit in a rather piecemeal fashion) the design and delivery of teaching and learning using new technologies which transcend national boundaries. Furthermore, as Teichler reminds us, higher education may increasingly need to respond to changes in the global labour market – no longer preoccupied with national considerations. Thus, as we move into the twenty-first century, we may be moving into a situation where the 'hold' that any one state currently has on its higher education system may be significantly loosened ... what then will we be able to say about the relationship between higher education and the state?

References

Cooper, W.M., Davis, W.G., Parent, A. M. and McConnell, T.R. (1966) *Governments and the University.* New York and Toronto: St Martin's Press.

Gibbons, M., Limoges, C., Nowotny, H., Schwartzman, S., Scott, P. and Trow, M. (1994) *The New Production of Knowledge: the dynamics of science and research in contemporary societies.* London: Thousand Oaks, New Delhi: Sage Publications.

Kogan, M. and Henkel, M. (1983) *Government and Research: the Rothschild Experiment in a Government Department.* London: Heinemann Educational Books.

McConnell, T.R. (1966) 'A comparative analysis.' In W. Cooper *et al.* (1966) (eds). *Governments and the University.* New York and Toronto: St Martin's Press.

Trist, E. (1972) 'Types of Output Mix of Research Organisations and their Complementarity.' In A.B. Cherns *et al.* (eds) *Social Science and Government: Policies and Problems.* London: Tavistock Publications.

The Contributors

Catherine Bargh is research associate at the Centre for Policy Studies in Education at the University of Leeds. She has worked on a range of research projects in the field of higher education including the governance of universities and is currently working on a study of the external role and responsibilities of UK vice-chancellors.

John Barnes lectures on executive government and policy making at the London School of Economics (LSE) and has twenty years experience in local government. Between 1992 and 1994 he was the Director of its Centre for Educational Research. He is a member of the LSE's Education Funding Group.

Marianne Bauer is Professor Emerita, University of Gothenburg, where she is currently engaged in international comparative research on higher education reforms. She was President of the European Association of Institutional Research (EAIR) from 1995–1997. Until 1994, she held national responsibilities in Swedish higher education, notably for national evaluation programmes, first at the Swedish National Board of Universities and Colleges, Stockholm, and then in the Office of the University Chancellor, Stockholm.

Jean Bocock is research associate at the Centre for Policy Studies in Education, University of Leeds. As research associate at Manchester Metropolitan University, she conducted a national evaluation study of student guidance and counselling systems in higher education. She has worked extensively in the fields of further and higher education partnerships, franchise provision and non-standard entry to higher education.

John Brennan is head of the Quality Support Centre, a centre for higher education research within the UK's Open University. His main research interests are in quality assurance and relations between higher education and the labour market and he has directed several research projects on both themes. Much of his research and writing has been in an international context and he has been involved in collaborative research projects in Eastern Europe and Latin America in recent years. He has published extensively on higher education policy themes.

Helen Connor is an independent labour market researcher whose main area of work is on graduates and the relationship between higher education and employment. Recent research has included a longitudinal survey of graduates investigating jobs and career development over six years. She is currently embarking on a large scale study of student choice in higher education at the Institute for Employment Studies (IES) where she is an Associate Fellow.

Rob Cuthbert is Assistant Vice-Chancellor at the University of the West of England, Bristol. He has worked as a teacher, researcher, manager and management consultant, in colleges, universities and government agencies in the UK, North America, Africa and China. He has published widely in the field of higher education policy and management; his books include *Going Corporate* and *Working in Higher Education*.

Peter Dolton is David Dale Professor of Economics at the University of Newcastle and has published widely in the field of labour economics. His particular research interests include the economics of education and training and the problems of youth labour market transitions.

Mary Henkel is Reader in the Department of Government, Brunel University. She has published in the fields of higher education policy, professional education and evaluation. She is currently researching the implications for academics of changing higher education and science policies, in collaboration with colleagues at Brunel, Gothenburg, and Bergen universities.

Sandra Jones conducted a number of major social policy research studies at University College, Cardiff, before moving to Brunel University in 1984. From 1989 she was Director of Enterprise and then a Senior Research Fellow in the Centre for the Evaluation of Public Policy and Practice at Brunel University. She is currently an Associate Senior Research Fellow at CEPPP and a partner in Helix Consulting Group.

Maurice Kogan is Professor of Government and Social Administration (Emeritus) and Joint Director of the Centre for the Evaluation of Public Policy and Practice at Brunel University. He is the author of several books and articles on higher education, local government, education, health, social services and science policy and is the editor of *Higher Education Management*.

Brenda Little is a researcher with the Quality Support Centre, a centre for higher education research within the UK's Open University. Her main area of interest is higher education and work, and in particular the relationship between work-based learning and higher education. She has conducted a number of projects funded by the Department for Education and Employment and is currently leading a project investigating the development of key skills in undergraduate work placements.

Ian McNay is Professor of Higher Education and Management and Head of the School of Post-Compulsory Education and Training at the University of Greenwich. His major research interests are in policy analysis and the response of institutions in terms of strategy and management. From 1995–97 he led a team, funded by the Higher Education Funding Council for England, researching the impact of the Research Assessment Exercise on institutions and their staff.

Christine Musselin works as chargée de recherche at the Centre de Sociologie des Organisations (CNRS) in Paris. For many years she led a programme on higher education systems in France and Germany and published with Erhard Friedberg En Quête d'universités (L'Harmattan) and L'Etate face aux universités (Anthropos). She is now leading a comparative study on the academic marketplace in France and Germany.

David Smith is a Senior Research Fellow in the School of Education, University of Leeds and Deputy Director at the Centre for Policy Studies in Education, University of Leeds. He has taught in schools, colleges and universities in England and was previously research fellow at the universities of East Anglia and Warwick. He has worked on a wide range of research projects concerning policy in post-compulsory education and training and has published widely in academic journals, books and the national press.

Peter Scott is Vice-Chancellor of Kingston University. From 1992 to 1997 he was Director of the Centre for Policy Studies in Education and Professor of Education at the University of Leeds. Before that he was Editor of *The Times Higher Education Supplement.* His main research interests are in the governance and management of higher education institutions and wider access to higher education.

Maivor Sjölund works for the National Agency for Higher Education in Sweden. She has a doctorate in Political Science and her main research interest is in the field of Public Administration. She has undertaken many studies for the National Agency, including the one reported on in this book.

Ulrich Teichler is Professor at the Centre for Research in Higher Education and Work, and the Department of Applied Sociology and Law of the University of Kassel, Germany. He has researched and written widely on higher education systems, education and employment, and international education. Major recent publications include *Higher Education and Work* (with J. Brennan and M. Kogan, London: Jessica Kingsley, 1996) and *The ERASMUS Experience* (with F. Maiworm; Luxembourg, Office of Official Publications of the European Community, 1997).

Jussi Välimaa is Head of the Higher Education Research Team at the Institute for Educational Research at the University of Jyväskylä,

Finland. His current research interests focus on the relationship between higher education and society. His most recent empirical research project looked at the relationship between Ph.Ds and labour market.

Anna Vignoles works at the University of Newcastle, and is currently investigating the labour market returns to education. She was a contributor to the review undertaken by the National Committee of Inquiry into Higher Education under the chairmanship of Sir Ron Dearing.

David Watson has been Director of the University of Brighton since 1990. His academic interests are in the history of ideas and higher education policy, and he has published widely in both fields. His latest book is *Lifelong Learning and the University: A Post-Dearing Agenda* (with Richard Taylor, Falmer Press 1998). He was a member of the National Committee of Inquiry into Higher Education, and is the current chair of the Universities Association for Continuing Education.

Gareth Williams is Professor of Educational Administration and Head of the Centre for Higher Education Studies at the Institute of Education, University of London. An economist by training he has written extensively on the economics of education both academically and for policy purposes. In recent years he has concentrated particularly on the finance of higher education. He has travelled widely as an exponent and a critic of market approaches to the funding and administration of higher education institutions and systems.

Subject Index

Author Index